T0224645

Automated Unit Testing with ABAP

A Practical Approach

James E. McDonough

Apress®

Automated Unit Testing with ABAP: A Practical Approach

James E. McDonough
Pennington, NJ, USA

ISBN-13 (pbk): 978-1-4842-6950-3   ISBN-13 (electronic): 978-1-4842-6951-0
https://doi.org/10.1007/978-1-4842-6951-0

Copyright © 2021 by James E. McDonough

This work is subject to copyright. All rights are reserved by the Publisher, whether the whole or part of the material is concerned, specifically the rights of translation, reprinting, reuse of illustrations, recitation, broadcasting, reproduction on microfilms or in any other physical way, and transmission or information storage and retrieval, electronic adaptation, computer software, or by similar or dissimilar methodology now known or hereafter developed.

Trademarked names, logos, and images may appear in this book. Rather than use a trademark symbol with every occurrence of a trademarked name, logo, or image we use the names, logos, and images only in an editorial fashion and to the benefit of the trademark owner, with no intention of infringement of the trademark.

The use in this publication of trade names, trademarks, service marks, and similar terms, even if they are not identified as such, is not to be taken as an expression of opinion as to whether or not they are subject to proprietary rights.

While the advice and information in this book are believed to be true and accurate at the date of publication, neither the authors nor the editors nor the publisher can accept any legal responsibility for any errors or omissions that may be made. The publisher makes no warranty, express or implied, with respect to the material contained herein.

Managing Director, Apress Media LLC: Welmoed Spahr
Acquisitions Editor: Susan McDermott
Development Editor: Laura Berendson
Coordinating Editor: Rita Fernando

Cover designed by eStudioCalamar

Cover image designed by Pixabay

Distributed to the book trade worldwide by Springer Science+Business Media New York, 1 New York Plaza, New York, NY 10004. Phone 1-800-SPRINGER, fax (201) 348-4505, e-mail orders-ny@springer-sbm.com, or visit www.springeronline.com. Apress Media, LLC is a California LLC and the sole member (owner) is Springer Science + Business Media Finance Inc (SSBM Finance Inc). SSBM Finance Inc is a **Delaware** corporation.

For information on translations, please e-mail booktranslations@springernature.com; for reprint, paperback, or audio rights, please e-mail bookpermissions@springernature.com.

Apress titles may be purchased in bulk for academic, corporate, or promotional use. eBook versions and licenses are also available for most titles. For more information, reference our Print and eBook Bulk Sales web page at http://www.apress.com/bulk-sales.

Any source code or other supplementary material referenced by the author in this book is available to readers on GitHub via the book's product page, located at www.apress.com/9781484269503. For more detailed information, please visit http://www.apress.com/source-code.

Printed on acid-free paper

*To Norman Edge, teacher and bassist extraordinaire,
whose benevolent guidance toward improving the
qualities of my musicianship also had a profound
influence on the qualities of my character.*

Table of Contents

About the Author

James E. McDonough received a degree in music education from Trenton State College. After teaching music for only 2 years in the New Jersey public school system, he spent the past 38 years as a computer programmer while also maintaining an active presence as a freelance jazz bassist between New York and Philadelphia. Having switched from mainframe programming to ABAP in 1997, he now works as a contract ABAP programmer designing and writing ABAP programs on a daily basis. An advocate of using the object-oriented programming features available with ABAP, he has been teaching private ABAP education courses over the past few years, where his background in education enables him to present and explain complicated concepts in a way that makes sense to beginners.

About the Technical Reviewer

Paul Hardy joined HeidelbergCement in the United Kingdom in 1990. For the first seven years, he worked as an accountant. In 1997, a global SAP rollout came along, and he jumped on board and has never looked back. He has worked on country-specific SAP implementations in the United Kingdom, Germany, Israel, and Australia.

After starting off as a business analyst configuring the good old IMG, Paul swiftly moved on to the wonderful world of ABAP programming. After the initial run of data conversion programs, ALV (ABAP List Viewer) reports, interactive Dynpro screens, and SAPscript forms, he yearned for something more and since then has been eagerly investigating each new technology as it comes out, which culminated in him writing the book *ABAP to the Future*.

Paul became an SAP Mentor in March 2017 and can regularly be found blogging on the SAP Community site and presenting at SAP conferences in Australia (Mastering SAP Technologies and the SAP Australian User Group annual conference), at SAP TechEd Las Vegas, and all over Europe at various SAP Inside Track events. If you happen to be at one of these conferences, Paul invites you to come and have a drink with him at the networking event in the evening and to ask him the most difficult questions you can think of, preferably about SAP.

Acknowledgments

I could not have done this project without the help of others.

I extend my gratitude to Chris Bostian, Larry Nansel, and Brian Brennan, who, after attending a presentation I gave on the subject of ABAP Unit testing to my colleagues in 2011, presented me with the opportunity to undertake a pilot project exploring how automated unit testing could be incorporated into the ABAP development process used at that site.

Thanks go to Dr. Juergen Heymann and Thomas Hammer, both of whom did a magnificent job of preparing and presenting the openSAP course **Writing Testable Code for ABAP** between March and May 2018, through which I realized that what I already knew on this topic was only the tip of the ABAP Unit testing iceberg.

I am very grateful to Paul Hardy for agreeing to undertake the task of reviewing the content of the book and for doing such a magnificent job at it, offering many suggestions for improvement.

Susan McDermott, Rita Fernando, and Laura Berendson, my editors at Apress Media, LLC, were of enormous help in guiding me through the publication process and resolving the technical glitches we encountered along the way.

Finally, it would have been much more difficult to complete this project without the love and understanding I received from my family for tolerating my absences during those long hours on weekends and holidays while I was secluded in deep thought about how to organize and present this content.

CHAPTER 1

Introduction

It is unlikely you still remember the first unit test you ever ran for an ABAP program you wrote. It is very likely you remember the most recent one. It is also very likely that the first and the last, and indeed all those tests in between, consisted of a manual effort executing the program over and over again using various combinations of values to insure the program produced the expected results. This seems to be the unit testing experience for the overwhelming majority of ABAP programmers, who remain pedestrians on the development superhighway when it comes to unit testing. For programmers coding in many other languages, it is commonplace for automated unit testing frameworks to be used as the vehicle whisking them along the software development expressway toward high-quality software.

Because so many ABAP-ers continue to use a unit testing process that is both horribly inefficient and woefully inadequate to the task, you might assume that there is no automated unit testing framework available to ABAP as there is for so many other languages. That would be a false assumption. Not only is there an automated unit testing framework for ABAP but unlike other languages it is seamlessly integrated into the development environment. It is known as the ABAP Unit Testing Framework, or simply ABAP Unit. It has been part of the ABAP tool set since 2004 but remains virtually unknown to many ABAP programmers.

For Whom This Book Is Applicable

This book is applicable to ABAP programmers having little or no familiarity with the concepts associated with automated unit testing for ABAP as well as to ABAP programmers who already are familiar with ABAP Unit testing but who want to explore further its testing capabilities. Though generally applicable to a wide range of programmers having various levels of experience writing ABAP code, from beginners to seasoned experts, and certainly to those who are familiar with object-oriented concepts,

© James E. McDonough 2021
J. E. McDonough, *Automated Unit Testing with ABAP*, https://doi.org/10.1007/978-1-4842-6951-0_1

it is particularly applicable to those ABAP programmers who have not yet become familiar with or comfortable using the object-oriented model for program design.

How This Book Should Be Used

This book is modeled on the "learn by doing" premise. Accordingly, **Appendix A** contains information about retrieving the requirements documentation for the accompanying comprehensive set of executable ABAP exercise programs, with each exercise program illustrating or reinforcing some new concept introduced in the book, from writing the most basic automated test to refactoring a program to enable comprehensive unit testing upon it. This provides for a multitude of options for using the book and doing the corresponding exercise programs, among them:

- Writing each new exercise program based solely on the information provided by the requirements documentation accompanying the collection of executable example ABAP exercise programs. This option might need an occasional supplement of performing comparisons of adjacent versions of the executable example ABAP exercise programs just to reinforce that the correct decisions have been made.

- Writing each new exercise program after looking at how the new concepts were implemented in the corresponding executable example ABAP exercise program. This option probably will require constantly performing comparisons of adjacent versions of the executable example ABAP exercise programs to identify the differences between them.

- Dispensing entirely with writing any code and simply relying on the corresponding executable example ABAP exercise programs to illustrate the implementation.

Consider the following before deciding among the options outlined here. Because there are more than 180 executable example ABAP exercise programs accompanying this book, the easiest of these options, by far, is the last one. It will allow you to proceed through the exercises at the quickest pace, reaching the last exercise program in the shortest period of time. Accordingly, this may be the most tempting option. However, it is most probable that you will learn more about automated unit testing by choosing one of the preceding options. This is because those options will force you to think about what you are doing and to actually write the unit tests, enabling you to try various options with each new exercise so that you can explore the nuances of how automated unit testing actually works. The best way to sharpen your testing skills and to acquire the knowledge and wisdom necessary to implement comprehensive automated unit tests is to experience the satisfaction that comes with wrestling the code into submission by your own hand. Surely it will be more arduous and tedious, and certainly it will take longer to complete all the exercises, but in the end you will have become much more adept at making the decisions required to insure that your program is flexible, robust, and correct.

Refer to **Appendix B** for instructions for retrieving the accompanying collection of executable example ABAP exercise programs and their corresponding diagrams.

Why This Book Was Written

In January 2011, I became aware of ABAP Unit, the automated unit testing feature provided with SAP releases and available directly from the ABAP editor. I began to explore the possibilities of writing these *automated* unit tests for programs in the hope that I could present a convincing case to management for allowing them as an alternative to what until then had been rigid requirements for writing a formal unit test plan using a cumbersome spreadsheet template in which manually executed test results were to be recorded and then saved as a permanent artifact to accompany the software release documentation.

By then I had concluded that the manual spreadsheet process for testing, converted from a text document format well over three years before and taking far too long to execute a single unit test, was ineffective in assessing the quality of the software simply because it left too much to chance whether the actual test would sufficiently cover most parts of the software. Worse, the test plan, prepared by the developer who wrote the software, often was written in a way that assumed much application knowledge on the part of the person running the test, making it virtually useless to some other developer unfamiliar with that application, a discovery I made when I found and tried to run a unit test plan that had been written by someone else years earlier.

MY "AHA!" MOMENT WITH UNIT TESTING

I had first heard about the Agile software development philosophy in late 2008. Over the next year or so, I devoured many of the articles on this topic available on the Internet. This eventually led me to articles about Test-Driven Development (TDD). These TDD articles constantly stressed the importance of writing the unit test prior to writing the corresponding production code, but I found the explanations to be somewhat lacking because my concept of writing the unit test was modeled after the process used at my site, where the unit test was written using a spreadsheet or similar text document, to be executed manually once the production code became available. It was only after months of reading such articles that it finally dawned on me that the tests being discussed in these TDD articles were *automated*, tests that could be executed by the push of a button and run to completion in seconds. It was my "Aha!" moment to realize that the significant characteristic of these unit tests was that they were automated, a word that curiously had been missing from all those articles.

In April 2011, I prepared and presented to my development colleagues a demonstration on the benefits to be gained by using ABAP Unit testing. Also in attendance were some management personnel I had invited. At the conclusion of the demo, I was approached by a few of the managers who asked me whether I could devise a pilot project using software I already had been developing through the current project pipeline. I jumped at the opportunity and in July 2011 made another presentation to three representatives of the combined development and support staff illustrating the ease by which software already flowing through the development process could be thoroughly unit tested *automatically*. Sadly, this presentation was not well received by all who attended.

One point raised was that it took some time to write the code to run the automated unit test, time not currently budgeted with our current process. To this I responded candidly that, yes, it took longer to write the ABAP Unit test code than it would take to prepare an equivalent spreadsheet-based unit test, perhaps an order of magnitude of two or three times as long. However, I continued, although it might take longer to write ABAP Unit test code, there was significant time to be saved because it often took *hours* to run the spreadsheet-based test compared with only *seconds* to run the automated test, pointing out that repeated executions of the spreadsheet-based test would consume the same number of *hours* with each test execution compared with only the same number of *seconds* with each repeated execution of the automated test. Furthermore, in contrast to the spreadsheet-based test plan usually glossing over specific application knowledge possessed by the person both writing and executing it, making it ill-suited for use by anyone other than the author, the automated unit test could be run by any developer, irrespective of their familiarity with the application.

Another point raised was that it would cause more work on the part of maintenance developers who now would need to learn to use this new capability and accommodate it in code where automated unit tests had been included by the original developer, going so far as to suggest that this should be considered grounds for not using automated unit tests. I did not challenge the point but merely agreed that, yes, it might require developers to learn and become more comfortable with this new feature. However, I was flabbergasted that anyone with the authority to manage a software development staff would raise what I considered to be such an indefensible position. Here was a representative of presumably capable developers insinuating that not only did those maintenance developers currently have no knowledge of ABAP Unit testing but neither should they be expected to make any effort to learn it.

Taking that reasoning to its logical conclusion, new software development should employ no technology, technique, or feature that might require a maintenance programmer to keep abreast of the technological improvements constantly being introduced in new releases. This would eliminate many features introduced in SAP releases *more recent than that familiar to the average maintenance developer* from ever being implemented in subsequent development efforts, from the simple use of ALV to the more advanced implications of using object-oriented design.

The three representatives in attendance would later consider the merits of my request for allowing ABAP Unit testing to be used as an alternative to the spreadsheet-based method already in place. About a week later, I received news of their final decision: not only would ABAP Unit testing *not be accepted* as an alternative to the current testing requirements but indeed the use of ABAP Unit testing *would be prohibited* for testing any code going to production. The reason for the draconian ruling, I was told, was due to concerns some of these managers had with perceived problems that ABAP Unit testing code introduces into the production environment.

Despite my attempt to improve the development process, I had succeeded in getting a useful automated testing tool blacklisted not only for myself but also for all the other members of my 30–odd person development staff. A few years later, another developer challenged the prohibition on the grounds that SAP itself recommended using ABAP Unit, and finally its prohibition was rescinded, but not before much new development that might have gained some benefit from its use already had gone to production. I took advantage of the revised policy and gradually began to include ABAP Unit tests with some of my development efforts.

Over time I found that writing ABAP Unit tests helped me to write better production code. My initial approach to using ABAP Unit testing was to write all the production code first and then write the associated automated unit test code later, similar to the process already established at that site where writing the spreadsheet-based test would not be started until after all the production code had been written. What I found was that the attempt to retrofit an automated unit test to my newly completed production code exposed deficiencies in the way the production code was written, requiring that I refactor it to enable a clean test. In other cases, a retrofitted automated unit test I implemented would encounter failures that I suspect I never would have found had I used the spreadsheet-based approach in preparing the test. I soon came to appreciate both the improved thoroughness of testing and the beneficial implications on software design arising from the use of automated unit testing. It is through this book that I want to sing those praises loudly to the ABAP development community.

Credentials of the Author

My formal training in the data processing industry consists of one year at a community college learning mainframe languages (IBM assembler, COBOL, and PL/I) and, nearly 15 years later, a six-week seminar on ABAP programming. Compared with some of my colleagues over the years, I have very little formal training in computer programming. Indeed, the only formal training I had undertaken on the subject of ABAP Unit testing was to attend the openSAP course "Writing Testable Code for ABAP" offered online during March–May of 2018. Everything beyond what I learned in that course I learned on my own. So what makes me think I am qualified to teach anyone else about the associated concepts?

Prior to getting into the data processing industry in 1982, I earned a college degree in music education and taught instrumental music for two years in two different public school districts in the state of New Jersey. During my college years, I made an effort to learn and gain some modicum of proficiency with all of the band and orchestra instruments. My perception then was that I could be a better music educator by understanding more about the struggles students endure when they endeavor to learn to play a musical instrument. How, I thought, could I presume to teach a seventh grader how to play the trombone if I were not able to play it myself?

This philosophy on education served me well those two years I taught in the public schools, and I have continued with this approach ever since. Accordingly, although my credentials in data processing may not be as impressive as those of some of my colleagues, my background as an educator enables me to perceive the problems students are likely to encounter when learning any new skill. So I have learned all I could about ABAP Unit testing, some through the openSAP course noted in the preceding text and some on my own, and over the past few years have been able to employ this feature with some of my ABAP development efforts. I believe that now, having gained a certain level of proficiency in this subject, I am ready to impart what I know to others who also wish to become familiar with this fascinating field of automated unit testing.

Summary

This chapter described how the book should be used as the reader is guided from a reliance upon manual testing of ABAP software to one based on automation. The audience is ABAP programmers. The approach to be used to convey the concepts is based on the "learn by doing" premise. In accordance with that premise, there are exercises the reader is urged to perform to reinforce those concepts, exercises based on a sizable collection of executable example ABAP exercise programs available for download. The reason for writing the book is based on the desire to share with others how they can reduce the time and effort involved in unit testing as well as to reveal the beneficial implications automated unit testing casts upon the design of software.

CHAPTER 2

Preparing to Take the First Step

Automated unit testing offers many new concepts for us to explore, so we will want to be certain we've taken the necessary precautions to insure a successful expedition into this new realm. Accordingly, let's take a moment to prepare ourselves for the adventure we are about to undertake, to pause and give consideration to both the journey itself and the expectations we have about what we will encounter along the way.

Road Map to Automated Unit Testing

A road map is a useful metaphor to illustrate the path we will take from our familiar surroundings of manual unit testing (MUT) to the unfamiliar new territory of automated unit testing. The road map shows us the way. We know we will need to travel the road between these two locations, eventually reaching our destination, but that each step along the way is dependent upon having taken the previous steps. That is, we move continuously in one general direction from our point of origin to our destination, covering each mile as we encounter it, not beginning to cover the tenth mile until after we already have passed through the ninth mile to get there. Accordingly, we become familiar with those parts of the road closest to our point of origin before those parts farther along. As with most such journeys, we find that the terrain associated with the first few steps is very similar to our starting location, but the terrain changes as we continue moving. This similarity of terrain between adjacent steps enables us to adapt gradually to the changes awaiting us along the road.

© James E. McDonough 2021
J. E. McDonough, *Automated Unit Testing with ABAP*, https://doi.org/10.1007/978-1-4842-6951-0_2

So, before we start on our journey from manual unit testing to automated unit testing, let us give some consideration toward preparing for a successful trip:

1. Where are we now?

2. Where are we going?

3. Why are we going there?

4. How are we going to get there?

Where We Are Now

If you are like many other programmers using SAP, you gained your experience writing ABAP programs before SAP introduced the feature known as ABAP Unit testing for facilitating automated unit testing of components written using the ABAP language, or if this feature had been introduced, your organization was not using a release where it was available to you. For most of us, the idea of unit testing never rose to the level of a topic worthy of education, training, and skill development during our careers, so generally we had been left to fend for ourselves when it came time to test a program. Over the years, each of us has collected useful techniques into our own personal bag of tricks to facilitate unit testing a program. Perhaps the one thing many of us share with each other is that unit testing has been and remains a dreaded and time-consuming *manual* process.

So here is where we find ourselves: capable ABAP developers, knowing very little about the new automated unit testing feature, ABAP Unit testing, and knowing even less about how to use it effectively to test ABAP components. It should come as no surprise that many ABAP programmers contemplating whether to learn and use this feature will choose to continue on with their manual testing techniques and avoid the automated unit testing feature so long as the standards in place at the site where they work do not require its use, but other ABAP programmers, who appreciate the significance of this new feature, who have become enlightened to the benefits of automating their unit testing efforts and want to leverage these new capabilities, will undertake to embrace this new feature and use it to their full advantage.

Where We Are Going

Automated unit testing facilities first emerged in the late 1980s when Kent Beck invented such a facility called SUnit for automatically unit testing programs written in the Smalltalk language and became further embraced in the late 1990s with the introduction of JUnit for automatically unit testing Java programs. Since then, a multitude of automated unit testing facilities have been created for various other programming languages.

In our quest to reach this district known as automated unit testing, we are headed for a place which was founded over a quarter century ago and has since grown into a thriving metropolis within the data processing landscape, so it is hardly new. However, it is new to us. This is a place where we will find we'll be able to use these automated unit testing techniques as freely and comfortably as we have with our current comfort level of writing programs using the ABAP language.

Why We Are Going There

We are going there primarily for *four* reasons:

1. Eliminate the drudgery associated with preparing and running manual tests.

    Most of us regard manually writing and running unit tests to be a process filled with dread and agony as we jump out of our comfort zone of programming and into the twilight zone of using spreadsheets and text editors to prepare a document to describe a unit test script. After that horrible experience, we then sit at a computer as we swap back and forth between the session presenting the unit test script and the session executing the software to be tested in a dizzying effort to execute in the software test session the instructions we are reading in the unit test script session. Such testing endeavors, where swapping between sessions is frequent, challenge our ability to pay attention to where we are and what we are intending to do with each swap. It is even worse if we are expected to update the unit test script with results as we step through it.

2. Shift the relatively long time it takes to manually run unit tests to more productive development pursuits.

   Hardly anyone would suggest that manually running a unit test script could be completed anywhere near as rapidly as an automated unit test could complete when one considers that an automated unit test typically runs to completion in a mere fraction of a second. If we were to aggregate all the time we have spent manually running unit tests over our careers, we might find that we have the time to complete all the component refactoring we had been unable to address, attend to all the technical debt that had accumulated over the years, and apply all the performance optimizations to those software components that have begun running more slowly in production and still have time left over for learning some new software feature or sharpening the skills we already possess.

3. Reap the benefits automated unit testing has on software design.

   In many cases, the very attempt to write an automated unit test for a component will reveal any weaknesses in the design of the production software. The inability to find a way to automatically test a component is a smell that should suggest there is a better way to design the software such that it is capable of being automatically tested. Accordingly, the production software design is improved when it is refactored to enable a passing automated unit test to be written for it. Code having such tests often gets better with each change, whereas code without such tests often gets worse with each change.

4. Instill confidence applying changes during maintenance.

   Statistics show that the initial development effort of writing a computer program consumes only a small fraction of the total time spent during its life cycle and that most of the time we devote to programming is in pursuit of maintenance efforts – change.[1]

---

[1]Software maintenance costs can be 75% of software total ownership costs. `https://galorath.com/software-maintenance-costs/`

A significant reason offered by many experts for using an automated unit testing facility is that the tests run so rapidly it encourages the developer to run them frequently. Since automated unit tests can be run at the push of a button and often will complete faster than the time it takes to reach for and push that button, running automated unit tests after applying a maintenance change instantly instills in the developer the confidence that the most recent changes applied have introduced no new bugs.

How We Are Going to Get There

We are going to start where we are most comfortable and familiar and then move slowly and methodically until we have mastered the fundamentals of automated unit testing. This means we shall start from the familiar surroundings of manual unit testing (MUT) as practiced in our hometown of Mutville and travel along the path of least resistance to the automated unit testing (AUT) as practiced at our destination of Autropolis.

Along the way from Mutville to Autropolis, we will pass through the following districts:

- Software Quality

- xUnit

- ABAP Unit

- Rudiments

- Design for Testability

- Test Doubles

- Service Locator

- Leveraging the Service Locator

- Test-Driven Development

- Configurable Test Doubles

- Cultivating Good Test Writing Skills

Each district will present its own unique landscape distinguishing it from the other districts. Although we will use this book primarily to provide the directions for navigating the new terrain, we also will take the opportunity to pause in each district long enough to become more familiar with the new concepts we will encounter by performing exercises designed to strengthen our grasp of the nuances and idiosyncrasies each district has to offer. In the same way that merely reading a book about swimming could not sufficiently prepare us for the experience of actually jumping into the water for the first time, merely reading this book without performing the accompanying exercises similarly would leave us less than sufficiently prepared for the experience of actually using what we will be learning.

The first district we will encounter along the road from Mutville to Autropolis is known as Software Quality, a region where we can learn about what it takes to build good-quality software and the methods through which the level of software quality can be assessed. This is first because it establishes the reasons why we subject software to testing, providing us with a solid foundation for our trek through the remaining districts. This district is covered in Chapter 3.

Once we've learned about the things the Software Quality district has to offer, we'll proceed on to the district known as xUnit, a territory where the residents have transformed the art of unit testing by inventing a way to automate this process. Since it was first established about 30 years ago, it has grown over that time to have a significant impact on many of the languages used throughout the software industry. This district is traversed in Chapter 4.

In Chapter 5, we will explore ABAP Unit, a particular neighborhood of the xUnit district where the primary language spoken is ABAP. The local residents have found ways to adapt the peculiarities of the ABAP language to the same laws, regulations, and customs underpinning the automated unit testing that made the xUnit district famous.

Upon departing ABAP Unit, we'll head for a place known as Rudiments, where the residents have established procedures for engaging in practical activities designed to strengthen our understanding of the basic concepts associated with automated unit testing. This district is explored in Chapter 6.

After leaving Rudiments, we will continue on our way until reaching the district known as Design for Testability, where the residents excel at reorganizing components in such a way that promotes cleaner code while at the same time maintaining the ability to utilize the automated unit testing techniques we learned in Rudiments. Chapter 7 will guide us through this sector.

Farther down the road, we will move through Test Doubles, where the residents have mastered the art of deception and illusion, masquerading as dummy objects, fake objects, mock objects, stubs, and spies. This district is featured in Chapter 8.

After Test Doubles, we will cross into Service Locator, a place where the residents have organized their shared municipal services (animal control, fire alarm certification, tax reassessment, etc.) in such a way that all it takes is a call to the services distributor to arrange for the requested service. In most cases, the requester of a service is oblivious of the entity providing the service. Chapter 9 takes us through this district.

Beyond Service Locator lies Leveraging the Service Locator, where the residents have instituted a process for establishing control over entities providing services to other entities, enabling a service to be provided by the most appropriate entity based on the circumstances of the requester. For instance, the town dog catcher can respond to a resident calling animal control about a stray dog, but a call about a prowling cougar in a neighborhood might elicit a response from both the local police department and the Division of Wildlife Resources to tranquilize and safely move the animal to a remote area. We'll be escorted through this district by Chapter 10.

Next, we will traverse through the TDD district, where we will explore a process known as Test-Driven Development, the skill for which is in abundant supply among the district residents, all of whom are familiar with and adherents of a process whereby an automated test is written even before writing the corresponding production code it is intended to test – effectively putting the cart (test) before the horse (production code). It will be Chapter 11 that leads us through this district.

We will then traverse through Configurable Test Doubles, where the residents have found ways to eliminate the need to write their own explicit test double classes and instead rely on a software framework capable of simulating the presence of actual test doubles. This district is covered in Chapter 12.

Chapter 13 will guide us through the next district, a place known as Obtaining Code Coverage Information. The residents here have developed ways to determine the extent of the code covered by unit tests, enabling them to identify those parts of programs that remain without unit tests.

Next, we will pass through a place known for Cultivating Good Test Writing Skills. The folks who live here have learned many lessons about what makes for good unit tests and are willing to share this wisdom with visitors on their way to Autropolis. This district is covered in Chapter 14.

In Chapter 15, we finally will have reached our destination of Autropolis, where all the things we've learned along the way will enable us to walk the walk and talk the talk with the residents who have contributed to raising automated unit testing into a high art form.

Legacy Code

Our journey to Autropolis will consist of many encounters with ABAP code. Since the year 2000, there have been two different programming paradigms available for writing ABAP: procedural and object-oriented. Perhaps it is because the bulk of customized programs at a site had been written before the object-oriented flavor of ABAP became available that much of the ABAP code we see today is procedural, referred to euphemistically as *legacy code.*

Some testing scholars point out that legacy procedural code presents a more formidable challenge to writing unit tests than would be found with object-oriented code:

> *Legacy code ... often refers to code that's hard to work with, hard to test, and usually even hard to read.*[2]

> *Anyone who has tried to retrofit automated unit tests onto legacy software can testify to the difficulty this raises.*[3]

Gerard Meszaros identifies six kinds of tests and lists them in approximate ascending order of difficulty, with "non-object-oriented legacy software" identified as most difficult:

> *As we move down the list, the software becomes increasingly more chal-lenging to test. The irony is that many teams "get their feet wet" by trying to retrofit tests onto an existing application. ... Unfortunately, many teams fail to test the legacy software successfully, which may then prejudice them against trying automated testing ...*[4]

---

[2]Osherove, Roy, *The Art of Unit Testing,* second edition, Manning, 2014, p. 9

[3]Meszaros, Gerard, *xUnit Test Patterns: Refactoring Test Code,* Addison Wesley, 2007, p. 40

[4]Ibid, p. 176

These quotations may seem alarming, but we will find that all things are relative.[5] My reason for including them is to set the context for how we are going to get to Autropolis. Although it may be much easier to write automated unit tests for object-oriented ABAP, it is far more likely that (1) the bulk of the code at your site is legacy procedural code and (2) there remain many ABAP programmers who have not yet become comfortable with the object-oriented paradigm, so even their new code still is being written in a procedural style. Accordingly, to appeal to the widest cross-section of ABAP programmers, the procedural programming paradigm is used intentionally for the ABAP code examples in this book and the accompanying exercises. Programmers already writing object-oriented code should have no problem adapting the concepts presented in this book to their everyday activities, while programmers unfamiliar with object-oriented programming will not find themselves trudging through code difficult to understand.

Calisthenics

Along the way from Mutville to Autropolis, we will pause occasionally to perform some calisthenics by completing a few of the more than 180 exercises associated with this book. Each exercise presents or reinforces some concept presented in this book by introducing minor code changes into an ABAP program and then executing both its production path and unit test path to observe the effects of those changes. Indeed, some exercises will introduce changes to the program that will become reversed or discarded by a subsequent exercise so that we can more fully understand why some seemingly appropriate implementation techniques should be avoided.

It will take some time, effort, and determination to complete all of the exercises, but the end result is to become comfortable with the techniques used for writing unit tests as well as to understand how a production program can be refactored to enable automated unit testing upon it. As you make your way through the exercises, you may find yourself questioning how a particular exercise is intended to help you understand anything associated with automated unit testing since its practical benefit is not obvious. Perhaps the following anecdote might help.

In the movie *The Karate Kid*, Mister Miyagi asks adolescent Daniel to agree to a pact: in order to learn karate, Daniel is to spend each training day at Miyagi's house

---

[5]A phrase often attributed to Albert Einstein

performing whatever physical training Miyagi asks of him, without question. Daniel agrees, and on the first day, Miyagi shows Daniel the technique he wants used to apply wax to his cars, which Miyagi describes using the phrases "wax on" and "wax off." Daniel complies and is exhausted after spending the day waxing all of Miyagi's many cars.

The next day Miyagi shows Daniel how to "sand the floor," and Daniel spends the day using this technique on all the wooden decks at Miyagi's house. The next day Miyagi introduces Daniel to "paint the fence" and the following day to "paint the house." With each day, Daniel grows more and more frustrated that he is not learning karate, as promised, but is simply spending his time making home improvements to Miyagi's house. Daniel confronts Miyagi, complaining bitterly about all the work he has completed yet still knowing nothing about karate. In a scene exquisitely capturing the essence of "learn by doing," Miyagi stands facing Daniel and asks him to show the motions for "wax on" and "wax off," which Daniel does as Miyagi simultaneously performs the corresponding offensive karate maneuver for which Daniel's motions are the defense. Miyagi continues, having Daniel show the motions for "sand the floor," followed by "paint the fence" and "paint the house," each time attacking Daniel with the corresponding offensive karate maneuver. Afterward, Miyagi bows to Daniel and walks away in silence, leaving Daniel dumbfounded by suddenly realizing how much he has learned about karate without even knowing he was learning it.

Similarly, it is recommended that you simply perform the exercises even though at the time you may not grasp the benefit of having done so. It may not improve your karate skills, though this is only speculation, but certainly it should reinforce and solidify your comprehension of the concepts associated with automated unit testing.

Summary

The road map for traveling from Mutville to Autropolis was presented, specifically that the reader will be traveling along a path leading from the familiar surroundings of their hometown of Mutville, a place where arduous and time-consuming manual unit testing (MUT) still reigns, to the less familiar but highly mechanized town of Autropolis, a place where automated unit testing (AUT) has displaced outdated manual efforts of testing. It has oriented and prepared the reader for the journey, explaining where we are, where we are going, why we are going there, and how we are going to get there. Primarily it will be procedural code used with the examples throughout the book and with the accompanying exercise programs in order to appeal to the largest cross-section of

ABAP programmers. The exercises will require some dedication to complete them all but will serve to improve the ability to design and write unit tests as well as to enhance the skills necessary to refactor code to facilitate automated testing. Some exercises will introduce code eventually discarded in a subsequent exercise, providing an effective illustration for why some testing solutions are not as attractive as they appear on the surface.

CHAPTER 3

Software Quality

Every software component has a quality; it may be low quality, high quality, or somewhere in between. Its level of quality will reflect how well the software component meets the needs of the organization using it. This chapter covers software quality and how it can be evaluated.

The Quality of Software

The capabilities incorporated into a component of software will reflect those characteristics the developer considers most important for the software to possess. These capabilities represent the quality of the software. Some of these qualities relate directly to the reason why the software was written, such as whether the software provides the service for which it was designed. Other qualities relate to the user experience it yields, such as whether interaction with it is intuitive and response time is reasonable. Still other qualities relate to the design of the software, such as whether it can be changed to provide additional features within a reasonable amount of time. Some of these qualities must be present in the software – certainly it must execute correctly – while other qualities can be missing; additional features might take a while to incorporate. Accordingly, we might perceive the quality of software as a hierarchy of levels, with each higher level providing an increase in the quality.

Perhaps the most minimal requirement to be met is that the software component must be capable of providing the correct outcome when it is called upon to perform its most basic and fundamental work. We might refer to this as being capable of providing the expected outcome for the happy path execution. Arguably this is the one thing the software should be able to do correctly even if it is written poorly – it must be *effective*, producing the correct result under the simplest of conditions. This is the lowest level of quality and typically is the first thing programmers will insure the software is capable of doing. There is no lower level because software that cannot do at least this would be regarded as useless.

21

© James E. McDonough 2021
J. E. McDonough, *Automated Unit Testing with ABAP*, https://doi.org/10.1007/978-1-4842-6951-0_3

The next level of quality is where the software is capable of handling invalid input, perhaps described as being able to cope with the unhappy paths of execution. It must be *robust*, able to determine that its basic processing should not be performed unless the input it has been provided is valid. Software that does not have this level of quality is not quite useless because it could still provide the correct processing so long as the input it is provided is valid. Software meeting this level of quality can accommodate more combinations of input and distinguishes between those that are valid and those that are invalid, processing or not processing accordingly. This also seems to be the next capability programmers will infuse into the software.

The next level of quality is where the software is easy to use and capable of diagnosing any invalid input it has been provided. Users will not be happy with software they find difficult to use. Software that does not alert the user of what it found to be incorrect also is not useless, but it can be frustrating to a user who has been provided no information about what the software determined to be faulty. A message such as "invalid input detected" is hardly helpful, so at this level of quality, the software must be *user-friendly* enough to provide the user with ease of use as well as feedback to suggest what the software considers to be incorrect. Programmers who have already insured the software meets the previous two levels of quality will generally select this as its next capability.

The next level of quality is where the software is capable of performing its processing within a reasonable response time. It must be *efficient*. Users will become frustrated and impatient with software that meets the previous three levels of quality but causes them to wait an exorbitantly long time before it completes its work. Programmers who have already insured the software meets the previous three levels of quality will usually find they are applying this level of quality next, perhaps initiated by user complaints of poor software response time.

The next level of quality is where the software is designed in such a way as to enable changes to be applied quickly and easily and without introducing any new problems in the process. The software needs to facilitate *easy maintenance*. Software that meets the previous four levels of quality reflects capabilities directly associated with the user experience, but at this level of quality, the user is indirectly affected. It is only after the user has made a request for a change and, after a reasonable wait, learns the change has not yet been implemented because of software difficult to change that things escalate, prompting the displeased user to squawk about the loss to the business caused by the delay. This level of quality reflects the skill of the programmer, who is or is not able to design the software to facilitate future changes easily, and usually requires a programmer to have many years of experience wrestling with software that was not originally designed to be easily maintainable in order to understand and recognize those software design flaws that prevent rapid change.

In summary, here is the hierarchy of levels of software quality just described:

- Capable of handling the happy path – Effective

- Capable of handling invalid input – Robust

- Easy to use and capable of diagnosing invalid input – User-friendly

- Having been optimized for performance – Efficient

- Conducive to applying changes quickly – Easily maintained

The first four of these quality levels seem to correspond to the sequence of activities specified in a software industry phrase attributed to Kent Beck:

Make it work, make it right, make it fast[1]

The pyramid shown in Figure 3-1 illustrates these levels graphically. The relative width of the various quality levels is intended to suggest that whereas virtually all software components at a site meet the quality standard of the lowest level, the percentage of software components meeting higher levels of quality diminishes with each next level.

---

[1] https://wiki.c2.com/?MakeItWorkMakeItRightMakeItFast

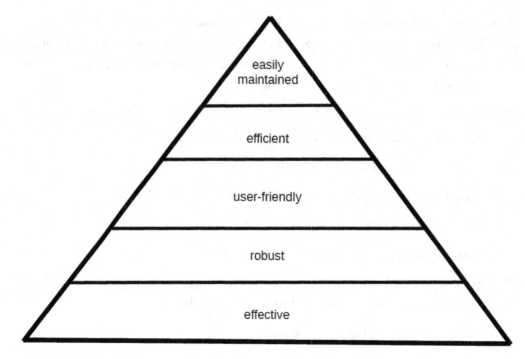

Figure 3-1. *Levels of software quality*

Assessing Software Quality

In the many years since the first computer program was written, a general consensus has emerged that performing unit testing is a necessary activity in the pursuit of insuring high-quality software. The phrase *unit testing* denotes the testing performed by software developers upon the specific components of software under their direct control. It typically is performed in a development environment where software can be changed at will. It gets its name from the fact that the associated testing is being applied to a distinct unit of software, one that cannot reasonably be subdivided into smaller units.

Hardly anyone in the software industry would argue against the need to perform some level of unit testing to assess the quality of software. However, it is the experience of many software developers that unit testing often gets performed in haste or is entirely omitted when tight deadlines are in jeopardy, milestones are being missed, schedules are slipping, and management personnel react to the pressure by urging developers to work longer and harder in an effort to get back on track.

Virtually all of us developers have found ourselves in situations where the delivery of finished software by the expected due date became jeopardized due to difficulties encountered during the development cycle. Under such circumstances, more than a few of us have had to make difficult decisions about where we would devote our attention in the time remaining until the finish date.

Many organizations have devised and published highly detailed development standards in their quest to assure the quality of homegrown software, often with detailed variable naming conventions to which developers are expected to adhere, enforced through manual code inspection procedures where a passing grade often is determined by how well the code reviewer feels the developer has observed the published development standards. Usually such development standards focus on establishing a style of coding intended to be used by all developers under the unquestioned assumption that the code base will be easier to maintain so long as all the code conforms to the same prescribed coding style, with any approach to its unit testing remaining unaddressed and left entirely to the discretion of the developer. Lacking any clear guidance on effective unit testing procedures in the development standards coupled with being assigned to work on a project falling behind schedule, software professionals frequently find themselves choosing thorough unit testing as the activity to be sacrificed at the altar of expediency, a decision perhaps made subconsciously, but regrettable nonetheless.

Indeed, unit testing as it is practiced in many software development organizations is a tedious, arduous manual process involving a lengthy test data preparation stage to be completed prior to running a test consisting of following a script describing the manual steps to be performed. Too often it becomes a burdensome task to be weathered as well as one possibly can as it challenges the stamina and endurance of even the most seasoned practitioners. It is not unusual for the same manual unit test to be run repeatedly as adjustments are made to the software to correct problems encountered during previous test executions.

Perhaps you have had this experience yourself, realizing during the third or fourth time through the same manual unit test that you no longer are reading the associated test script but simply performing by rote what you believe to be the next activity after having become so accustomed to the sequence of steps, later regretting having fallen into this trap once you reach the point where the software is not behaving as expected because you accidentally skipped a step in the test script. When accounts such as these describe the typical experiences developers have with the unit testing procedures at their disposal, then it is no mystery why unit testing becomes one of the first casualties of a development cycle where the scheduled completion date becomes jeopardized.

Whether a development cycle is one in which unit testing activities are partially or fully curtailed or one in which the amount of time allocated toward unit testing activities is regarded as sufficient, it follows that software quality is a consequence of the comprehensiveness of the unit testing to which it had been subjected. To paraphrase Portia's soliloquy in Act IV, Scene I, of William Shakespeare's *The Merchant of Venice*

> *The quality of software is not constrained. It relateth directly to the effort the developer doth invest toward insuring the software is effective, robust, user-friendly, efficient, and easily maintained.*

In short, it is primarily the responsibility of the developer to insure the quality of software, but that quality can be affected by the level of support the developer receives from management for preparing and executing unit tests. At development sites where the developers enjoy substantial management support for their testing efforts, having been allocated the necessary time and resources to reach the goal of high-quality software, it can be expected that the quality would be higher than at sites where management support is weak or absent. So although the developer bears primary responsibility for the quality of the software, the entire team contributes to the level of quality that can be attained.

Much of the drudgery and mistakes normally associated with manual unit testing can be avoided when the unit testing itself is *automated*. This is the idea behind automated unit testing:

> *A unit test is an automated piece of code that invokes the unit of work being tested, and then checks some assumptions about a single end result of that unit. A unit test is almost always written using a unit testing framework. It can be written easily and runs quickly. It's trustworthy, readable, and maintainable. It's consistent in its results as long as production code hasn't changed.*[2]

The computer is capable of executing a unit test far faster than could be achieved manually by a developer sitting at a workstation, and the computer does not suffer from the same attention deficit episodes plaguing developers, so there is no chance it could accidentally skip a step due to having becoming disoriented. Indeed, the whole reason there is a computer industry is to automate what most of us consider to be boring repetitive manual tasks. The next chapter explores further the topic of automated unit testing.

---

[2]Osherove, Roy, *The Art of Unit Testing*, second edition, Manning, 2014, p. 11

Summary

Software quality can be categorized along five ascending levels:

- Capable of handling the happy path – Effective

- Capable of handling invalid input – Robust

- Easy to use and capable of diagnosing invalid input – User-friendly

- Having been optimized for performance – Efficient

- Conducive to applying changes quickly – Easily maintained

The quality of software has been and continues to be assessed through the process of unit testing, an exhausting and time-consuming process when performed manually and fraught with challenges when software delivery schedules are jeopardized. Many of the deficiencies inherent in manual unit testing can be eliminated when such testing can be automated.

CHAPTER 4

The Origins of Automated Unit Testing

ABAP Unit is one of the many automated unit testing frameworks falling under the umbrella term xUnit. This chapter covers what xUnit is and how it came to be.

In the Beginning …

In the 1980s, a fellow by the name of Kent Beck began to experiment with various ways to facilitate automating the task of unit testing programs he had written in the Smalltalk language. By 1989, he had succeeded in creating an automated unit testing framework for Smalltalk programs. This framework was described in a paper he wrote titled "Simple Smalltalk Testing: With Patterns," which in 1998 became Chapter 30 in the book *Kent Beck's Guide to Better Smalltalk*.[1] He named this framework SUnit – "S" for Smalltalk and "Unit" for unit testing framework.

According to Martin Fowler in an article he posted on the Internet, Kent Beck and Erich Gamma found themselves on the same flight from Zurich to Atlanta to attend the 1997 OOPSLA conference. The two pair-programmed during the flight to create the first version of an automated unit testing framework for Java, which came to be known as JUnit. As Fowler states, although SUnit was little known outside the Smalltalk community, "JUnit took off like a rocket – and was essential to supporting the growing movement of Extreme Programming and Test Driven Development."[2]

---

[1]Beck, Cambridge University Press, December 1998
[2]https://martinfowler.com/bliki/Xunit.html

© James E. McDonough 2021
J. E. McDonough, *Automated Unit Testing with ABAP*, https://doi.org/10.1007/978-1-4842-6951-0_4

The Emergence of xUnit

Since then, various other languages have had comparable automated unit testing frameworks created for them, each of which is named following the same convention used with both SUnit and JUnit – the characters preceding the "Unit" portion denote the associated language. Some examples are shown in Table 4-1.

Table 4-1. *Automated unit testing frameworks and their associated languages*

Framework name	Associated language
ABAPUnit	ABAP
CUnit	C
COBOLUnit	COBOL
CppUnit	C++
NUnit	.NET
PHPUnit	PHP

Because all the automated unit testing frameworks for these languages share the same traits, capabilities, and characteristics, they are collectively known by the term *xUnit*, where "x" denotes a generic designation for the associated language.

Features of xUnit

Perhaps the most appealing feature of xUnit automated unit testing frameworks is that the language used to write the unit tests *is the same language used to write the code being tested*. It is therefore out of necessity that we need to distinguish between code intended for production and code used to test the code intended for production.

Other than prototype code, written in a development environment and serving only as the basis for demonstrations and experimenting with capabilities the language provides, code intended for production and having no associated unit testing code never needed such a distinction because there simply was no other type of code. Terms to describe this type of code are

- Production code

- Productive code

- Code intended for production

- System code

Meanwhile, productive code for which there *is* a corresponding unit test also may be described using these additional terms when referenced in the context of running the unit tests:

- Code being tested

- Code under test or component under test (CUT[3])

- Object under test

- System under test (SUT[4])

Finally, the code used to write the unit test itself is referred to as

- Test code

- Unit test code

- Unit test

Having both the productive code and the unit test code written using the same language presents many advantages.

For one, programmers can call upon their vast knowledge and experience of the programming language when writing the unit tests. The structure and syntax of the unit test code must comply with the demands the compiler already places upon the code being tested.

Another advantage is that the unit test code is an integral part of the file containing the code to be tested. This means there is no way for the unit test code to become separated from the code it tests – it is retained in the code repository. How often have you found yourself tasked with making changes to code with which you are not familiar and then trying to find its corresponding unit test? If your experience is anything like

---

[3]This acronym is used prominently in much of the documentation covering unit testing with ABAP

[4]This acronym is used throughout the book *xUnit Test Patterns: Refactoring Test Code* (Meszaros, Addison Wesley, 2007) which presents concepts independent of any specific language

mine, the corresponding unit test, if one had been created, was written using either a text editor (bad enough) or a spreadsheet application (even worse); and it is buried in a separate document repository which offers little hope for finding it easily, if it exists at all.

Yet another advantage is that the automated unit testing code provides working examples of how to invoke the code being tested. Indeed, such unit tests represent the most accurate and up-to-date documentation describing the functionality of the tested software because the tests must always pass. Again, if your experience is anything like mine, that unit test text document or spreadsheet that you have been lucky enough to find in the separate document repository was probably prepared by your predecessor in a way that made sense to the author but is perhaps unintelligible to you. Frequently, programmers will write such unit tests and omit important information which to them seems obvious, leaving others trying to interpret the unit test document to wonder how to proceed with the tests. A good example might be a unit test step which states something like the following:

> *Use transaction ZYX987 to create a rabblefrang document that contains a combination of compatible values for the tillimux and zamitrope attributes.*

If you happen to be familiar with the area of expertise required to understand what is needed to create such a document, then you are in luck, but too often a statement like this is such a showstopper to the next programmer as to render the unit test useless. However, when the automated unit test is written in the language of the code to be tested, it is easy to determine how to create a rabblefrang document because the unit test actually performs this step. As a consequence, one can learn from the unit test itself how to do this, even though knowing the process no longer is necessary since the unit test already is quite capable of performing that step without any help at all from the next programmer.

Another feature of xUnit automated unit testing frameworks is that the tests themselves are *self-checking*. Gerard Meszaros, author of *xUnit Test Patterns: Refactoring Test Code*, describes the self-checking characteristic of unit tests this way:

> *A Self-Checking Test has encoded within it everything that the test needs to verify that the expected outcome is correct. Self-Checking Tests apply the Hollywood principle ("Don't call us; we'll call you") to running tests. That is, the Test Runner "calls us" only when the test did not pass; as a consequence, a clean test run requires zero manual effort.*[5]

---

[5]Meszaros, Gerard, *xUnit Test Patterns: Refactoring Test Code*, Addison Wesley, 2007, p. 26

The Test Runner appearing in the preceding statement is a reference to a component of the automated unit testing framework capable of running the tests for the language in which the tests are written.

xUnit testing frameworks enable testing at an individual module level. That is, each of their tests focuses on the validity of a small fragment of code and not on the validity of an entire integrated system. As such, these tests may be written for software elements such as classes, subroutines, and functions. Taken together, all the unit tests written for the software elements contained within the same source code file represent a *test harness* capable of asserting the validity of all the associated software elements.

Perhaps the most important feature of xUnit testing frameworks is that they facilitate fast test execution. How fast? *Very, very fast!!* In the simplest case of a small module with a few unit tests, it might return a message that all the tests had run and passed before the user is even able to focus their eyes on the message. In more complicated cases, it might take a few seconds. It depends on many factors, not the least of which are how well structured the production program modules are for performance optimization, how well the tests are written, how much load is on the computer at the time the tests are run, whether any required resources to complete running a unit test are available and functioning, and perhaps even whether the Moon is in the seventh house and Jupiter is aligned with Mars.

Robert C. Martin says the following about how fast automated unit tests should run:

Tests should be fast. They should run quickly.[6]

Yes, it will take some time to write the automated unit tests. Occasionally, it will take the same amount of time as it takes to write a unit test script counterpart in the form of a text document or spreadsheet. In other instances, it may take twice or three times as long to write the automated unit testing code. Indeed, you may find that a comprehensive unit test for a module contains far more testing code than the production code it is testing. But the point is that once the automated unit test is written, it takes far, far less time to execute than possibly could be attained through a manual execution. Accordingly, when the unit tests run rapidly, the developer is much more likely to execute them not only more frequently but also *while the development is underway*, gaining valuable feedback about the module at a time when it is easiest to implement design changes.

---

[6]Martin, Robert C., *Clean Code: A Handbook of Agile Software Craftsmanship*, Prentice Hall, 2009, p. 132

I have my own tale of having written a long and comprehensive unit test script as a text document in 2007 to test new ABAP software I had written. The test script was long and excruciatingly detailed because I not only wanted to enable some other developer to run this same unit test (which eventually became necessary) without having to know anything about the application but was also afraid that over the next few years I would need to run it again and might have forgotten so much about it that I would have to relearn how to prepare its test data. Manually running the unit test script took an exhausting *10 hours* to complete, which included preparing much of the test data that would be consumed by the test. I recall that I had to run this unit test about eight times before I found the software to be satisfactory. So you could say that it took all of 2 weeks of 8-hour workdays for me to run this unit test the number of times necessary for it to pass everything as I had expected. I feel certain that had I known at the time about the xUnit testing feature available with ABAP, it might have taken about 4 days to write the necessary unit tests and then I might have been able to run the tests to completion in a few seconds. Indeed, I believe it would have taken less time to write all of the xUnit tests than it took for me to write that excruciatingly detailed unit test script as a text document.

xUnit also is well suited to facilitate Test-Driven Development (TDD). TDD is one of the Agile software development methodologies and consists of a short cycle of activities designed to produce a test for some fragment of production code prior to actually writing the production code itself:

1. Write a new executable test.

2. Run all tests to confirm the new test fails.

3. Write production code to make the new test pass.

4. Run all tests to confirm they all pass.

5. Refactor production code as necessary and rerun all tests.

6. Repeat from step 1.

We will explore TDD further in a subsequent chapter.

Phases of xUnit Tests

One of the ways unit tests resemble the production components they test is that they contain a series of statements executed to produce a desired result. The desired result should be easily discernible to a reader of the unit test. A test containing complicated logic to establish all the conditions necessary for a successful test or to confirm its results can have a detrimental effect on the ability of the reader to quickly understand the purpose of the test. A unit test should clearly impart its intent. Gerard Meszaros addresses this issue of clarity with xUnit tests:

> *How do we structure our test logic to make what we are testing obvious? We structure each test with four distinct parts executed in sequence.*[7]

Meszaros goes on to describe what he calls the Four-Phase Test consisting of the following phases[8]:

- Setup

- Exercise

- Verify

- Teardown

The Setup phase consists of establishing the conditions necessary to insure that the component under test will exhibit the behavior expected of it. This may include acquiring or creating test data to be used during the test, setting global variables to specific starting values, and making it possible to examine the result of running the test. It establishes a starting state for the component under test and those components with which it will interact during the course of the test.

The Exercise phase is where the unit test interacts with the component under test. This typically involves the unit test causing the component under test to be executed.

The Verify phase consists of confirming whether the Exercise phase produced the expected results.

The Teardown phase consists of setting the environment back to the same state it was in prior to the start of the Setup phase, effectively reestablishing a clean slate.

---

[7]Meszaros, Gerard, *xUnit Test Patterns: Refactoring Test Code*, Addison Wesley, 2007, p. 358
[8]Ibid

Organizing an xUnit test this way enables readers to determine at a glance what is being verified by the test, contributing to the goal of having the unit test serve as documentation for the component under test, clearly identifying how the component can be used as well as what results can be expected from it.

Roy Osherove offers a similar sequence of steps he refers to as *Arrange-Act-Assert*. According to him, a unit test usually comprises three main actions:

1. Arrange objects, creating and setting them up as necessary.

2. Act on an object.

3. Assert that something is as expected.[9]

Writing xUnit Tests

Each xUnit test framework provides its own protocol through which unit test authors can assert the validity of a software module. Usually this consists of a set of assertion methods, defined by a single class supplied with the framework, that can be called by the test author. These assertion methods typically test the relationship between an actual value and an expected value to determine whether the code that produced the actual value passes or fails the assertion. When the assertion is true, the test passes; when false, the test fails.

For example, let's say we have the following pseudo-code for a fragment of production code

```
subroutine getSign
  if number is greater than 00
    sign = '+'
  else
    if number is less than 00
      sign = '-'
    else
      sign = ' '
    endif
  endif
endsubroutine
```

---

[9]Osherove, Roy, *The Art of Unit Testing*, second edition, Manning, 2014, p. 27

along with the following pseudo-code for its corresponding unit test:

```
testPositive
  set thisNumber = 55
  call subroutine getSign sending thisNumber receiving sign
  call xUnitAssert.isEqual actualValue = sign
                          expectedValue = '+'
                          failureMessage = 'Sign assertion failed'
```

The production code of subroutine *getSign* inspects a *number* parameter it has been sent and, based on whether the number is positive, negative, or zero, will set the corresponding *sign* parameter accordingly.

Meanwhile, the test code of *testPositive* sets the variable *thisNumber* to 55. It then calls the *getSign* subroutine sending the parameter *thisNumber* and receiving the parameter *sign*. This is followed by a call to method *isEqual* of static class *xUnitAssert* which asserts whether *actual* value in variable *sign* is equal to the *expected* value '+'. When the value in variable *sign* is equal to '+', then the assertion passes, and the *failureMessage* parameter is ignored. This is the result we should expect with the pseudo-code as written in the preceding text.

Let's suppose instead that the test pseudo-code had been written as follows:

```
set thisNumber = 55
call subroutine getSign sending thisNumber receiving sign
call xUnitAssert.notEqual actualValue = sign
                         expectedValue = '+'
                         failureMessage = 'Sign assertion failed'
```

The only difference between this example and the previous one is that the test code invokes method *notEqual* of class *xUnitAssert* instead of method *isEqual*. In this case, we should find that the assertion fails and that the xUnit testing framework will present some type of report to include the message "Sign assertion failed."

Accordingly, the user is presented with an assertion failure report only when one or more of its self-checking tests have failed. Otherwise, the user typically is presented with some simple message indicating that all tests have passed.

Those unit tests which require some special preparation to be executed can specify what is known as a *fixture*. A fixture consists of a set of actions to be taken to prepare one or more tests for execution. This could include setting values for global variables, reading and applying configuration settings, preparing test data for the test to use, and any other type of activity required to establish the preconditions necessary to test the assertion.

The general sequence of steps for executing a unit test consists of the following:

1. Setup – Establish the fixture.

2. Run a unit test.

3. Teardown – Restore to a pre-setup state.

A collection of unit tests all using the same fixture is known as a *test suite*.

Often a single module of production code will require multiple tests to thoroughly assert its validity. Let's see this with an example using the same production pseudo-code from the preceding text with the following three unit tests defined to test every possible path through subroutine *getSign*:

```
testPositive
  set thisNumber = 55
  call subroutine getSign sending thisNumber receiving sign
  call xUnitAssert.isEqual actualValue = sign
                           expectedValue = '+'
                           failureMessage = 'testPositive assertion failed'

testZero
  set thisNumber = 00
  call subroutine getSign sending thisNumber receiving sign
  call xUnitAssert.isEqual actualValue = sign
                           expectedValue = ' '
                           failureMessage = 'testZero assertion failed'

testNegative
  set thisNumber = 00 - 55
  call subroutine getSign sending thisNumber receiving sign
  call xUnitAssert.isEqual actualValue = sign
                           expectedValue = '-'
                           failureMessage = 'testNegative assertion failed'
```

As you can see in the preceding code, we now have defined

- A test named *testPositive*, which will assert that the value '+' is returned from subroutine *getSign* when it is sent a *positive* number

- A test named *testZero*, which will assert that the value ' ' is returned from subroutine *getSign* when it is sent a number *equal to zero*

- A test named *testNegative*, which will assert that the value '-' is returned from subroutine *getSign* when it is sent a *negative* number

The number of logical paths defined within a module will determine the number of tests required to execute each of those logical paths.

xUnit testing frameworks require the freedom to run the tests of a test suite in any order. As such, the unit test author has no control over the sequence in which unit tests will be run. This imposes upon the unit test author the discipline to insure that there are no dependencies between individual unit tests. That is, the unit test author should not structure unit tests in such a way that the execution of unit test *testB* is dependent upon unit test *testA* having been run first and leaving something behind for *testB* to use. To do so, whether intentionally or not, exposes the tests to failures occurring from what Gerard Meszaros calls *Interacting Tests*:

> *Every test needs a starting point. As part of our testing plan, we take care that each test sets up this starting point, known as the test fixture, each time the test is run. This … helps us avoid Interacting Tests by insuring that tests do not depend on anything they did not set up themselves.*[10]

Advantages of xUnit Tests

A policy of implementing and running xUnit tests at a site as opposed to a policy of writing and executing manual unit tests will offer the following advantages:

- All unit tests are *automated* – the tests can be run at the press of a button.

- The unit tests are embedded with the production code – they cannot get lost or misplaced.

---

[10]Meszaros, Gerard, *xUnit Test Patterns: Refactoring Test Code*, Addison Wesley, 2007, p. 5

- No need to have any special application knowledge to prepare the unit test for execution.

- No need to have any special application knowledge to be able to run the unit test.

- No need to remember what should be the result of each unit test.

- No need to inspect a report of test results to determine simply that all tests have passed.

Summary

The xUnit philosophy, embraced by many of those in the software industry, has laid the foundation for the features and characteristics incorporated into automated unit testing frameworks adhering to its principles. Its origin is traced from the Smalltalk SUnit testing framework first conceived and developed by Kent Beck to the Java JUnit framework that popularized this approach to unit testing to the central role it plays in Test-Driven Development (TDD). Its concept of fixtures enables establishing a fresh unit testing environment for multiple unit tests. Its foundation of four phases – Setup, Exercise, Verify, and Teardown – provides a viable model for writing and organizing *self-checking rapidly executing* unit tests using the same language and code repository as used to develop the code to be tested. When compared with manual unit testing, the advantages xUnit provides include tests embedded with the production code, preventing them from getting lost, and alleviating the person running the tests from needing to know anything about how to prepare, run, and determine the results of the tests.

Quiz #1: xUnit Concepts

Now that you are familiar with the concepts associated with xUnit, test your knowledge by completing the following quiz. See Appendix B for the answers when you're done.

Multiple Choice: Select the Best Answer

1. xUnit describes

    A. Manual code–driven testing frameworks

    B. Automated code–driven testing frameworks

    C. Consolidated code–driven testing frameworks

2. xUnit enables testing at the

    A. Internet level

    B. System level

    C. Module level

3. xUnit facilitates

    A. Test-Driven Development

    B. Extreme programming

    C. Seat-of-the-pants development

4. xUnit tests are implemented as

    A. Breakpoints

    B. Conditions

    C. Assertions

5. xUnit facilitates preparing a test through

    A. Dynamic definition

    B. Fixture

    C. Collection

6. The order in which xUnit tests are executed

    A. Is the order in which they appear

    B. Is dependent on test attributes

    C. Should not matter

True or False

Advantages of using xUnit testing include

1. No need to remember what the test result should be
2. Elimination of user testing
3. Tests are automated
4. Reduction in requests for changes
5. No need to think about how to implement logic
6. No need to write the same test more than once
7. Can substitute for design discussions
8. Enables testing of peripheral systems

The phases of xUnit can be described using the word sequence

9. Ready, Set, Go
10. Arrange, Act, Assert
11. Setup, Exercise, Verify, Teardown
12. Open, Test, Close

CHAPTER 5

Automated Unit Testing with ABAP

With the concepts underlying xUnit now familiar to us, this next chapter covers how ABAP Unit provides the xUnit capabilities to the ABAP language.

ABAP Unit

ABAP Unit is the implementation of xUnit testing for the ABAP language. It first became available with ABAP release 6.40 (2004). These tests may be written for the following types of components containing ABAP code:

- Executable programs
- Class pools
- Function groups
- Module pools
- Subroutine pools

In conformance with the principles of xUnit testing frameworks, unit tests for ABAP are written using the ABAP language, are embedded with the object containing the production code, and may specify a testing fixture. Although the Code Inspector (transaction SCI) and the ABAP Unit Browser (an option available via SE80) provide options for executing ABAP Unit tests, perhaps the most common way to do this is via the editor used to create the ABAP code to be tested. For instance, while an ABAP report is being edited via the ABAP editor (transaction SE38), the corresponding unit tests can be run via a simple selection from the menu or through its designated keyboard shortcut. The advantage of this is that the unit tests can be run without having to leave

© James E. McDonough 2021
J. E. McDonough, *Automated Unit Testing with ABAP*, https://doi.org/10.1007/978-1-4842-6951-0_5

the editor to do so – passing tests will be noted so with a status message appearing at the bottom of the screen, while failing tests will cause the ABAP Unit Result Display report to be presented. Accordingly, the developer can, in only a few seconds, make a change to a report, activate those changes, and then run the associated unit tests to confirm that nothing has been broken by the most recent change.

Because they are written in ABAP, unit tests are subject to the same syntax requirements for production code, and because the tests are embedded with the production code, they also are subject to the same policies and constraints established for source code management. By default, ABAP Unit test code *is not* compiled into a production environment. Why not? Well, it would be unwise to enable in a production environment the execution of testing components which can leave behind permanent changes to configuration, new financial postings, deletion of master data, and other such persistent changes made to the environment by the unit tests themselves. An incidental benefit of this default is that the unit test code does not contribute to the size of modules in production.

Further information about ABAP Unit can be obtained from within the SAP environment itself by following these simple steps:

- From any ABAP editor (SAP ECC 6.0 onward)

1. Click the "Help on..." button appearing on the ABAP editor button bar.

2. Select ABAP Glossary.

3. Select the entry for ABAP Unit.

4. Click the "More" button appearing at the end of the definition.

The ABAP Unit Testing Framework

The implementation of the ABAP Unit automated testing feature is provided through the set of components comprising the *ABAP Unit Testing Framework*. This testing framework consists of a collection of executable programs along with a set of global static classes through which the author of a unit test may invoke the assertion services offered by the testing framework.

Conceptually, the ABAP Unit Testing Framework is composed of the following components:

- Unit test preparation components

    - ABAP Language Extensions

    - Testing Framework Test Assertion Interface

- Unit test execution components

    - ABAP Unit Test Environment Configuration

    - ABAP Unit Test Runner

    - ABAP Unit Test Results Report

Figure 5-1 illustrates this arrangement graphically.

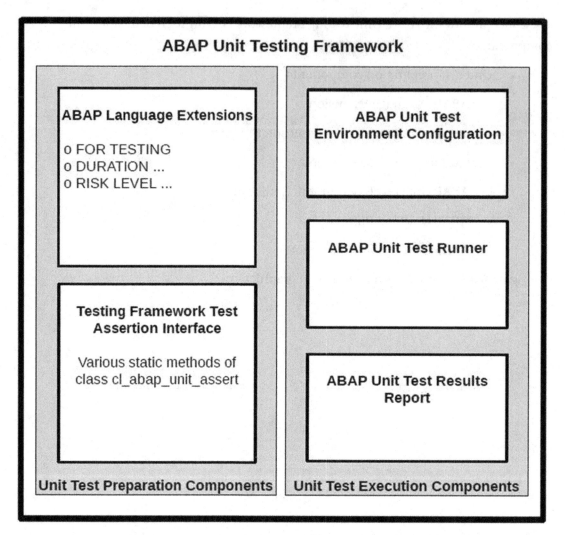

Figure 5-1. *Graphical illustration of the ABAP Unit Testing Framework components*

Each of these components is explained in further detail in subsequent sections.

Requirements for Writing ABAP Unit Tests

Among the requirements for writing ABAP Unit tests is that the tests themselves must be written as local classes which are designated specifically as test classes. This is so that the ABAP Unit Testing Framework can recognize them as ABAP unit tests and run them accordingly. Let's explore each of these requirements in more detail:

Classes

> The object-oriented model of programming must be used to
> define an ABAP Unit test.

Local

> Not only must the tests be defined using classes but those classes
> must be written as *local classes*, meaning the tests cannot be
> created using the Class Browser (SE24) but only by using the same
> editor as used to create the associated code to be tested.[1]

Designated specifically as test classes

> The class definition statement needs to include the additional
> clause FOR TESTING to denote that the local class is an ABAP
> Unit test class.

Before continuing, let me put many of you at ease. It has been my experience that the term "object-oriented," when used in discussions with developers of ABAP code, elicits various levels of fear, anxiety, and revulsion by those unfamiliar with this programming model, despite its availability with the language since R/3 4.6 (1999). Although writing ABAP Unit tests will require that the object-oriented ABAP statements be used to define classes and their respective methods, writing such tests will not require an intimate familiarity with every concept and nuance of object-oriented design. If unfamiliar with the object-oriented design concepts available to ABAP programming, refer now to **Appendix C** for an overview of the subset of object-oriented ABAP statements and syntax necessary for writing ABAP Unit tests.

Note   If you have no experience using object-oriented concepts and language syntax with ABAP programs, then you certainly will gain some after you have completed all of the exercises associated with this book.

Not only do the unit tests need to be written as local classes but the methods of those unit test classes that are to be invoked by the Test Runner need to be designated

---

[1]Except, of course, the Class Browser is used to define the local test classes used for testing global classes

specifically as test methods having no signature. Let's explore each of these requirements in more detail:

Designated specifically as test methods

The METHODS statement needs to include the additional clause FOR TESTING to denote that the method is an ABAP Unit test method to be invoked by the Test Runner.

Method having no signature

A method designated as an ABAP Unit test method will be invoked directly by the Test Runner of the ABAP Unit Testing Framework. When the Test Runner calls the method, it cannot be expected to provide any appropriate values for any of the arbitrary parameters the author might want to include in the method signature. As such, methods designated as test methods cannot have a signature.

Types of Components Applicable to Unit Testing

Another misconception associated with writing ABAP Unit tests is that these tests are capable of testing only ABAP components which also are written using the object-oriented model. This is false, false, false! In fact, ABAP Unit tests can be defined for any of the following types of ABAP components:

- Executable programs
- Class pools
- Function groups
- Module pools
- Subroutine pools

Though the tests themselves must be written as local object-oriented classes, the components those classes are capable of testing can be written using any valid ABAP program design, including a component using only those ABAP statements that were available in the release preceding the introduction of classes with ABAP. That is, a simple report, written long before the Great Pyramids of Egypt were built, composed only of a start-of-selection event block and a few FORM-ENDFORM subroutines certainly can be retrofitted with newly defined ABAP Unit tests. Indeed, the example programs associated with this book show exactly this capability by describing how to provide automated ABAP Unit tests to a simple report program originally written with no object-oriented statements at all.

Testable ABAP Modularization Units

In their book *Official ABAP Programming Guidelines,* authors Horst Keller and Wolf Hagen Thümmel state the following about modularization units:

> *The key modularization units or callable units within an ABAP program are referred to as processing blocks. In this context, you distinguish between procedures on one side and dialog modules and event blocks on the other side. While dialog modules and event blocks are called from the dynpro flow logic or from the event processing of the ABAP runtime environment, procedures are provided for a direct call from an ABAP program.*[2]

They subsequently clarify the scope of what is included in procedures:

- "Procedures include the following

  - *Methods*

  - *Function modules*

  - *Subroutines*"[3]

It is these *procedures* that are the modularization units that can be tested through automated unit tests because it is procedures that can be called directly by an ABAP Unit test. So let's expand upon the list of component types and describe what it is within these components that can be tested:

- Executable program

  This type of ABAP component is capable of containing procedures defined as both subroutines and methods of local classes. Both its subroutines and its methods of the local classes are eligible candidates for testing by automated unit tests.

---

[2]Keller, Horst and Thümmel, Wolf Hagen, *Official ABAP Programming Guidelines*, Galileo Press, 2010, p. 287
[3]Ibid

- Class pool

   This type of ABAP component is capable of containing procedures defined as methods of the global class as well as methods for any local classes it may contain. Its methods defined for both the global class and local classes are eligible candidates for testing by automated unit tests.

- Function group

   This type of ABAP component is capable of containing procedures defined both as function modules and as subroutines. Both its function modules and its subroutines are eligible candidates for testing by automated unit tests.

- Module pool

   This type of ABAP component is capable of containing procedures defined as both subroutines and methods of local classes. Both its subroutines and its methods of the local classes are eligible candidates for testing by automated unit tests.

- Subroutine pool

   The purpose of a subroutine pool has changed since it was first introduced:

   Subroutine pools were – as their name suggests – originally intended for subroutines that were called from other programs. Because subroutines, and particularly their external call, are declared as obsolete within these programming guidelines, this intended use for subroutine pools is no longer given. Instead, subroutine pools are proposed as independent containers for local classes because they are hardly impacted by the implicit processes of the ABAP runtime environment otherwise.[4]

   The new purpose of subroutine pools is to serve as containers for the local classes associated with an OO transaction. Regardless of whether a subroutine pool still contains subroutines written

---

[4]Keller, Horst and Thümmel, Wolf Hagen, *Official ABAP Programming Guidelines*, Galileo Press, 2010, p. 54

a long time ago by a programmer now far, far away or contains a collection of local classes to service an OO transaction, both its subroutines and the methods of the local classes are eligible candidates for testing by automated unit tests.

Having been so clearly defined in the book *Official ABAP Programming Guidelines*, the term *procedures* is what will be used throughout the remainder of this book to refer generically to subroutines, function modules, and methods of a class when the discussion about the automated unit testing of ABAP components is applicable to all three of them. Also, just to make it abundantly clear and unmistakable what is meant by these three terms

- A subroutine is composed of a set of ABAP statements appearing between the statements FORM and ENDFORM.

- A function module is composed of a set of ABAP statements appearing between the statements FUNCTION and ENDFUNCTION.

- A method is composed of a set of ABAP statements appearing between the statements METHOD and ENDMETHOD.

Automatic Generation of ABAP Unit Test Classes

Test classes may be generated automatically for global classes and function modules. The corresponding editor provides a test class generation wizard that can be invoked to guide the programmer through this process:

- For function modules

  On the Function Builder initial screen, select Utilities ➤ Test Classes ➤ Test Class Generation.

- For global classes

  On the Class Builder: Change ... screen, select Utilities ➤ Test Classes ➤ Generate.

Unfortunately, automatic test class generation is not available for any other types of components, and even the test class generation wizard for function modules and global classes only partially automates this task:

- The wizard only generates calls to method assert_equals.

- After the wizard generates the code for the unit test class, the author manually must perform the following tasks:

  - Complete the code for invoking the code under test.

  - Specify the expected value to be compared with actual value produced by the code under test.

  - Specify any text of message to be issued with an assertion failure.

TALKIN' 'BOUT MY GENERATION

Although I have used the Class Builder wizard only occasionally over the years, I have retained virtually none of its generated code. Instead, I have chosen only to allow the wizard to generate the code into the corresponding unit test containers associated with the class, saving me the trouble of having to select them manually via the menu. Then once the code was generated, I discarded all of it and wrote the unit test the way I felt it should be written. For the most part, I found the generated code to consist mainly of incomprehensible comments formatted using html tags and only a few associated ABAP statements, statements usually not pertinent at all to the type of test I intended to write.

One of the problems associated with using such unit test class generators, aside from the need to manually modify the generated code anyway, is that they depend on the existence of function modules in a function group or methods of a global class in order to determine the content of the generated code. This may be acceptable if you are retrofitting legacy code with unit tests or you are using the development model of writing the production code before writing the associated tests. If, however, you are using the development model of writing the unit test code prior to production code, such as the Test-Driven Development (TDD) model, described in further detail in a subsequent chapter, then these wizards are simply not applicable since the code they generate depends upon the corresponding production code existing already.

ABAP Language Statements Related to Unit Testing

The ABAP language has been enhanced to enable a programmer to clearly distinguish between classes that are for production code and classes that are intended to facilitate automated ABAP Unit testing. In the latter category, we already have seen that the FOR TESTING clause was added to the ABAP language for use with both the class definition statement and the METHODS statement. This is only one of the ways in which the ABAP language has changed to accommodate the xUnit testing capabilities afforded by the ABAP Unit Testing Framework. Here is a more complete description of the ABAP language statements related to unit testing:

- FOR TESTING

    This clause is applicable to both the class definition statement and methods statement. When applied to a methods statement, it denotes a method that is to be recognized by the ABAP Unit Testing Framework as a method to be invoked by the Test Runner. When applied to a class definition, it denotes a class that is relegated solely for use by the ABAP Unit Testing Framework.

    A class that defines a method containing this clause also must contain this clause on its class definition statement.

    A class having this clause on its class definition statement will be subject to the following:

    - None of its members will be accessible by productive code.

    - Unless overridden by a system start-up value, it will not be compiled into a production system.

- RISK LEVEL <level>

    This is an optional clause to be included on the class definition statement. It indicates a relative level of risk associated with the execution of the unit test class. It is to be followed by a word designating the associated risk of running all of its unit test methods. The value <level> may indicate any of the following words:

    - CRITICAL (default)

    - DANGEROUS

    - HARMLESS

53

Each risk level word indicates a risk level severity relative to the other two words. The SAP online documentation suggests the following explanations for these levels[5]:

- CRITICAL – Such as changes to system settings or customizing

- DANGEROUS – Such as changes to persistent data

- HARMLESS – No effects on persistent data or system settings

- DURATION <relative length of time>

   This also is an optional clause to be included on the class definition statement. It indicates a relative duration of the time it should take to complete the execution of all the unit tests defined for the class. It is to be followed by a word designating the cumulative time to execute all its unit test methods. The value <relative length of time> may indicate any of the following words:

- SHORT (default)

- MEDIUM

- LONG

Each duration word indicates a length of elapsed time relative to the other two words. The SAP online documentation suggests the following explanations for these durations[6]:

- SHORT – Within the blink of an eye.

- MEDIUM – Take a sip of tea.

- LONG – Get another cup.

There are actual ABAP Unit Testing Framework configuration settings associated with both the RISK LEVEL and DURATION clauses, settings that will be discussed in a subsequent section.

---

[5]ABAP Keyword Documentation ➤ CLASS ➤ class_options ➤ FOR TESTING ➤ Test properties
[6]Ibid

Writing an ABAP Unit Test

So how is a local ABAP Unit test class defined? In the example to follow, we will see both a procedural and object-oriented version of the same production code to be tested by a local ABAP Unit test class, but will start with the object-oriented version. First, let's see an example of what might be considered the most minimal local class of any kind that can be defined, as shown in Listing 5-1.

Listing 5-1. Minimal local class

```
class some_local_class definition.
  public section.
    class-methods do_something.
endclass.
class some_local_class implementation.
  method do_something.
  endmethod.
endclass.
```

Here we see the complementary definition and implementation components of a class named some_local_class which has a single empty static method named do_something. This class is hardly usable as it is written, so let's update it so that its sole method will provide the sum of two numbers, as shown in Listing 5-2.

Listing 5-2. Local class with method providing sum of two numbers

```
class some_local_class definition.
  public section.
    class-methods get_sum
                  importing
                    addend_01
                      type i
                    addend_02
                      type i
                  exporting
                    sum
                      type i
```

```
endclass.
class some_local_class implementation.
  method get_sum.
    sum = addend_01 + addend_02.
  endmethod.
endclass.
```

That's much better! This class now is providing the service of returning the sum of two numbers. This shall be considered our *code under test* (CUT). To write a unit test for this code, we'll start with the same complementary class definition and implementation components, as shown in Listing 5-3.

Listing 5-3. Local class with only complementary class definition and implementation components

```
class some_test_class definition.
endclass.
class some_test_class implementation.
endclass.
```

Add to that the FOR TESTING clause on the class definition statement, as shown in Listing 5-4 with changes highlighted in bold.

Listing 5-4. Local class identified as one to be used for testing

```
class some_test_class definition for testing.
endclass.
class some_test_class implementation.
endclass.
```

Add to that the RISK LEVEL clause on the class definition statement, as shown in Listing 5-5 with changes highlighted in bold.

Listing 5-5. Local class for testing identified with minimal risk level

```
class some_test_class definition for testing risk level harmless.
endclass.
class some_test_class implementation.
endclass.
```

Add to that a private, empty method definition having no signature, as shown in Listing 5-6 with changes highlighted in bold.

Listing 5-6. Test class defining empty private method

```
class some_test_class definition for testing risk level harmless.
  private section.
    methods test_for_get_sum.
endclass.
class some_test_class implementation.
  method test_for_get_sum.
  endmethod.
endclass.
```

Add to that the FOR TESTING clause on the METHODS statement, as shown in Listing 5-7 with changes highlighted in bold.

Listing 5-7. Test class indicating its method is identified as one to be used for testing

```
class some_test_class definition for testing risk level harmless.
  private section.
    methods test_for_get_sum for testing.
endclass.
class some_test_class implementation.
  method test_for_get_sum.
  endmethod.
endclass.
```

Provide its method implementation with some code to invoke the productive code, as shown in Listing 5-8 with changes highlighted in bold.

Listing 5-8. Unit test method with implementation for calling static method get_sum of class some_local_class

```
class some_test_class definition for testing risk level harmless.
  private section.
    methods test_for_get_sum for testing.
endclass.
```

```
class some_test_class implementation.
  method test_for_get_sum.
    constants addend_01 type i value 17.
    constants addend_02 type i value 30.
    data       sum        type i.
    call method some_local_class=>get_sum
      exporting
        addend_01 = addend_01
        addend_02 = addend_02
      importing
        sum        = sum.
  endmethod.
endclass.
```

And finally provide its method implementation with some code to apply an assertion test on the result of invoking the productive code, as shown in Listing 5-9 with changes highlighted in bold.

Listing 5-9. Unit test method containing assertion against value returned by static method get_sum of class some_local_class

```
class some_test_class definition for testing risk level harmless.
  private section.
    methods test_for_get_sum for testing.
endclass.
class some_test_class implementation.
  method test_for_get_sum.
    constants addend_01 type i value 17.
    constants addend_02 type i value 30.
    data       sum        type i.
    data       expected_sum type i.
    call method some_local_class=>get_sum
      exporting
        addend_01 = addend_01
        addend_02 = addend_02
      importing
        sum        = sum.
```

```
      expected_sum = addend_01 + addend_02.
      call method cl_abap_unit_assert=>assert_equals
        exporting
          act = sum
          exp = expected_sum
          msg = 'Unexpected sum'.
    endmethod.
endclass.
```

The statement calling static method *assert_equals* of class *cl_abap_unit_test* is requesting an assertion that the actual value (parameter *act*) returned from the call to static method *get_sum* of class *some_local_class* is equal to the expected value (parameter *exp*). Also included on this statement is a message (parameter *msg*) to be written to the ABAP Unit Result Display report in the event the assertion fails, and the ABAP Unit Result Display report is presented.

Now let's combine the code under test from Listing 5-2 and the unit test class from Listing 5-9 into a real executable program, the source code for which is shown in Listing 5-10, with new lines highlighted in bold.

Listing 5-10. Executable program containing production class and its corresponding unit test

```
report.
class some_local_class definition.
  public section.
    class-methods get_sum
                    importing
                      addend_01
                        type i
                      addend_02
                        type i
                    exporting
                      sum
                        type i
endclass.
class some_local_class implementation.
  method get_sum.
```

```
    sum = addend_01 + addend_02.
  endmethod.
endclass.

parameters: addend01 type int4
          , addend02 type int4
          .

data      : sum type int4
          .

start-of-selection.
    call method some_local_class=>get_sum
      exporting
        addend_01 = addend01
        addend_02 = addend02
      importing
        sum       = sum.
    message i000(OK) with 'Sum is' sum.

class some_test_class definition for testing risk level harmless.
  private section.
    methods test_for_get_sum for testing.
endclass.
class some_test_class implementation.
  method test_for_get_sum.
    constants addend_01 type i value 17.
    constants addend_02 type i value 30.
    data      sum        type i.
    data      expected_sum type i.
    call method some_local_class=>get_sum
      exporting
        addend_01 = addend_01
        addend_02 = addend_02
      importing
        sum        = sum.
    expected_sum = addend_01 + addend_02.
    call method cl_abap_unit_assert=>assert_equals
```

```
      exporting
        act = sum
        exp = expected_sum
        msg = 'Unexpected sum'.
    endmethod.
endclass.
```

Here we have done the following:

- Preceded the "code under test" class (some_local_class) with a report statement

- Followed the definition of some_local_class with the definition of an initial selection screen (parameters statement) defining two signed integer fields to be used to accept from the user the values to be added together

- Followed that with the definition of a global data field (sum) to receive the sum of the specified numbers

- Followed that with the classic ABAP event block start-of-selection containing two statements:

  - The first statement invokes method get_sum of class some_local_class and places the result into data field sum.

  - The second statement issues an information message showing the sum just calculated.

- Followed that with the "unit test" class (some_test_class)

This defines both an executable program and one that contains an automated unit test. From within the ABAP editor (SE38), it can be executed by clicking Execute (F8) and can have its automated unit tests run by selecting the appropriated menu path (Ctrl-Shift-F10).

When this unit test is executed and there is no failure of the assertion, the user will see a status message at the bottom of the screen such as (in this case)

```
Processed: 1 program, 1 test classes, 1 test methods
```

Accordingly, a successful unit test will result in a status message appearing at the bottom of the screen, whereas a failing unit test will result in presenting the ABAP Unit Result Display report, allowing the developer to see which unit tests have failed and why.

Let's examine this unit test class more closely. The FOR TESTING clause appearing on the class definition statement is a proclamation to the ABAP Unit Testing Framework that this class contains no production code. The RISK LEVEL HARMLESS clause appearing on the class definition statement is a proclamation to the ABAP Unit Testing Framework that this class does not affect configuration or persistence repositories or leave behind permanent changes that would affect subsequent operation of the SAP environment. The FOR TESTING clause on the METHODS statement is a proclamation to the ABAP Unit Testing Framework that this method should be invoked by its Test Runner. Together, these clauses defined on the class definition and methods statements enable the ABAP Unit Testing Framework to do the following:

- Read the definitions of all the test classes contained in the ABAP component.

- Identify those methods of test classes that are to be invoked by the Test Runner of the ABAP Unit Testing Framework.

- Recognize that no permanent change will result from running the associated unit tests (via RISK LEVEL HARMLESS) and compare this with the unit testing framework environmental settings to determine whether the unit test class may be executed.

- Invoke each of the methods designated FOR TESTING, one after the other, retaining any information arising from assertion failures.

- At the completion of running all unit tests, depending on whether any assertion failures had been encountered, present either a success status message or the ABAP Unit Result Display report.

To run the test described in the preceding text exactly as it is written should take less time than it would take you to snap your fingers. How's that for fast unit test execution?! Try it for yourself and see.

Also, just to prove the point that automated unit tests can be written for classic ABAP procedural components and not just those written using the object-oriented statements, let's convert the process performed by the "code under test" – some_local_class – into a corresponding subroutine. Listing 5-11 shows what the code would look like, with differences highlighted in bold.

Listing 5-11. Executable program containing single subroutine and its corresponding unit test, with changes highlighted

```
report.
class some_local_class definition.
  public section.
    class-methods get_sum
                       importing
                         addend_01
                           type i
                         addend_02
                           type i
                       exporting
                         sum
                           type i
endclass.
class some_local_class implementation.
  method get_sum.
    sum = addend_01 + addend_02.
  endmethod.
endclass.

parameters: addend01 type int4
          , addend02 type int4
          .
data      : sum type int4
          .

start-of-selection.
    call method some_local_class=>get_sum
      exporting
        addend_01 = addend01
        addend_02 = addend02
      importing
```

```
    sum          = sum.
    perform get_sum using addend_01
                          addend_02
               changing sum.
    message i000(OK) with 'Sum is' sum.

form get_sum using addend_01 type int4
                   addend_02 type int4
          changing sum        type int4.
    sum = addend_01 + addend_02.
endform.

class some_test_class definition for testing risk level harmless.
  private section.
    methods test_for_get_sum for testing.
endclass.
class some_test_class implementation.
  method test_for_get_sum.
    constants addend_01 type i value 17.
    constants addend_02 type i value 30.
    data      sum        type i.
    data      expected_sum type i.
    call method some_local_class=>get_sum
      exporting
        addend_01 = addend_01
        addend_02 = addend_02
      importing
        sum          = sum.
    perform get_sum using addend_01
                          addend_02
               changing sum.
    expected_sum = addend_01 + addend_02.
    call method cl_abap_unit_assert=>assert_equals
      exporting
        act = sum
        exp = expected_sum
```

```
      msg = 'Unexpected sum'.
  endmethod.
endclass.
```

Here we have done the following:

- Discarded class some_local_class.

- Defined a new subroutine (form-endform) named get_sum and
  placed it after the start-of-selection event block; its single statement
  adds the two numbers of its using clause parameters and places the
  result in its changing clause parameter, just like what had been done
  in method get_sum of the discarded class some_local_class.

- Discarded the statement in the start-of-selection event block
  invoking method get_sum of class some_local_class and replaced it
  with a statement to perform subroutine get_sum.

- Discarded from method "test_for_get_sum" of unit test class "some_
  test_class" the statement invoking method get_sum of class some_
  local_class and replaced it with a statement to perform subroutine
  get_sum.

Listing 5-12 shows how the code would look without all the highlighting and stricken
lines.

Listing 5-12. Executable program containing single subroutine and its
corresponding unit test, without changes highlighted

```
report.

parameters: addend01 type int4
          , addend02 type int4
          .

data      : sum type int4
          .

start-of-selection.
    perform get_sum using addend_01
                          addend_02
                 changing sum.
```

```
    message i000(OK) with 'Sum is' sum.

form get_sum using addend_01 type int4
                   addend_02 type int4
         changing sum       type int4.
    sum = addend_01 + addend_02.
endform.

class some_test_class definition for testing risk level harmless.
  private section.
    methods test_for_get_sum for testing.
endclass.
class some_test_class implementation.
  method test_for_get_sum.
    constants addend_01 type i value 17.
    constants addend_02 type i value 30.
    data      sum        type i.
    data      expected_sum type i.
    perform get_sum using addend_01
                          addend_02
                 changing sum.
    expected_sum = addend_01 + addend_02.
    call method cl_abap_unit_assert=>assert_equals
      exporting
        act = sum
        exp = expected_sum
        msg = 'Unexpected sum'.
  endmethod.
endclass.
```

If you were to create a program like that shown in Listing 5-12, you would find that it produces the same result as the previous version either when executed or its unit tests are run. Although we have seen with this simple example the same new functionality of production code to be tested written using both the procedural and object-oriented models, the recommendation for writing new code destined for production is to use the object-oriented model as it offers greater flexibility with both program design and unit testing, as will become evident in subsequent chapters.

Using Fixture Methods

As unit tests become more comprehensive in testing the productive code, it may be necessary to define a fixture to facilitate establishing a known test state on behalf of each unit test prior to its execution. This can be achieved through the use of the following reserved method names defined for a unit test class:

```
class_setup
setup
teardown
class_teardown
```

None of these fixture methods are required. A unit test does not require a fixture, but when defined for a unit test class, they are invoked automatically by the ABAP Unit Testing Framework. Their intent is to establish or reset the preconditions necessary for invoking the unit test methods defined for the unit test class in which they appear. They are shown in the same logical sequence they would be invoked during the life of a unit test class execution:

- class_setup

  This static fixture method is automatically invoked only once, prior to invoking the first unit test method executed for the unit test class. It enables establishing fixture preconditions applicable to all unit test methods defined within the same class. A good example of its use might be to create an internal table of records intended to be used by all of the unit test methods, an activity that would only need to be done once and not each time a unit test method is executed. It bears a conceptual similarity to the static constructor method (class_constructor) defined for a class in that it is automatically invoked only once before any other activity of the class occurs.

- setup

  This instance fixture method is automatically invoked prior to invoking each unit test method defined for the unit test class. It enables establishing fixture preconditions just prior to the execution of each individual unit test method defined within

the same class. A good example of its use might be to set global
variables to specific values such that each unit test method
starts its execution with the same global variable values, an
activity that would need to be done each time a unit test method
is about to be executed. It bears a conceptual similarity to the
instance constructor method (constructor) defined for a class in
that the setup method is automatically invoked first with each
unit test execution, just as the instance constructor method is
automatically invoked first with each new class instantiation.

- teardown

  This instance fixture method is automatically invoked upon
  completion of each unit test execution. It enables restoring the
  SAP environment to its state prior to invoking the most recently
  executed unit test method.

- class_teardown

  This static fixture method is automatically invoked only once
  upon completion of the last unit test method executed for the unit
  test class. It enables restoring the SAP environment to its state
  prior to invoking the first unit test method.

Just to reinforce how these fixture methods are invoked automatically by the ABAP
Unit Testing Framework. Listing 5-13 shows an example of a unit test class named tester
having definitions for three unit tests simply named unit_test_01 through unit_test_03
along with definitions for all of the fixture methods described previously.

Listing 5-13. Example of unit test class defining all fixture methods and three
unit test methods

```
class tester definition for testing risk level harmless.
  private section.
    class-data    class_setup_calls     type i.
    class-data    class_teardown_calls type i.
    data          setup_calls           type i.
    data          teardown_calls        type i.
    class-methods class_setup.
```

```
      class-methods class_teardown.
      methods        setup.
      methods        teardown.
      methods        unit_test_01 for testing.
      methods        unit_test_02 for testing.
      methods        unit_test_03 for testing.
endclass.
class tester implementation.
  method class_setup.
    add 01 to class_setup_calls.
  endmethod.
  method setup.
    add 01 to setup_calls.
  endmethod.
  method unit_test_01.
    break-point.
  endmethod.
  method unit_test_02.
    break-point.
  endmethod.
  method unit_test_03.
    break-point.
  endmethod.
  method teardown.
    add 01 to teardown_calls.
  endmethod.
  method class_teardown.
    add 01 to class_teardown_calls.
  endmethod.
endclass.
```

Notice that each of the unit test methods contains only a break-point statement, whereas the fixture methods contain only a statement to increment a corresponding counter. When an ABAP component containing this unit test definition is subjected to a unit test execution, it will cause each of the break-point statements to present the ABAP debugger. With the ABAP Unit Testing Framework, we cannot be certain of the order in which the unit test methods of this unit test class will be invoked, but let us assume for the moment that they are called in the sequence shown in Table 5-1. If, upon encountering each break-point statement, we were to use the debugger to inspect the values for each of the attributes defined for this unit test class, we would find the following attribute values for the following unit test method executions.

Table 5-1. *Unit test method execution call counts to fixture methods*

Unit test method execution	Value of attribute class_setup_calls	Value of attribute setup_calls	Value of attribute teardown_calls	Value of attribute class_teardown_ calls
unit_test_01	1	1	0	0
unit_test_02	1	2	1	0
unit_test_03	1	3	2	0

Notice that when the break-point statement presents the debugger during the execution of test method unit_test_01, the fixture methods class_setup and setup already have been called once. This confirms that these fixture methods are automatically called by the Test Runner because we provided no explicit calls to these fixture methods within the unit test method. Notice also that when the break-point statement presents the debugger during the execution of test method unit_test_02, fixture method class_setup still has been called only once, but fixture method setup now has been called twice and fixture method teardown has been called once. Finally, notice that when the break-point statement presents the debugger during the execution of test method unit_test_03, fixture method class_setup still has been called only once, but fixture method setup now has been called three times and fixture method teardown has been called twice. With this example, there are no calls registered for fixture method class_teardown when any of the break-point statements are encountered because that method will not be called until after the last unit test method of the unit test class has completed its execution.

Roy Osherove advises caution when choosing whether to use fixture methods:

The setup method is easy to use. In fact, it's almost too easy – enough so that developers tend to use it for things it wasn't meant for, and tests become less readable and maintainable as a result. Also, setup methods have limitations, which you can get around using simple helper methods ...[7]

Osherove continues afterward to qualify the several ways that programmers abuse the setup method, including using it to initialize objects used by only some of the test methods, writing code in the setup method that is difficult to understand due to its length, and using it for the instantiation of fakes and mock objects. He states he no longer uses the setup method with his tests, disparaging it as a relic that arose during an era of unit testing that has since faded into history, superseded by more modern approaches made possible by advances in technology. He offers the following conclusion:

Setup and teardown methods in unit test can be abused to the point where the tests or the setup and teardown methods are unreadable. Usually the situation is worse in the setup method than the teardown method. ... I've several times written full test classes that didn't have a setup method, only helper methods being called from each test, for the sake of maintainability. The classes were still readable and maintainable.[8]

Invoking the Services of the ABAP Unit Testing Framework

In the preceding section, we saw in Listing 5-9 a glimpse of how a unit test determines whether or not the test has passed or failed. This was through the call to static method *assert_equals* of class *cl_abap_unit_test*. Class cl_abap_unit_assert is the primary mechanism by which unit tests are determined to have passed or failed. Through the methods of this class, the unit test author is provided with a way to communicate with the Test Runner during test execution. Depending on which method of class cl_abap_unit_assert is called and the values provided for its parameters, the Test Runner will determine whether the result of the call represents a passing or failing condition for the

---

[7]Osherove, Roy, *The Art of Unit Testing*, second edition, Manning, 2014, p. 166
[8]Ibid, p. 184

unit test. When a failure condition is detected, the Test Runner will collect and retain information about the unit test, information to be presented in the ABAP Unit Result Display report at the conclusion of the unit test run.

Class cl_abap_unit_assert has a multitude of static methods that can be used to determine whether the unit test passes or fails. Table 5-2 shows the name of the static method along with its returning parameter name (if any) and its importing parameters.

Table 5-2. *Static methods of class cl_abap_unit_assert*

Method	Returning	Importing							
ABORT				MSG		QUIT	DETAIL		
ASSERT_BOUND	ASSERTION_FAILED	ACT		MSG	LEVEL	QUIT			
ASSERT_CHAR_CP	ASSERTION_FAILED	ACT	EXP	MSG	LEVEL	QUIT			
ASSERT_CHAR_NP	ASSERTION_FAILED	ACT	EXP	MSG	LEVEL	QUIT			
ASSERT_DIFFERS	ASSERTION_FAILED	ACT	EXP	MSG	LEVEL	QUIT	TOL		
ASSERT_EQUALS	ASSERTION_FAILED	ACT	EXP	MSG	LEVEL	QUIT	TOL	IGNORE_HASH_SEQUENCE	
ASSERT_EQUALS_FLOAT	ASSERTION_FAILED	ACT	EXP	MSG	LEVEL	QUIT	RTOL		
ASSERT_FALSE	ASSERTION_FAILED	ACT		MSG	LEVEL	QUIT			
ASSERT_INITIAL	ASSERTION_FAILED	ACT		MSG	LEVEL	QUIT			
ASSERT_NOT_BOUND	ASSERTION_FAILED	ACT		MSG	LEVEL	QUIT			
ASSERT_NOT_INITIAL	ASSERTION_FAILED	ACT		MSG	LEVEL	QUIT			
ASSERT_NUMBER_BETWEEN	ASSERTION_FAILED			MSG	LEVEL	QUIT	LOWER	UPPER	NUMBER
ASSERT_SUBRC	ASSERTION_FAILED	ACT	EXP	MSG	LEVEL	QUIT	SYSMSG		
ASSERT_TABLE_CONTAINS	ASSERTION_FAILED			MSG	LEVEL	QUIT	LINE	TABLE	
ASSERT_TABLE_NOT_CONTAINS	ASSERTION_FAILED			MSG	LEVEL	QUIT	LINE	TABLE	
ASSERT_TEXT_MATCHES	ASSERTION_FAILED			MSG	LEVEL	QUIT	PATTERN	TEXT	
ASSERT_THAT	ASSERTION_FAILED	ACT	EXP	MSG	LEVEL	QUIT	SYSMSG		
ASSERT_TRUE	ASSERTION_FAILED	ACT		MSG	LEVEL	QUIT			
FAIL				MSG	LEVEL	QUIT	DETAIL		

The importing parameters appearing in **bold** are not optional. Notice how every method has a message parameter (MSG) and a flow control parameter (QUIT) and that every method other than ABORT has a failure severity level parameter (LEVEL).

The value specified for the failure severity level (LEVEL) parameter may be any of the following:

Value	Description	Corresponding constant
0	Tolerable	IF_AUNIT_CONSTANTS=>TOLERABLE
1	Critical	IF_AUNIT_CONSTANTS=>CRITICAL (default)
2	Fatal	IF_AUNIT_CONSTANTS=>FATAL

The value specified for the flow control (QUIT) parameter may be any of the following:

Value	Description	Corresponding constant
0	Continue with test	IF_AUNIT_CONSTANTS=>NO
1	Quit the current test method	IF_AUNIT_CONSTANTS=>METHOD (default)
2	Skip/quit all tests of current test class	IF_AUNIT_CONSTANTS=>CLASS
3	Skip/quit all tests of current program	IF_AUNIT_CONSTANTS=>PROGRAM

Methods FAIL and ABORT seemingly serve the same purpose and have nearly identical signatures. The SAP online help text explains the distinction between these methods as follows:

> *[Method abort()] raises an unconditional alert, similar to the fail() method. The semantics are however different. abort() is used to tell ABAP Unit that a test case was not executed due to a failed prerequisite to perform the test. fail() is used to signal a failed test case.*[9]

---

[9]SAP online help text. To access via SE38, locate or create a call to method abort of class cl_abap_ unit_assert in one of the unit test methods, place the cursor on the method name, and press F1.

For those methods providing a returning parameter, checking the returning value can be used to determine whether some additional processing is to be performed based on whether the assertion passed or failed. This would be applicable only to those methods called with the parameter "quit = no" since any other value for the quit parameter would cause the unit test code to be exited immediately, providing no opportunity for the unit test to perform any additional processing.

Calls to the appropriate static methods of class cl_abap_unit_assert should appear in the unit tests after the corresponding productive code has been invoked, such as shown in the preceding section in Listing 5-10 where the following call to static method assert_equals is invoked after the call to static method get_sum of productive code class some_local_class:

```
call method cl_abap_unit_assert=>assert_equals
  exporting
    act = sum
    exp = expected_sum
    msg = 'Unexpected sum'.
```

Despite the completely valid use of the "call method" statement shown in the preceding code to invoke the services of the ABAP Unit Testing Framework, it is more likely that you will find such calls using the functional method call format, as shown in the following:

```
cl_abap_unit_assert=>assert_equals(
  act = sum
  exp = expected_sum
  msg = 'Unexpected sum'
  ).
```

TOLERATION

All the unit tests I have written were at client sites where there were two different development clients in the same SAP instance: one client was used for the creation and maintenance of the ABAP software, and the other client was used solely for testing. The testing client had much more robust test data available for unit testing, in some cases having records in customized tables for which its counterpart client would have no records at all in those same tables.

Accordingly, I found it handy to issue a tolerable failure message when the unit tests were run in the environment where there were no records available in the customized tables used by the unit tests, along with a corresponding message indicating that there was no test data available in that client. This made it easy to spot that I had mistakenly run the unit test in the wrong client – because it issued tolerable (yellow) failure messages – as opposed to running it in the correct client and getting critical (red) failure messages because the unit tests were actually failing.

When deciding whether a failing assertion should be accompanied by a level of tolerable (so it appears as a warning) or a message providing further clarification, consider that the users who will see these failures are ABAP programmers. Accordingly, message severity and content should reflect the level of technical expertise associated with programmers and not be restricted to the type of messages issued through production code which typically assumes a user with a less technical background.

KNOW YOUR AUDIENCE

In 2019, in pursuit of a dual-language requirement for customized programs, I wrote a utility program to automatically retrofit ABAP components by converting their text literals into text elements. The utility produced a set of ALV reports describing all of the changes applied. I provided for the ability to run in simulation mode so that the programmer could first see what would be changed before actually choosing to commit those changes. Some report messages, such as "component ZYX is not locked under an active transport," were reported as warnings when run in simulation mode but as errors when run in update mode. This was only one of a set of language conversion utilities written by others and me to be used by all the programmers on the development staff.

After this utility had been available for a while, I began getting calls from other programmers who were getting failure messages during runs in update mode. I asked whether the utility was run first in simulation mode. "Yes," was the answer, "but I got no failures during that run." The discussion continued using a screen-sharing application where both of us could see what was happening. After running the utility again in simulation mode, the report contained a series of warning messages indicating that some of the components of the program that would require updating were not locked on a transport. These same warnings subsequently were being displayed as errors during the update run.

It has been my experience that ABAP programmers have learned to ignore warnings, whether issued during activation of components or a transport process or via the extended program check utility. In the preceding case, the programmer was ignoring the warnings issued during a simulation mode run of the text literals retrofitter utility. Accordingly, your audience for ABAP Unit testing will be ABAP programmers, so use the level=tolerable qualifier with caution.

ABAP Unit Test Runner

In the game of baseball, a player who manages to get on base is known as a *base runner*. The term is a specific reference to a person playing for the team at bat. In contrast, when it comes to unit testing, the term *test runner* does not refer to the person who initiates a unit test, but instead refers to a component of the unit testing framework.

The ABAP Unit Test Runner is the component of the ABAP Unit Testing Framework responsible for executing a unit test. Typically, it is triggered via a menu path selected or a keyboard shortcut issued from within the ABAP editor. When invoked, it will

1. Identify all the unit test classes within the compilation unit.

2. Invoke each of the unit test methods of each of the unit test classes, accumulating information about each one.

3. Present one of the following:

   A. A **status message** indicating the number of compilation units, test classes, and test methods found within the body of the source code. Such a message, if issued, is an indication that all unit tests have passed.

   B. The **ABAP Unit Result Display** report, a set of reports indicating, among others, the names of the test classes found and their respective test methods, a status associated with each unit test invoked, and one or more messages associated with each of those. If this set of reports is presented, it is an indication that invoking one or more of the specified unit test methods resulted in a warning or a failure.

The Test Runner will identify unit test classes as those having the FOR TESTING clause on their class definition and will identify unit test methods as those having the FOR TESTING clause on their method definitions.

The unit test class definition clause RISK LEVEL will determine whether or not its unit tests are run during a unit test execution. This value will be compared with the ABAP Unit testing environment settings to determine whether it is safe to run the unit tests in that environment. These environment settings are configurable via the transaction SAUNIT_CLIENT_SETUP, which will be covered in a subsequent section.

The unit test class definition clause DURATION will determine whether the elapsed time during the execution of a specific unit test class exceeds a threshold and accordingly should be discontinued. If so, it will cause the ABAP Unit Result Display report to be presented along with an applicable warning message for the corresponding unit test class.

In describing the properties of a good unit test, Roy Osherove states "It should run quickly."[10]

I have found that the Test Runner of the ABAP Unit Testing Framework is very fast indeed, typically executing a complex set of unit test classes in only a fraction of a second. Accordingly, it seems to provide the necessary speed for complying with the properties Roy Osherove lists for a good unit test, enabling us to run the unit tests often and not suffer for having to wait for them to finish.

Unit Test Results Report

The ABAP Unit Test Runner will collect information about each unit test it executes. When it has completed running the final unit test, it will determine whether there had been any test execution failures. If so, it will present the ABAP Unit Result Display report. This full-screen report will show information about all unit test methods for all the unit test classes contributing to the test run.

---

[10]Osherove, Roy, *The Art of Unit Testing*, second edition, Manning, 2014, p. 6

Figure 5-2 shows an example of an ABAP Unit Result Display report presented for one of the accompanying example unit test programs.

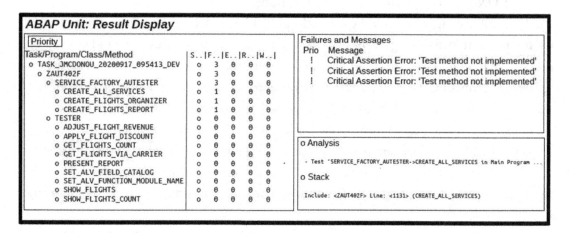

Figure 5-2. *Example of an ABAP Unit Result Display report presented for one of the accompanying example unit test programs*

As illustrated in Figure 5-2, a tree structure appears on the left side of the screen which, when fully expanded, contains four node levels. The top node indicates in its name the userid, system, date, and time of execution. Beneath that is a node indicating the name of the component containing unit test classes that have been run. The next node level indicates the names of each participating unit test class, and the next indicates the names of the associated unit test methods. Each node is accompanied by columns indicating its status, number of failed assertions, number of exception errors, number of runtime aborts, and number of warnings. The status is indicated by an LED icon: green indicates passed; red indicates failure; yellow indicates a warning.

The right side of the screen is divided into an upper and lower area. The upper area shows the messages associated with the selected tree node, and the lower area shows further analysis and navigation capability to the associated code for the message selected in the upper area. The content of the tree structure and the areas to the right of it are presented using ALV within containers that may be resized to fit the preferences of the user through dragging and dropping the separating bars.

Clicking once an entry in the tree structure will change the content of the areas to the right. Clicking once a message in the upper-right area will change the content of the lower-right area. Clicking once an entry appearing in the Stack section of the lower area will present the associated lines of code where the message was issued.

Initiating ABAP Unit Test Execution

There are a variety of ways to initiate the execution of ABAP Unit tests. Probably the most typical way to do so is through an ABAP editor, whether the standard ABAP editor used to create and maintain programs and reports (SE38 and SE80) or one of the more specialized ABAP editors, such as those associated with the Function Builder (SE37) or the Class Builder (SE24). Why is this probably the most typical? It is because executing unit tests while within an ABAP editor will provide the most timely and useful feedback for your development efforts. Whereas ABAP Unit tests can be executed through utilities that do not involve an ABAP editor, software developers who would use *only* such utilities to run automated unit tests would be imposing upon themselves an unnecessary handicap.

Initiating Unit Tests from Within an ABAP Editor

The ABAP Unit Testing Framework has been seamlessly integrated into the ABAP editors so that unit tests can be run without having to leave the editor. Here are the ways to initiate executing the associated ABAP Unit tests from within the various ABAP editors:

- From the ABAP editor (SE38)

  Select from menu: Program ➤ Test ➤ Unit Test.

- From the Function Builder (SE37)

  Select from menu: Function Module ➤ Test ➤ Unit Test.

- From the Class Builder (SE24)

  - When in the method editor

    Select from menu: Method ➤ Unit Test.

  - When not in the method editor

    Select from menu: Class ➤ Unit Test.

- From the Object Navigator (SE80)

  Right-click the component in the Repository Browser to present the context menu. Then ...

  - For programs, select

    Execute ➤ Unit Test

  - For function groups, select

    Unit Test

  - For classes/interfaces, select

    Test ➤ Unit Test

Once the unit tests initiated through the ABAP editor have completed executing, the Test Runner will present one of the following:

- When all unit tests have run successfully, a status message will appear at the bottom of the screen indicating what was executed. Here are some examples of such messages, with their differences attributable to different releases of the ABAP Unit Testing Framework producing them:

  - Unit tests processed successfully; 1 programs, 2 classes, 7 methods

  - Processed: 1 programs, 2 classes, 7 methods

  When any one of the unit tests fails, then the **ABAP Unit Result Display** report is presented.

Initiating Unit Tests from Outside an ABAP Editor

The ABAP Unit Testing Framework also has been seamlessly integrated into other utilities associated with analyzing and reporting on ABAP code, utilities not dependent upon an ABAP editor for their use. Here are some of the ways to initiate executing the associated ABAP Unit tests from outside an ABAP editor:

- From the Code Inspector (SCI)

  - On the Code Inspector initial screen, click the **Create** button appearing in the Inspection block.

- On the Code Inspector Inspection screen, in the Object Selection block, select the **Single** radio button, in the slot to the right of that indicate **Program**, and in the slot to the right of that supply the **name of the program** to be unit tested.

- In the Check Variant block, select the **Temporary Definition** radio button.

- On the next Check Variant screen, select the **Temporary Definition** radio button and place a checkmark only in the checkbox associated with **Dynamic Tests** (first uncheck the checkbox for List of Checks to uncheck all other checkboxes).

- On the next Code Inspector Inspection screen, click the **Execute** icon.

- From the ABAP Unit Browser

  - Invoke Object Navigator (SE80).

  - Select **ABAP Unit Browser** from among the pushbuttons in the upper-left section of the screen.

Note   To make the ABAP Unit Browser pushbutton available, do the following:

- Select from the Object Navigator menu: Utilities ➤ Settings.

- Select tab Workbench.

- Select the checkbox for ABAP Unit Browser.

  - **Select a component** which has ABAP Unit code written for it.

  - To **execute a specific test class**, right-click the test class name to present the context menu and then select **Execute Test Class**.

  - To **execute all test classes**, right-click the component name to present the context menu and then select **Execute Test**.

These utilities offer the capability to execute the associated unit tests by personnel other than the author of the code. In the case of the Code Inspector, it can be configured to run the unit tests for multiple programs, function modules, and classes in a single execution. Accordingly, it might be considered most useful in performing a final mass unit test execution before a collection of associated components is released for subsequent quality assurance testing.

Evolution of the ABAP Unit Testing Framework

With its introduction in 2004, SAP has since updated, refined, and improved the ABAP Unit Testing Framework. Releases since 2009 (7.0 EhP2 and later) include the static class `cl_abap_unit_assert` and its methods through which the unit test author can invoke the services of the testing framework. This class is relatively recent and was not included with version 1.0 of the ABAP Unit Testing Framework. Instead, the first release of the ABAP Unit Testing Framework provided the author with access to its services via this class: `cl_aunit_assert`.

It seems that over time the folks at SAP might have had second thoughts about the name of this class, deciding that perhaps "aunit" was not as descriptive as "abap_unit," and so defined a completely new class with the more descriptive name.

The original class cl_aunit_assert is still available in releases where class cl_abap_unit_assert is available. The implementation of each method defined in class cl_aunit_assert delegates its respective processing to its counterpart method defined in class cl_abap_unit_assert. Accordingly, tests written using the methods of either of these static classes will provide the same processing.

Class cl_aunit_assert also provides aliases for public static constants not defined in class cl_abap_unit_assert, such as these operands applicable to the level parameter

- tolerable
- critical
- fatal

and these operands applicable to the quit parameter:

- no
- method
- class
- program

These are actually aliases for the constants defined in interface if_aunit_constants, which also could be used to specify operands on these parameters.

Also, the newer releases since 2009 provide the class definition clauses RISK LEVEL and DURATION. These were not part of the ABAP language with the first release of the ABAP Unit Testing Framework. Prior to 2009, the way these values were specified was through the use of ABAP pseudo-comments placed after the class definition statement. So, for instance, the following class definition statement that can be written using releases since 2009

```
class some_test_class definition
                      for testing
                      risk level harmless
                      duration short.
```

would need to have been written the following way with releases prior to 2009:

```
class some_test_class definition
                      for testing.
                      "#AU Risk_Level Harmless
                      "#AU Duration Short
```

The pseudo-comments still may be used, but it is recommended to use the new class definition clauses instead. They are explained here only so that they could be recognized for the role they play in unit testing if they were to be encountered with unit test classes written using a release prior to one where RISK LEVEL and DURATION have become valid clauses for the class definition statement.

Challenges to Effectively Testing ABAP Code

Many of the xUnit testing frameworks are associated with purely object-oriented languages. This means that those testing frameworks benefit from the constraints the associated object-oriented language imposes upon program design. In conformance with the basic xUnit principle that a unit test is written in the same language as the productive code, the unit tests executed by their respective xUnit testing frameworks also can only have been written and designed using the same object-oriented language as the productive code tested by those unit tests.

In contrast, ABAP is not a purely object-oriented language. Accordingly, the structure of programs made possible by the ABAP compiler presents challenges to effectively testing the ABAP code. This section covers some of those challenges, specifically those presented by

- Classic ABAP event blocks

- Global variables

- The MESSAGE statement

- ALV reports

- Classic list processing statements

- Open SQL statements

Challenges Presented by Classic ABAP Event Blocks

Perhaps the most significant of these challenges is that an ABAP Unit test cannot directly invoke the code contained within an ABAP classic event block, such as the classic event blocks for *initialization* and *start-of-selection*. A unit test can, however, invoke a subroutine written using the FORM-ENDFORM construct. This means that in order to provide a unit test for any code contained within an ABAP classic event block, it first would be necessary to refactor the program such that the code currently residing within the ABAP classic event block is moved into a subroutine, which then can be called from both the ABAP classic event block from which it was moved and an ABAP Unit test.

Challenges Presented by Global Variables

Global variables are capable of retaining values set by the procedure tested by a unit test method. Accordingly, it presents the possibility of Interacting Tests, such as when one unit test method sets the value of a global variable, explicitly or as a result of calling the procedure it tests, and a subsequent unit test accesses that changed value or perhaps causes it to be changed again so that yet another subsequent unit test has access to the newly changed value. These are examples of Interacting Tests; the test may pass sometimes and fail at other times simply due to the values of global variables as the tests are run. Since it is typically not known the order in which unit test methods will be executed, the values contained in global variables when they are accessed during a unit test will be indeterminate unless they had been explicitly set to some initial value at the start of the unit test.

Consider that the term "global variables" casts a wide shadow which includes not only data definitions that occur outside of subroutines but also the parameters and select-options statements available for initial selection screen definitions as well as data definitions defined within subroutines using the STATICS statement.

Challenges Presented by the MESSAGE Statement

Depending on the severity (message type) of the message, the ABAP MESSAGE statement can have an effect on the flow of control of the program during normal execution:

- Messages of severity exit (message type "X") will cause an immediate program termination accompanied by a short dump.

- Messages of severity abort (message type "A") also will cause an immediate program termination but will be accompanied by a Cancel message instead of a short dump.

- The effect caused by messages of severity error (message type "E") will depend upon which classic ABAP event block is in control at the time they are issued and whether the program is running in foreground or background. When the event block is any of the event blocks that precede the start-of-selection event block, such as initialization and the varieties of at selection-screen, then in foreground executions the associated error message will appear at the bottom of the screen and provide the user the chance to change values on the selection screen to alleviate the error message. Once the program reaches the start-of-selection event block, an error message will cause the program to terminate processing.

- The effect caused by messages of severity warning (message type "W") will depend upon which classic ABAP event block is in control at the time they are issued and whether the program is running in foreground or background. When the event block is any of the event blocks that precede the start-of-selection event block, then when running in foreground, the warning message is issued and provides the user the opportunity to continue program execution; and when running in background, the message simply is registered in the resulting job log. Once the program reaches the start-of-selection event block, a warning message will be treated the same as an error message, causing the program to terminate processing.

- The effect caused by messages of severity information (message type "I") will depend upon whether the program is running in foreground or background. When running in foreground, a popup message will appear to the user who must respond by clicking one of the buttons on the popup window to cause the program to resume. When run in background, the message simply is registered in the resulting job log.

- Messages of severity status (message type "S") will cause a message to appear at the bottom of the screen when running in foreground and simply is registered in the resulting job log when running in background.

The ABAP Unit tests typically are run in foreground, so the preceding explanations for background execution will not apply, but message statements also behave differently when encountered in the code under test during a unit test execution. For one thing, there is no classic ABAP event block in control during unit test executions, so the flow of control through the program does not necessarily observe the same rules as when a program is executed in foreground mode. In addition, you will find that messages of severities status, information, and warning will not appear during the execution of a unit test. Also, messages of severities error, abort, and exit will be intercepted by the Test Runner and logged either as an exception error, for severities error and abort, or runtime error for severity exit.

Accordingly, a unit test execution that encounters the ABAP MESSAGE statement for a message of severity error will result in the failure of the unit test, regardless of whether issuing such a message would have been the correct action to be taken by the code under test. This means that to enable testing of programs with ABAP MESSAGE statements scattered throughout the code, we will need a way to intercept and prevent such failures. This consideration will be explored further in a subsequent chapter and through the accompanying exercise programs.

Challenges Presented by ALV Reports

One of the more notable features SAP has made available over the years is the ABAP List Viewer, abbreviated ALV, which enables an ABAP program to present output simply as rows and columns of content to be displayed to a user in a fashion similar to a spreadsheet. Its initial release facilitated this capability through SAP-supplied function modules. It has since been made available through the use of SAP-supplied classes.

Regardless of whether an ABAP program makes use of the function modules or the classes, when the ALV report is presented, it will interrupt program processing until the user issues a command to allow the program to continue. This behavior is the same for both the production path and the automated unit testing path, meaning that when a unit test encounters the ALV component responsible for displaying the report, the unit test will be suspended. Test execution will resume when the person who initiated the test clicks Back, Exit, or Cancel or presses the Escape key.

This is totally unacceptable since it would require the test initiator to remain on standby to explicitly press a key every time an ALV report is presented by the Test Runner, violating one of the most basic tenets of automated unit tests – that they run to completion with no assistance by the test initiator. In subsequent chapters, we will explore ways to mitigate the effects of ALV during the execution of automated unit tests.

Challenges Presented by Classic List Processing Statements

Since the advent of the ABAP List Viewer (ALV) in the 1990s, there no longer seems to be any need for new ABAP programs to use the classic list processing statements, such as new-line, write, skip, uline, and so on. Indeed, the book *Official ABAP Programming Guidelines* states the following regarding classic lists:

> ### Rule 5.20: Use the SAP List Viewer
>
> *Do not use classic lists. If you still deploy dynpro-based, classical UI technologies, you should use the SAP List Viewer (ALV) or other GUI control-based technologies instead of classical lists in live programs.*[11]

---

[11]Keller, Horst and Thümmel, Wolf Hagen, *Official ABAP Programming Guidelines*, Galileo Press, 2010, p. 204

Unfortunately for us, there are thousands of legacy programs that were written prior to the availability of ALV, and they generate reports formatted as classic lists using classic list processing statements. Classic lists cause the same problem for automated unit tests that ALV reports do – specifically, they cause the execution of the unit test to be suspended until the user presses a key to enable resumption of the test. This suspension is just as unacceptable with classic lists as it is with ALV reports, but when classic list processing statements are encountered during an automated unit test, the Test Runner will present the report to the screen looking similar to what is shown in Figure 5-3 before it suspends test execution.

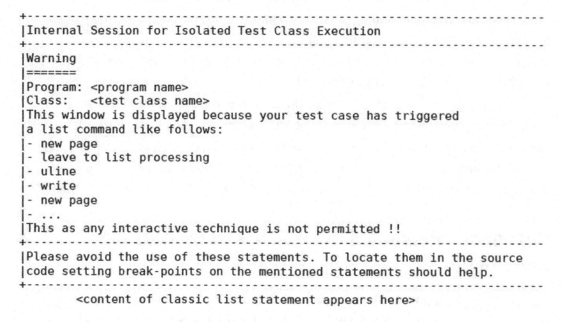

```
+-------------------------------------------------------------------------
|Internal Session for Isolated Test Class Execution
+-------------------------------------------------------------------------
|Warning
|=======
|Program: <program name>
|Class:   <test class name>
|This window is displayed because your test case has triggered
|a list command like follows:
|- new page
|- leave to list processing
|- uline
|- write
|- new page
|- ...
|This as any interactive technique is not permitted !!
+-------------------------------------------------------------------------
|Please avoid the use of these statements. To locate them in the source
|code setting break-points on the mentioned statements should help.
+-------------------------------------------------------------------------
        <content of classic list statement appears here>
```

Figure 5-3. *Report presented when automated unit test encounters a classic list processing statement*

Notice in Figure 5-3 that the content of the report is presented starting on the final line shown, after a series of introductory lines the test runner presents ahead of those produced by the tested procedure. These introductory lines do not appear when ALV reports are presented during a unit test. Furthermore, these introductory lines include the word "Warning" and the phrase "is not permitted !!" and some lines are formatted using red highlighting, giving the impression that the unit test has failed. In subsequent chapters and through the exercise programs, we will explore ways to circumvent this presentation during the execution of automated unit tests.

Challenges Presented by Open SQL Statements

There are few other modern programming languages that have their own statements for performing database access. The ABAP language has had such statements since its first release, and these statements can appear in the code at virtually any location. While the Open SQL statement *select* is virtually harmless, the same cannot be said for the Open SQL statements *insert, modify, update*, and *delete*, each of which will leave the corresponding persistence repository in a permanently changed state.

The intent with ABAP Unit testing is to leave the SAP environment in which it runs unchanged after the execution of the unit tests. To achieve this when the language itself provides statements that could leave the persistence repositories permanently changed will require some additional diligence on the part of the author of any unit tests where such statements could be encountered. While it might be acceptable for customized repositories to be explicitly reset to their pre–unit test state at the conclusion of the unit test, the same process of directly updating persistence repositories supplied by SAP is *not recommended*, either for production code or for unit testing code. Accordingly, some extra work will be required to insure the SAP environment is reset back to a pre–unit test state.

Controlling the ABAP Unit Testing Framework

One of the hallmarks of SAP software is that it is configurable to the requirements of the site for which it runs. Just issue transaction SPRO, and you will be presented with a multitude of options for configuring virtually every area of the Enterprise Resource Planning (ERP) Central Component (ECC). This type of system configuration is not an area in which the typical software developer spends much time.

The ABAP Unit Testing Framework also is a feature for which site-specific configuration is applicable. In this section, we explore the various site configuration settings applicable to this feature.

Client Category

As mentioned previously, ABAP components that are marked FOR TESTING are, by default, not compiled into production systems. So what denotes whether or not a system is a production system? It is table T000, which contains records indicating the various attributes of each client in the SAP system. One of its fields is known as the Client Control Category (T000-CCCATEGORY) which denotes the role of the corresponding client and can be set to "P" for production or "T" for test. SAP clients where ABAP development is performed are set as test clients.

It is in test clients where the ABAP Unit Testing Framework will be enabled, by default, to compile and execute components marked for unit testing. Attempts to run unit tests in clients where the ABAP Unit Testing Framework is not enabled will result in receiving a warning message indicating

```
The system settings prevent the use of unit tests in this client
```

CHANGING THE CLIENT CONTROL CATEGORY

I once worked at a site where a person in the Basis group, who had obtained the requisite permission to do so, changed for me the client control category of the quality assurance client from production to test, which enabled me momentarily to run my unit tests in that system before resetting it back to a production system.

Client Category Override

As already noted, unit test code is, by default, not compiled into production systems. The operative phrase here is *by default*. The default setting can be overridden via the SAP system profile parameter

```
abap/test_generation
```

which will control whether the ABAP Unit Testing Framework is enabled to run in production systems.

It is probably not a good idea to change this in the production system where your users are performing all their day-to-day activities. In contrast, it is often the case that such a production system is periodically copied to what might be called a quality assurance system, an environment containing the latest copy of real production data and also capable of accepting new and improved software for the purpose of thoroughly testing it before it can be moved into the definitive production system. It is in such quality assurance systems that are marked as production systems where overriding the default setting of unit testing prohibition might be most applicable.

The usefulness of enabling unit test executions in a production system is debatable. It certainly is to be expected that there would be far more test data available to such unit tests in the various persistence repositories, test data that would not be available in a typical development environment. From this we might conclude that a unit test would benefit from having such a comprehensive and robust set of test data at its disposal.

Here are two reasons why this might be undesirable:

1. There is a unit testing school of thought embracing the premise that unit tests should not depend upon the existence of records in persistence repositories. To depend on the presence of such test data would expose the test to the smell known as Resource Optimism,[12] a variety of Erratic Test,[13] passing at some times and failing at other times due solely to the presence or absence of such records.

2. All unit tests should pass in development, and if they do, then there is no reason they need to be run in any other environment. Unit tests should build and use their own test data if that is what is required for them to pass. A unit test failing in development due to lack of unit test data should not be dismissed with the rationale that it will pass once it is run in a quality assurance system where applicable test data exists.

Note   The process of defining unit tests capable of creating and using their own fabricated test data is covered in the accompanying exercises.

Unit Testing Configuration

The ABAP Unit Testing Framework can be further configured using transaction SAUNIT_ CLIENT_SETUP. This transaction enables configuring both the client and the associated application server associated with the development environment. Upon invoking this transaction, a screen similar to that shown in Figure 5-4 is presented.

---

[12]Meszaros, Gerard, *xUnit Test Patterns: Refactoring Test Code*, Addison Wesley, 2007, p. 233
[13]Ibid, p. 228

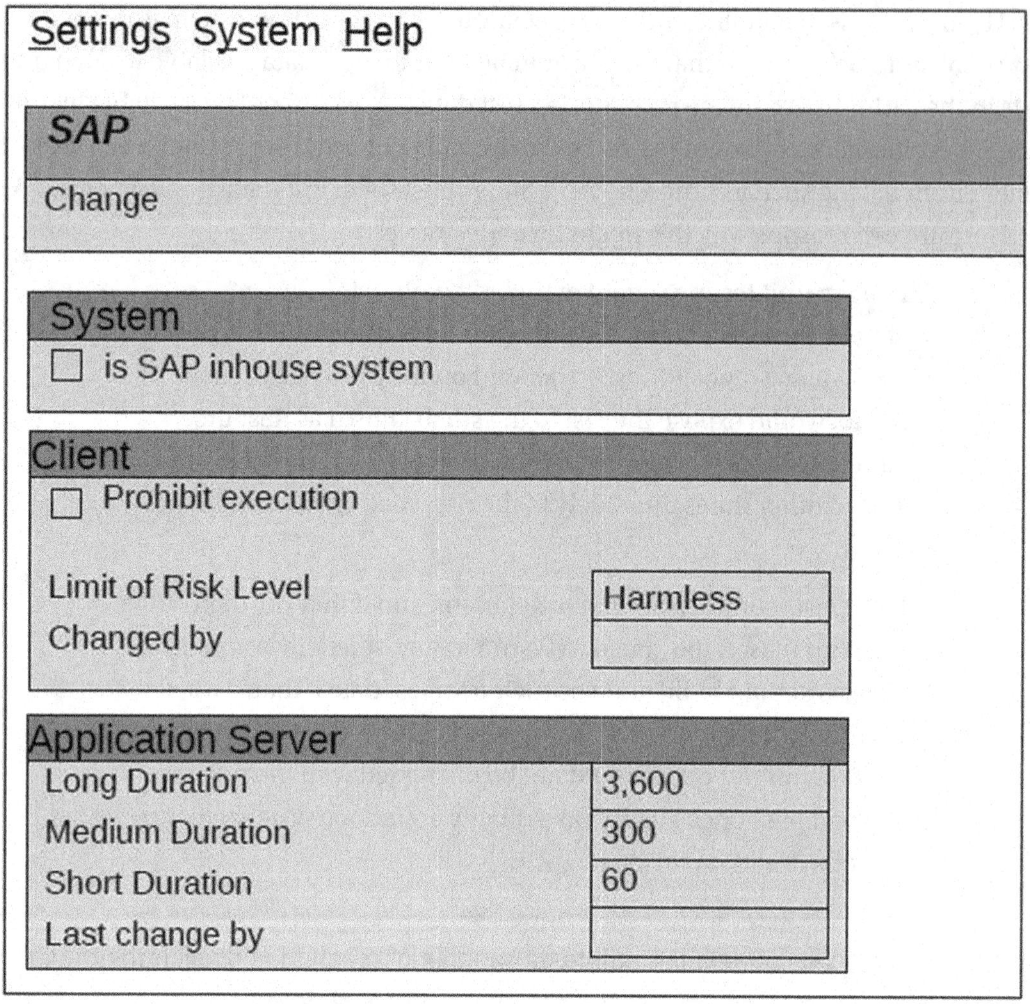

Figure 5-4. *Initial screen presented by transaction SAUNIT_CLIENT_SETUP*

Clicking the Change button enables updates to the respective settings, as shown in Figure 5-5.

```
 Settings  System  Help

┌──────────────────────────────────────────────────────┐
│ SAP                                                    │
├──────────────────────────────────────────────────────┤
│ Proposal                                               │
└──────────────────────────────────────────────────────┘

┌──────────────────────────────────────────────────────┐
│ System                                                 │
│  ☐  is SAP inhouse system                              │
└──────────────────────────────────────────────────────┘

┌──────────────────────────────────────────────────────┐
│ Client                                                 │
│    ☐  Prohibit execution                               │
│                                                        │
│  Limit of Risk Level        ┌─────────────────┐        │
│                             │ Harmless        │        │
│  Changed by                 │                 │        │
│                             └─────────────────┘        │
└──────────────────────────────────────────────────────┘

┌──────────────────────────────────────────────────────┐
│ Application Server                                     │
│  Long Duration              ┌─────────────────┐        │
│                             │ 3,600           │        │
│  Medium Duration            │ 300             │        │
│  Short Duration             │ 60              │        │
│  Last change by             │                 │        │
│                             └─────────────────┘        │
└──────────────────────────────────────────────────────┘
```

Figure 5-5. Appearance of screen from Figure 5-4 after clicking the Change button

The values shown in the preceding figure are the default values. Static class cl_aunit_ customizing is responsible for providing these default values: those for the client settings are set via method __init_client_setup, and those for the application server are set via method __init_host_setup.

If the default values are changed at the site, the new client settings will be retained in table TAUNIT_CLT_SETUP, and the new application server settings will be retained in table TAUNIT_SRV_SETUP. As you might expect, table TAUNIT_CLT_SETUP is client-dependent, while table TAUNIT_SRV_SETUP is not.

These settings apply to all developers in the respective client and application server. Changing the settings will affect all developers equally.

Client Settings

The Client block checkbox for the Prohibit execution setting already will be set to checked for a production client and cannot be overridden via this transaction. Otherwise it can be toggled between checked and unchecked to control whether developers will be permitted to run unit tests in that client.

The Limit of Risk Level setting can be raised from its default Harmless to either Dangerous or Critical. Its value correlates to the values that can be specified on the RISK LEVEL clause of a unit test class definition statement. This setting will determine the highest risk level that can be associated with the corresponding unit test classes included in the unit test execution. Say, for example, this setting is set to Harmless and one of the unit test classes in your source code indicates a risk level of Dangerous. This would be sufficient to disqualify this unit test class from being executed. If this client setting is subsequently raised from Harmless to Dangerous, then the same unit test class now would be accepted for execution.

EVOLVING HABITS

At one point in my development career, I had defined unit tests that resulted in new records created in standard SAP persistence repositories, identified accordingly via some banner such as "ABAP Unit testing" emblazoned in the description of the new records. For these unit test classes, I had indicated a risk level of Dangerous due to the fact that running the tests would leave behind permanent changes in the persistence repositories. I have since abandoned the use of that technique after some introspection through which I concluded that it is not a good idea for unit tests to create and leave behind such records.

Application Server Settings

The three Duration settings available in the Application Server block correlate to the values that can be specified for the DURATION clause of a unit test class definition statement. Here is where they are set to the number of seconds that may elapse between starting the first unit test method of a class and finishing the last one. If the elapsed time exceeds the setting for the DURATION clause associated with the unit test class, then the execution is interrupted after the specified duration time expires, and an applicable warning is issued for the unit test class upon presenting the ABAP Unit Result Display report.

Clicking the Proposal button (Calculate Proposal) will determine a different set of duration values based on an analysis it performs.

In my estimation, the default value of 60 seconds for Short Duration is too high even for Long Duration. Just consider for a moment that the default value for Long Duration is 3600 seconds – one hour! It strains my imagination to think of a case where I would ever want a single unit test class to run for one hour. Indeed, I want unit tests to run to completion in mere fractions of a second. Waiting even a few seconds for the unit test run to finish still would be too long for me. Robert C. Martin eloquently explains why tests should be fast:

> *When tests run slow, you won't want to run them frequently. If you don't run them frequently, you won't find problems early enough to fix them easily. You won't feel as free to clean up the code. Eventually the code will begin to rot.*[14]

Who wants rotten code?! Accordingly, default configuration settings that would result in waiting an hour for a single unit test class to finish seem as though inviting poorly written unit tests and, by extension, poorly written production code. Indeed, I would want all the developers at my site to strive for sub-second unit test execution times every time the tests are run and to provide a convincing justification for why these duration settings should be set any higher than a few seconds each.

Summary

The ABAP Unit Testing Framework, also known as ABAP Unit, is the xUnit automated unit testing framework applicable to the ABAP language and is applicable to testing *procedures* found in executable programs, class pools, function groups, module pools, and subroutine pools. The framework itself is divided into components providing test preparation activities and components providing test executions. Using this framework requires that unit tests are written as local object-oriented classes designated specifically as test classes. Global classes and function modules both may have the skeleton of their unit tests automatically generated for them but will still require the programmer to provide the details of the test.

---

[14]Martin, Robert C., *Clean Code: A Handbook of Agile Software Craftsmanship*, Prentice Hall, 2009, p. 132

The ABAP language was enhanced with the clauses FOR TESTING, DURATION, and RISK LEVEL added to the ABAP class definition statement and the clause FOR TESTING added to the methods statement. The use of the application programming interface supplied by the ABAP Unit Testing Framework makes it possible to assert whether a unit test passes or fails. The reserved method names class_setup, setup, teardown, and class_teardown represent the fixture methods automatically called by the framework to establish a fresh testing environment.

The ABAP Unit Result Display report is presented when any one of the unit tests fails and provides information to enable resolving the failure; otherwise, a simple status message appears indicating a successful execution of all unit tests. Unit test executions can be initiated from within the ABAP editor used to write the tests as well as from the Code Inspector (SCI) and ABAP Unit Browser.

The ABAP Unit Testing Framework has evolved from its first release in 2004 to the upgraded version released in 2009 which introduced the clauses DURATION and RISK LEVEL of the class definition statement superseding their pseudo-comment counterparts.

There are some ABAP statements and features to be found in the production code presenting challenges with writing automated unit tests, among them:

- Classic ABAP event blocks

- Global variables

- The MESSAGE statement

- ALV reports

- Classic list processing statements

- Open SQL statements

In accordance with the flexibility SAP provides for configuring a production system, the ABAP Unit Testing Framework also can be configured through transaction SAUNIT_CLIENT_SETUP to the development and testing needs of the site at which it is used.

Quiz #2: ABAP Unit Testing Concepts

Now that you are familiar with the concepts associated with ABAP Unit testing, test your knowledge by completing the following quiz. The answers can be found in Appendix B.

Multiple Choice: Select the Best Answer

1. ABAP Unit tests are written in

   A. SAPScript

   B. Java

   C. ABAP

2. ABAP Unit tests

   A. Must be implemented as local classes

   B. Must be implemented as global classes

   C. May be implemented as either local or global classes

3. ABAP Unit tests can be executed

   A. Only from the editor

   B. Only from the Code Inspector

   C. From either the editor or the Code Inspector

4. An ABAP Unit test class definition requires the class to be

   A. Marked as "for testing"

   B. Inherited from a globally defined static class provided by SAP

   C. Defined in a separate module

5. An ABAP Unit test validity is asserted by

   A. Using an ASSERT statement

   B. Invoking static methods of the class cl_abap_unit_assert

   C. Calling function module ASSERT_THIS

6. An ABAP Unit test may test

   A. Only code written using classes and methods

   B. Only classic procedural ABAP code

   C. Classic procedural ABAP code and code written using classes and methods

True or False

An ABAP Unit test may be defined for

---

1. Executable programs

2. Class pools

3. Interface pools

4. Module pools

5. Function groups

6. Configuration

7. Subroutine pools

8. Type groups

An ABAP Unit test

---

9. By default is compiled into all environments

10. Accommodates using a fixture

11. Is embedded with the object to be tested

12. Can generate the source code to comply with the test

13. May accept parameters

14. Is transported along with its tested object

EXERCISES

At this point, take a break from reading and shift into exercise preparation mode. Refer to the accompanying exercise workbook to prepare your ABAP programming environment for performing the associated exercises as described in workbook **Section 1: Overview of exercise programs** and **Section 2: Organization of requirements**.

CHAPTER 6

Rudiments

Since the ABAP Unit Testing Framework is modeled on the xUnit testing design characteristics, it is capable of providing unit testing for the type of program design applicable to virtually all of the languages providing xUnit testing facilities, meaning it is quite capable of handling the unit testing requirements for components written using the object-oriented design model. It would hardly provide any value if that had been the extent of its capabilities due to the fact that most ABAP code was written well before the object-oriented design features had been introduced into the ABAP language. Fortunately for us, the ABAP Unit Testing Framework is capable of providing unit testing for ABAP components using a non-object-oriented program design as well. In this chapter, we will start at the beginning, first exploring how to apply ABAP Unit testing to legacy programs, working our way through the transformations and improvements implemented into the language until eventually reaching the point where we have become proficient writing unit tests for ABAP components written using either a procedural design or the object-oriented paradigm.

Introducing a Simple Unit Test

The short ABAP program shown in Listing 6-1, written using none of the object-oriented language statements, will be our starting point for demonstrating how to retrofit a legacy program with ABAP Unit tests.

Listing 6-1. Simple message presentation program

```
report z_issue_message.
  constants  valid_severities  type string value 'SIWEAX'.
  data       severity_is_valid type abap_bool.
  parameters severity          type symsgty obligatory.
at selection-screen.
```

99

© James E. McDonough 2021
J. E. McDonough, *Automated Unit Testing with ABAP*, https://doi.org/10.1007/978-1-4842-6951-0_6

```
  perform validate_message_severity.
  if severity_is_valid ne abap_true.
    message e000(0k) with 'Select a message severity from the values'
                          valid_severities.
  endif.
start-of-selection.
  message 'Hello World!' type severity.
form validate_message_severity.
  if severity ca valid_severities.
    severity_is_valid = abap_true.
  else
    severity_is_valid = abap_false.
  endif.
endform.
```

Notice that it contains a single parameters statement defined as type symsgty representing the type of a message issued via the ABAP MESSAGE statement and that the start-of-selection event block contains the MESSAGE statement using the severity (message type) value specified by the user in the parameters field. The at selection-screen classic ABAP event block includes a perform statement to a subroutine to validate that the specified message severity is one of the valid values for a MESSAGE statement, and if not one of these, then an error message is to be displayed providing the valid values from which the user should choose a severity.

When this program is executed, there will be a simple selection screen presented on which the user is to specify a message severity. Then after having provided a valid value and clicking Execute, they will see the message 'Hello World!' displayed using whichever type of message severity the user had specified.

Certainly this simple program does not rise to the level of industrial-strength legacy code, but it is simple enough to use as a basis for applying unit testing since it uses only statements that might be found in ABAP legacy programs.

As it is currently written, those portions of the program that can be subjected to unit testing are limited to the statements in subroutine validate_message_severity. Why is that? It is because all the remaining executable ABAP statements appear in classic ABAP event blocks, blocks of code which are not subject to testing by the ABAP Unit Testing Framework. So let's provide a unit test class capable of testing this subroutine. The code shown in Listing 6-2 represents about the briefest definition of a class we might be able to write for such a unit test.

Listing 6-2. Unit test for simple message presentation program

```
class unit_tester definition for testing risk level harmless.
  private section.
    methods validate_message_severity_s for testing.
endclass.
class unit_tester implementation.
  method validate_message_severity_s.
    severity = 'S'.
    perform validate_message_severity.
    call method cl_abap_unit_assert=>assert_equals
      exporting
        act = severity_is_valid
        exp = abap_true
        msg = 'Unexpected result for severity S'.
  endmethod.
endclass.
```

Let's analyze this unit test class to identify what it is intended to do. We see on the "class ... definition ..." statement that this class name is "unit_tester," with the clause "for testing" designating it as a class applicable to unit testing, with the clause "risk level harmless" indicating that its effect upon the execution environment is minimal, and with the default value of "short" for "duration" indicating that it is not expected to take long to execute. Within the class definition component is the definition of a private method called validate_message_severity_s which is designated as a method applicable to unit testing due to its clause "for testing."

The class implementation component includes an implementation for method validate_message_severity_s, which does the following:

1. Sets the selection screen parameter named severity to the value 'S'

2. Invokes subroutine validate_message_severity

3. Invokes the static method assert_equals of class cl_abap_unit_assert to assert that the actual Boolean value resulting from the call to subroutine validate_message_severity is the same as the expected Boolean value abap_true

This unit test class would be appended to the end of the source code object containing the source for report z_issue_message either directly, as shown in Listing 6-3, or via an INCLUDE statement naming another object that contains the code of this unit test class.

Listing 6-3. Simple message presentation program with unit test

```
report z_issue_message.
  constants  valid_severities  type string value 'SIWEAX'.
  data       severity_is_valid type abap_bool.
  parameters severity          type symsgty obligatory.
at selection-screen.
  perform validate_message_severity.
  if severity_is_valid ne abap_true.
    message e000(Ok) with 'Select a message severity from the values'
                         valid_severities.
  endif.
start-of-selection.
  message 'Hello World!' type severity.
form validate_message_severity.
  if severity ca valid_severities.
    severity_is_valid = abap_true.
  else
    severity_is_valid = abap_false.
  endif.
endform.

class unit_tester definition for testing risk level harmless.
  private section.
    methods validate_message_severity_s for testing.
endclass.
class unit_tester implementation.
  method validate_message_severity_s.
    severity = 'S'.
    perform validate_message_severity.
    call method cl_abap_unit_assert=>assert_equals
      exporting
```

```
      act = severity_is_valid
      exp = abap_true
      msg = 'Unexpected result for severity S'.
  endmethod.
endclass.
```

When this unit test is executed, it will cause the test runner to do the following:

1. Scan the code and resolve the presence of unit test class "unit_tester."

2. Identify method validate_message_severity_s of class unit_tester as a method to be invoked during the test run.

3. Invoke method validate_message_severity_s of class unit_tester.

4. Report on the result of having invoked this unit test method.

In this case, we should expect to see the following status message appearing at the bottom of the screen:

```
Processed: 1 program, 1 test classes, 1 test methods
```

Great!! We now understand the minimum requirements for defining a unit test class for a legacy program containing a single subroutine.

EXERCISES

At this point, take a break from reading and shift into exercise mode. Refer to the accompanying workbook to perform the six exercises associated with workbook **Section 3: ABAP Unit Testing 101 – Creating Your First Unit Test**.

Expanding Unit Test Coverage

Upon closer inspection of our simple program shown in Listing 6-3, we see that we have provided validation for only a single one of the six valid values applicable to a message severity. Can we adjust the unit test to facilitate testing all of them?

Yes, we can! Simply change the implementation of the unit test method to check each of the six valid values. Listing 6-4 shows one way to do it.

Listing 6-4. Unit test for simple message presentation program enhanced to test all valid message severities

```
method validate_message_severity_s.
  data valid_severity_values type c length 06.
  data failure_message type string.
  valid_severity_values = valid_severities.
  while valid_severity_values is not initial.
    severity = valid_severity_values.
    perform validate_message_severity.
    concatenate 'Unexpected result for severity'
                severity
           into failure_message separated by space.
    call method cl_abap_unit_assert=>assert_equals
      exporting
        act = severity_is_valid
        exp = abap_true
        msg = failure_message.
    shift valid_severity_values left by 01 places.
  endwhile.
endmethod.
```

Now the method iterates through all of the valid severity values and checks that subroutine validate_message_severity returns abap_true for each one of them. The name of the method no longer implies what the unit test does, so it should be renamed to something more appropriate, such as validate_valid_severities. At this point, we still have a single unit test class with a single unit test method, but now it accommodates validating all the valid message severities.

Wonderful! We've expanded the unit testing to cover more validation without introducing any new unit test methods. However, our unit test is capable only of validating that subroutine validate_message_severity will return abap_true when we provide it with valid message severity values. We have not made any arrangements for validating that it would return abap_false if we were to provide it with an invalid message severity value. Can we adjust the unit test to do that as well?

Yes, we can! Simply clone the current unit test method testing for valid values to one that will test for invalid values. Listing 6-5 shows one way to do it, with changes highlighted in bold.

Listing 6-5. Unit test for simple message presentation program enhanced to test for invalid message severities

```
class unit_tester definition for testing risk level harmless.
  private section.
    methods validate_valid_severities for testing.
    methods validate_invalid_severities for testing.
endclass.
class unit_tester implementation.
  method validate_valid_severities.
    data valid_severity_values type c length 06.
    data failure_message type string.
    valid_severity_values = valid_severities.
    while valid_severity_values is not initial.
      severity = valid_severity_values.
      perform validate_message_severity.
      concatenate 'Unexpected result for severity'
                  severity
              into failure_message separated by space.
      call method cl_abap_unit_assert=>assert_equals
        exporting
          act = severity_is_valid
          exp = abap_true
          msg = failure_message.
      shift valid_severity_values left by 01 places.
    endwhile.
  endmethod.
  method validate_invalid_severities.
    data invalid_severity_values type c length 06 value '123456'.
    data failure_message type string.
    valid_severity_values = valid_severities.
    while invalid_severity_values is not initial.
```

```
      severity = invalid_severity_values.
      perform validate_message_severity.
      concatenate 'Unexpected result for severity'
                  severity
           into failure_message separated by space.
      call method cl_abap_unit_assert=>assert_equals
        exporting
          act = severity_is_valid
          exp = abap_false
          msg = failure_message.
      shift invalid_severity_values left by 01 places.
    endwhile.
  endmethod.
endclass.
```

Splendid! We've expanded the unit testing to cover both the valid path and the invalid path of subroutine validate_message_severity, providing full coverage for its processing logic. We can now confidently state that we've provided sufficient unit testing for this subroutine.

Notice how much easier it was to write the second unit test method for this unit test class. You'll typically find that the first test written for a class takes the most effort because it requires the unit test class itself to be defined. Once the unit test class is defined, creating additional test methods is quicker. Roy Osherove agrees:

> *Good tests against the system should be easy and quick to write ... Small warning: even experienced unit testers can find that it may take 30 minutes or more to figure out how to write the very first unit test against [code] they've never unit tested before. This is part of the work, and is expected. The second and subsequent tests on that [code] should be very easy to accomplish.*[1]

Using this same process, we should be able to take other legacy programs written over the years and similarly provide unit tests for their various classic ABAP subroutines. There are some caveats to this since these programs were not originally written to accommodate unit testing, but with some modest refactoring, we should be able to retrofit these programs with thorough automated unit tests.

---

[1]Osherove, Roy, *The Art of Unit Testing*, second edition, Manning, 2014, p. 10

```
┌─────────────────────────────────────────────────────────────────┐
│                           EXERCISES                             │
└─────────────────────────────────────────────────────────────────┘
```

At this point, take a break from reading and shift into exercise mode. Refer to the accompanying workbook to perform the 12 exercises associated with workbook **Section 4: ABAP Unit Testing 102 – Expanding Unit Test Coverage**.

Implementing Unit Tests for Function Modules

Perhaps the ABAP repository at your site has a large collection of customized function groups. This has been my experience with every SAP site at which I have worked. Function modules defined for many of these function groups also can have automated unit tests defined for them.

Note   There are some types of function modules which present a challenge with automated unit testing. Among them are those that are marked for remote procedure call, those marked to execute in an update task, and those that are designed to be containers for the screen definition and presentation processing required by corresponding dialog programs. In this section, we will restrict the discussion to the implementation of automated unit tests for simple function modules – those that are invoked to provide a synchronous functional service unrelated to any update task and which would not cause screens to be presented for the purpose of collecting user input.

The same process already described for creating a local unit test class for testing the code in subroutines defined for a simple report program also is applicable to creating a unit test class for a function module. Each unit test method of a local unit test class defined for testing a function module simply would invoke the function module instead of invoking a subroutine. Indeed, with function modules, the process might even be considered simpler due to the fact that a function module necessarily requires a specific signature defining its input and output parameters, avoiding the exposure associated with signature-less subroutines necessarily referring directly to various types of global variables for their input and output.

The main program of a function group is composed of a set of INCLUDEd container objects following a prescribed naming convention designated by SAP. For instance, function group Z123 will be composed of main program SAPLZ123, which itself will include a set of objects using the naming convention LZ123xxxx. There will be LZ123TOP to define the global data components for the function group, LZ123UXX to define the various function modules of the function group, and others. The developer may choose to place the various unit tests for a function module into the SAP-designated component intended to hold them, which for function group Z123 would be in container objects with the naming convention LZ123UNITT99.

The Function Builder (SE37) has its own testing capability through which parameter values used for testing a function module can be saved and recalled to be run at a later time. Such a test can be created by clicking the Test/Execute button, specifying values for the function module parameters on the input screen provided, and then clicking the Save Data Records button, which enables the programmer to assign a name and corresponding comment by which to save the specified parameter values. This same test can be recalled later by clicking the Test Data Directory button and selecting from the catalog of tests the one to be run again. This testing feature does not provide the same capability for testing function modules as found with the ABAP Unit Testing Framework; it merely records function module testing values so the programmer does not need to enter them manually each time the function module is to be run again in test mode with the same values.

EXERCISES

At this point, take a break from reading and shift into exercise mode. Refer to the accompanying workbook to perform the two exercises associated with workbook **Section 5: ABAP Unit Testing 103 – Writing Unit Tests for Function Modules**.

Implementing Unit Tests for Global Classes

The global class repository is another category of the ABAP repository for which automated unit tests can be defined. Due to the stricter syntax requirements applicable to classes, the task of providing global classes with associated unit tests is even easier than doing so for function modules. Global classes do not present the same types of challenges with regard to remote procedure calls, update tasks, and screen handling that function modules present because they cannot do any of those things.

The same process already described for creating a local unit test class for testing the code in subroutines defined for a simple report program also is applicable to creating a local unit test class for a global class. Each unit test method simply would invoke a method defined for the global class instead of invoking a subroutine. Also, as explained for unit tests with function modules, the methods of global classes require a specific signature defining their input and output parameters, avoiding the exposure associated with signature-less subroutines necessarily referring directly to various types of global variables for their input and output.

Unlike function modules, classes come in two flavors: static and instance. A static class is composed solely of static members, whereas an instance class has at least one instance member. A static class declares its members using the statements class-data and class-methods, whereas an instance class declares its members using the data and methods statements, respectively.

Invoking methods of classes from a unit test method is no different from invoking those methods from production code. For instance, when it comes to writing a unit test for it, the call to the method of the static class would be qualified with the name of the class, as in

```
call method some_static_class=>some_static_method ...
```

In contrast, when writing a unit test for an instance class, first, the class would need to be instantiated, and then the call to its method would be qualified by the corresponding instance reference variable, as in

```
data some_instance_class type ref to some_instance_class.
create object some_instance_class.
call method some_instance_class->some_instance_method ...
```

The main program of a global class is composed of a set of INCLUDEd container objects following a prescribed naming convention designated by SAP. For instance, global class ZCL_123 will be composed of main program name starting with "ZCL_123," followed by a series of equal signs ("=") to extend the name to 30 characters in length, followed by "CP," denoting class pool, which itself will include a set of objects using the same 30-character prefix followed by a suffix to denote the type of ABAP code to be found in that container object. There will be a container with suffix "CU" for public section,

"CI" for private section, "CCDEF" for local class definitions, "CCIMP" for local class implementations, "CMnnn" for method names, and so on. The container designated for holding the local unit test classes for a global class is the one with suffix "CCAU."

EXERCISES

At this point, take a break from reading and shift into exercise mode. Refer to the accompanying workbook to perform the two exercises associated with workbook **Section 6: ABAP Unit Testing 104 – Writing Unit Tests for Global Classes**.

ABAP Statements and Features Affecting Automated Unit Testing

The Chapter 5 section titled "Challenges to Effectively Testing ABAP Code" discussed the challenges associated with effectively testing ABAP code. This section explores three of those challenges in more detail.

- The MESSAGE statement

- ALV reports

- Classic list processing statements

Exploring the Effects of the MESSAGE Statement

It was previously explained that encountering a MESSAGE statement during a production execution causes a result attributable to a combination of factors: the severity of the message, whether the program is running in the foreground or background, and the classic ABAP event block in effect when the MESSAGE statement is encountered. Some of these factors in combination with each other will determine whether the associated message also is accompanied by a change to the program flow. For instance, a message issued through a MESSAGE statement during the execution of the start-of-selection classic ABAP event block will cause the program to be exited immediately when the severity of the message indicates "error" (type "E"), but the program will continue on with the next executable ABAP statement when it indicates "status" (type "S").

Included in that explanation was that the ABAP MESSAGE statement will not behave the same way when encountered during a unit test path execution as it will during a production path execution. Table 6-1 summarizes the valid message severity values and the corresponding behavior taken by the test runner of the ABAP Unit Testing Framework upon encountering a MESSAGE statement during a unit test.

Table 6-1. *Summary of message severity values and corresponding behavior by test runner when MESSAGE statement is encountered during a unit test*

Message severity	Description of severity	Behavior by test runner of the ABAP Unit Testing Framework when encountered
S	status	Message is not detectable
I	information	Message does not pop up as it would during foreground production path execution
W	warning	Message is not detectable and does not interfere with ABAP Unit test running to completion
E	error	ABAP Unit Result Display report appears showing exception error <CX_AUNIT_UNCAUGHT_MESSAGE>
A	abort	ABAP Unit Result Display report appears showing exception error <CX_AUNIT_UNCAUGHT_MESSAGE>
X	exit	ABAP Unit Result Display report appears showing runtime error <MESSAGE_TYPE_X>

Notice that the first three message severity values – S, I, and W – will neither cause a unit test failure nor will their associated message be displayed during a unit test, while the last three, E, A, and X, will cause a unit test failure.

It is reasonable that status, information, and warning messages should not appear during a unit test. Since the unit tests are run in random sequence, a user who might see these messages appear during a test run would have no context to relate to what unit test is causing them to be produced. Worse, interruptions by the test runner to present information and warning messages would require the user to press a key for the test to continue, defeating the purpose of having *automated* unit tests, requiring no user attention during their execution.

Table 6-1 shows that messages of severity exit encountered during a unit test will cause the test to fail and will be accompanied by runtime error <MESSAGE_TYPE_X>. This would suggest that there is no way to write a passing unit test which would encounter a MESSAGE statement with severity exit. We will revisit this issue in a subsequent chapter.

Table 6-1 also shows that messages of severities error and abort encountered during a unit test also will cause the test to fail but will be accompanied by exception error <CX_AUNIT_UNCAUGHT_MESSAGE>. This might suggest that it is possible to write a passing unit test which would encounter a MESSAGE statement with severity error or abort since CX_AUNIT_UNCAUGHT_MESSAGE is an SAP-supplied exception class that can be caught in a try-endtry block. Let's explore this further.

Listing 6-6 shows a simple subroutine and its associated unit test.

Listing 6-6. Simple subroutine and its associated unit test using write statement

```
form issue_error_message using text_01 type symsgv
                               text_02 type symsgv
                               text_03 type symsgv
                               text_04 type symsgv.
   message e000(OK) with text_01 text_02 text_03 text_04.
endform.

class unit_tester definition for testing risk level harmless.
  private section.
    methods issue_error_message for testing.
endclass.
class unit_tester implementation.
  method issue_error_message.
    clear sy-msgty.
    perform issue_error_message using 'This 'is' 'a' 'test'.
    call method cl_abap_unit_assert=>assert_equals
      exporting
        act = sy-msgty
        exp = 'E'
        msg = 'Unexpected result'.
  endmethod.
endclass.
```

Upon subjecting the preceding code to a unit test run, the ABAP Unit Result Display report would be presented and show that unit test method issue_error_message of class unit_tester failed. Its associated message would indicate exception error <CX_AUNIT_UNCAUGHT_MESSAGE>. So let's change the unit test to intercept this exception and avoid a unit test failure, as shown in Listing 6-7, with changes from Listing 6-6 highlighted in bold.

Listing 6-7. Simple subroutine and its associated unit test, including interception of class-based exception

```
form issue_error_message using text_01 type symsgv
                               text_02 type symsgv
                               text_03 type symsgv
                               text_04 type symsgv.
  message e000(OK) with text_01 text_02 text_03 text_04.
endform.

class unit_tester definition for testing risk level harmless.
  private section.
    methods issue_error_message for testing.
endclass.
class unit_tester implementation.
  method issue_error_message.
    clear sy-msgty.
  try.
    perform issue_error_message using 'This 'is' 'a' 'test'.
  catch cx_aunit_uncaught_message.
  endtry.
    call method cl_abap_unit_assert=>assert_equals
      exporting
        act = sy-msgty
        exp = 'E'
        msg = 'Unexpected result'.
  endmethod.
endclass.
```

Notice that the perform statement in the unit test method is now enclosed within a try-endtry block to catch class-based exception cx_aunit_uncaught_message. This should be sufficient to allow the unit test to intercept this class-based exception when it is thrown as a result of encountering a MESSAGE statement, enabling the unit test to gracefully continue on to the assertion call and avoid the unit test failure.

Upon subjecting the preceding code to a unit test, the results would be exactly the same as before: a failure accompanied by a message indicating exception error <CX_AUNIT_UNCAUGHT_MESSAGE>. How can that be?! Didn't we explicitly indicate that we wanted the unit test to intercept exactly this class-based exception when it is thrown? This might suggest that intercepting any class-based exception is beyond the capability of a simple unit test. Let's find out for certain. Listing 6-8 shows how we might test for this possibility, with changes from Listing 6-7 highlighted in bold.

Listing 6-8. Unit test both raising and intercepting a class-based exception

```
method issue_error_message.
  clear sy-msgty.
try.
  raise exception type cx_aunit_uncaught_message.
  perform issue_error_message using 'This 'is' 'a' 'test'.
catch cx_aunit_uncaught_message.
  cl_abap_unit_assert=>fail(
    msg = 'Caught exception in test method issue_error_message'
    ).
endtry.
  call method cl_abap_unit_assert=>assert_equals
    exporting
      act = sy-msgty
      exp = 'E'
      msg = 'Unexpected result'.
endmethod.
```

Notice that we have preceded the call to the subroutine with a RAISE EXCEPTION statement to deliberately raise the very same exception caught by the catch clause. Notice also that now the catch clause contains a call to method fail of class cl_abap_unit_assert. This will mean that now the subroutine we're trying to test will not be invoked. Instead, we expect to find that the catch clause now intercepts the class-based exception raised within the try block. We still expect the ABAP Unit Result Display report to be presented and show a failure for this unit test method, but now its associated failure message should indicate "Caught exception in test method issue_error_message."

Upon subjecting the preceding code to a unit test, we would indeed find that the failure message indicates the text we provided for the call to method fail of class cl_abap_unit_assert placed in the catch clause. This confirms that a unit test method is capable of intercepting such an exception within the unit test code. The conclusion we can draw here is that the test runner of the ABAP Unit Testing Framework raises this class-based exception during its own processing but the runtime environment does not allow the exception to be propagated back to the try block established in the test method. Accordingly, we cannot use the try-endtry block in a unit test to circumvent the failure issued by the test runner upon encountering message statements with severity values error and abort, despite that such messages would represent a successful unit test execution.

This means that messages issued with severities error, abort, and exit appearing in the executable code would present challenges to running clean tests if such messages were to be encountered during an ABAP Unit test execution. We will address this issue further in a subsequent chapter.

Exploring the Effects of ALV Reports

It already has been noted that the presentation of ALV reports will present challenges to running automated unit tests. One characteristic of ALV distinguishing it from classic lists is that the report is presented by an explicit call to a function module or a method of a class. Compare this with classic list output produced by an executable program, which has no explicit statement to present the report – it is simply presented by default following the completion of executing the end-of-selection classic ABAP event block, if one exists, or otherwise following the completion of executing the start-of-selection block.

Listing 6-9 has been copied from Listing 6-6 and adjusted accordingly to illustrate a simple subroutine that produces an ALV report of messages, along with its associated unit test, with changes highlighted in bold.

Listing 6-9. Listing 6-6 adapted to have subroutine present messages via ALV report

```
form issue_message_report using text_01 type symsgv
                                text_02 type symsgv
                                text_03 type symsgv
                                text_04 type symsgv.
                          changing messages type message_list.
   message e000(OK) with text_01 text_02 text_03 text_04.
   data alv_report type ref to cl_salv_table.
   try.
     call method cl_salv_table=>factory
       importing
         r_salv_table = alv_report
       changing
         t_table      = messages.
   catch cx_salv_msg.
     return.
   endtry.
   alv_report->display( ).
endform.

class unit_tester definition for testing risk level harmless.
  private section.
    methods issue_message_report for testing.
endclass.
class unit_tester implementation.
  method issue_message_report.
    data messages type message_list.
    append 'This is message 1' to messages.
    append 'This is message 2' to messages.
    append 'This is message 3' to messages.
    clear sy-msgty.
    perform issue_message_report using 'This 'is' 'a' 'test'.
                                 changing messages.
    call method cl_abap_unit_assert=>assert_equals
      exporting
```

```
      act = sy-msgty
      exp = space 'E'
      msg = 'Unexpected result'.
  endmethod.
endclass.
```

Notice that the name of the subroutine was changed from issue_error_message to issue_message_report and that its signature now accepts only a list of messages. Notice also that the message statement has been replaced with a comparable set of method calls to components of the ALV Object Model to produce an ALV report containing the messages supplied by the caller.

In addition, the name of the unit test method was changed to match the name of the subroutine it is calling, it now builds the list of messages to be sent on the call to the subroutine, and its assertion call expects the value of system variable sy-msgty to remain unchanged.

Listing 6-10 shows this same code but without the highlighting and stricken lines.

Listing 6-10. Listing 6-9 without highlighting and stricken lines

```
form issue_message_report changing messages type message_list.
  data alv_report type ref to cl_salv_table.
  try.
    call method cl_salv_table=>factory
      importing
        r_salv_table = alv_report
      changing
        t_table      = messages.
  catch cx_salv_msg.
    return.
  endtry.
  alv_report->display( ).
endform.

class unit_tester definition for testing risk level harmless.
  private section.
    methods issue_message_report for testing.
endclass.
```

```
class unit_tester implementation.
  method issue_message_report.
    data messages type message_list.
    append 'This is message 1' to messages.
    append 'This is message 2' to messages.
    append 'This is message 3' to messages.
    clear sy-msgty.
    perform issue_message_report changing messages.
    call method cl_abap_unit_assert=>assert_equals
      exporting
        act = sy-msgty
        exp = space
        msg = 'Unexpected result'.
  endmethod.
endclass.
```

Subjecting the code of Listing 6-10 to a unit test run while in the ABAP editor would result in a corresponding full-screen ALV report appearing to the user containing three rows of messages:

```
This is message 1
This is message 2
This is message 3
```

The user would need to press a key to cause the unit test execution to continue, resulting in a return to the ABAP editor with a status message appearing at the bottom of the screen indicating a successful unit test execution.

Whereas the unit test passes, for the unit test method to run to completion, it requires intervention by the user to press a key when the report appears. This same result would occur regardless of how the ALV report is produced, whether via the ALV function modules, using the ALV classes that are the forerunners of the ALV Object Model (cl_gui_alv*), or using the classes of the ALV Object Model as shown in the example.

This means that the presentation of ALV reports in the executable code would present challenges to running unattended tests if calls to the respective function modules or class methods were to be encountered during an ABAP Unit test execution. We will address this issue further in a subsequent chapter.

Exploring the Effects of Classic List Processing Statements

Also noted previously was that encountering classic list processing statements, such as write and skip, will present challenges to running automated unit tests. Presentation of a classic list can be made explicitly via the LEAVE TO LIST-PROCESSING statement for dialog programs, but it is called implicitly for executable programs (those that can be initiated via the SUBMIT statement). In both cases, the content presented in the classic list consists of the output associated with the classic list processing statements that had been encountered until that point.

Listing 6-11 has been copied from Listing 6-6 and adjusted accordingly to illustrate a simple subroutine that issues messages using a write statement instead of a message statement, along with its associated unit test, with changes highlighted in bold.

Listing 6-11. Simple subroutine and its associated unit test

```
form issue_message using severity type symsgty
                         text_01 type symsgv
                         text_02 type symsgv
                         text_03 type symsgv
                         text_04 type symsgv.
  message e000(OK) with text_01 text_02 text_03 text_04.
  write / severity, text_01, text_02, text_03, text_04.
endform.

class unit_tester definition for testing risk level harmless.
  private section.
    methods issue_message for testing.
endclass.
class unit_tester implementation.
  method issue_message.
    clear sy-msgty.
    perform issue_message using 'S' 'This' 'is' 'a' 'test'.
    call method cl_abap_unit_assert=>assert_equals
      exporting
        act = sy-msgty
        exp = space 'E'
```

```
        msg = 'Unexpected result'.
  endmethod.
endclass.
```

Notice that the name of the subroutine was changed from issue_error_message to issue_message and that its signature now accepts as its first parameter the severity indicator for the message to be issued. Notice also that the message statement has been replaced with a comparable write statement.

In addition, the name of the unit test method was changed to match the name of the subroutine it is calling, it now provides the value 'S' as the severity of the message to be issued upon calling the subroutine, and its assertion call expects the value of system variable sy-msgty to remain unchanged.

Listing 6-12 shows this same code but without the highlighting and stricken lines.

Listing 6-12. Listing 6-11 without highlighting and stricken lines

```
form issue_message using severity type symsgty
                        text_01 type symsgv
                        text_02 type symsgv
                        text_03 type symsgv
                        text_04 type symsgv.
  write / severity, text_01, text_02, text_03, text_04.
endform.

class unit_tester definition for testing risk level harmless.
  private section.
    methods issue_message for testing.
endclass.
class unit_tester implementation.
  method issue_message.
    clear sy-msgty.
    perform issue_message using 'S' 'This 'is' 'a' 'test'.
    call method cl_abap_unit_assert=>assert_equals
      exporting
        act = sy-msgty
```

```
      exp = space
      msg = 'Unexpected result'.
  endmethod.
endclass.
```

Subjecting the code of Listing 6-12 to a unit test run while in the ABAP editor would result in the full-screen classic list report appearing to the user as shown in Figure 6-1.

Only the last line is a result of the processing performed by the subroutine. The lines above that are generated by the test runner. The user would need to press a key to cause the unit test execution to continue, resulting in a return to the ABAP editor with a status message appearing at the bottom of the screen indicating a successful unit test execution.

```
+-------------------------------------------------------------------------
|Internal Session for Isolated Test Class Execution
+-------------------------------------------------------------------------
|Warning
|=======
|Program: <program name>
|Class:   <test class name>
|This window is displayed because your test case has triggered
|a list command like follows:
|- new page
|- leave to list processing
|- uline
|- write
|- new page
|- ...
|This as any interactive technique is not permitted !!
+-------------------------------------------------------------------------
|Please avoid the use of these statements. To locate them in the source
|code setting break-points on the mentioned statements should help.
+-------------------------------------------------------------------------
S This is a test
```

Figure 6-1. *Report presented when automated unit test shown in Listing 6-12 is executed*

Whereas the unit test passes, for the unit test method to run to completion, it requires intervention by the user to press a key when the list appears. Even worse, the classic list presented to the user has red highlighting throughout the lines generated by the test runner, suggesting a failure has occurred.

This means that classic list processing statements appearing in the executable code would present challenges to running unattended tests if such statements were to be encountered during an ABAP Unit test execution. We will address this issue further in a subsequent chapter.

EXERCISES

At this point, take a break from reading and shift into exercise mode. Refer to the accompanying workbook to perform the 15 exercises associated with workbook **Section 7: ABAP Unit Testing 105 – How Certain ABAP Statements Affect Unit Testing**.

How Automated Unit Testing Enables Confident Refactoring

The term "refactoring" has appeared sporadically in previous chapters, but perhaps it is a term unfamiliar to some readers. Roy Osherove describes it this way:

> *Refactoring means changing a piece of code without changing its functionality. If you've ever renamed a method, you've done refactoring. If you've ever split a large [procedure] into multiple smaller [procedures], you've refactored your code. The code still does the same thing, but it becomes easier to maintain, read, debug and change.*[2]

Once we have a collection of unit tests covering most or all of the production code to be found in an ABAP component, we now have at our disposal a way to periodically check the validity of any maintenance or refactoring changes we might apply. If we are applying refactoring changes, then it is likely none of the unit tests will require any changes but simply would need to be run again to confirm that the refactoring changes have not caused any previously successful unit tests now to fail. In contrast, if we are applying maintenance changes in pursuit of new business requirements, then it is likely at least one of the corresponding unit test classes will need corresponding changes to provide unit testing for the newly changed production code.

Suppose in response to a new business requirement we have been given the task to implement some minor change to a program for which we already had written several unit tests covering virtually the entire program. The first thing we should do before applying any code changes is to run all of the unit tests to determine that they all pass.

---

[2]Osherove, Roy, *The Art of Unit Testing*, second edition, Manning, 2014, p. 16

If any of them fail, then first we should address those failures and make the necessary changes until they all pass.

Suppose the necessary changes to the production code to satisfy the new business requirement are applicable only to a single subroutine for which we have provided unit tests to cover all its execution paths. Indeed, let's assume that this subroutine requiring changes checks a document type and determines the type of subcode to be associated with it. Perhaps our subroutine is written like what we see in Listing 6-13.

Listing 6-13. Example of subroutine to determine subcode to be associated with document type

```
form identify_document_subcode using document_type
                                      type blart
                         changing document_subcode
                                      type subcode.
  if document_type eq 'Z9'.
    document_subcode = 'W560'.
  else
    document_subcode = space.
  endif.
endform.
```

Let's also assume that the new business requirement calls for associating subcode 'Q050' with document type 'Z8'. Before we even change the code, we are faced with a decision about how we might want to implement this change into this subroutine. We could insert another "if" statement to handle the new document type, or we could replace the current "if" statement with a "case" statement. A quick chat with our business analyst confirms our suspicion that over the next few months, there will be additional document types requiring subcode assignments, so let's convert this existing "if" statement into a "case" statement that more easily can be extended as new document type/subcode combinations become required.

Accordingly, we would refactor the subroutine to look like what is shown in Listing 6-14, with changes highlighted in bold.

Listing 6-14. Example of refactored subroutine to determine subcode to be associated with document type

```
form identify_document_subcode using document_type
                                        type blart
                             changing document_subcode
                                        type subcode.
  case document_type.
    when 'Z9'.
      document_subcode = 'W560'.
    when others.
      document_subcode = space.
  endcase.
endform.
```

Notice that all we did was refactor the subroutine – to make it produce the same result it had produced before but with changes to how that result is determined. We have not yet applied any new processing to satisfy the new business requirement.

We should be able to run the unit tests at this point and find that all of them still pass, which would suggest that the refactoring changes we applied to this subroutine have not caused it to produce a result it was not already producing. Accordingly, simply having associated unit tests to run afterward, executable at the push of a button and completing in virtually no time at all, provides us with the confidence that our refactoring efforts have not introduced any new problems with the changed code. Not only that, but these refactoring changes required no counterpart changes to any of the existing unit tests.

Now that the unit tests are still passing after having refactored this subroutine to enable easier maintenance, we now can apply the changes associated with the new business requirement. Listing 6-15 shows the result, with changes highlighted in bold.

Listing 6-15. Example of subroutine changed to accommodate new business requirement

```
form identify_document_subcode using document_type
                                        type blart
                             changing document_subcode
                                        type subcode.
  case document_type.
```

```
    when 'Z8'.
      document_subcode = 'Q050'.
    when 'Z9'.
      document_subcode = 'W560'.
    when others.
      document_subcode = space.
  endcase.
endform.
```

Notice that the only change required was an additional "when" condition to the existing case statement along with its corresponding subcode assignment statement. Running the unit tests at this point should still result in all unit tests passing, but now we have introduced a new logic path into this changed subroutine. Accordingly, to continue to maintain unit test coverage for all logic paths through this subroutine, we should define a new unit test method specifically written to check that subcode 'Q050' is returned when this subroutine is called with document type 'Z8'.

EXERCISES

At this point, take a break from reading and shift into exercise mode. Refer to the accompanying workbook to perform the one exercise associated with workbook **Section 8: ABAP Unit Testing 106 – How Unit Testing Enables Confident Refactoring**.

Diagnosing the Absence of Sufficient Test Data

With a language like ABAP, it is commonplace to find locations within the code where records are retrieved from various persistence repositories with subsequent processing dependent upon the content of those records. Often it is the case that the development environment where program creation and maintenance is performed does not have a sufficient collection of records to accommodate the associated automated unit tests, but a development environment dedicated only to testing will have more than enough records to facilitate the necessary automated testing.

This seems to be the development scenario in which many ABAP programmers find themselves working. In such cases, the changes to the code would be applied using the development environment allocated to program creation and maintenance, while the development environment dedicated to testing would be the environment in which the unit tests would be run. In such a scenario, it is easy to accidentally run the unit tests in the wrong environment and see them fail simply because there is a lack of applicable records in the persistence repositories.

Unit test failures of any kind can induce feelings of dread and anxiety accompanied by dry mouth, cold sweat, and stomach knots, so it might be helpful to distinguish between unit tests that fail due to lack of records in the persistence repositories and unit tests genuinely failing due to the production code not processing correctly. A distinction can be made between these by including the "level = tolerable" parameter on the assertion performed by the unit test detecting a lack of records available from a persistence repository. This causes the associated failure diagnostics presented by the ABAP Unit Result Display report to be marked as warnings instead of errors, enabling the programmer to breathe a sigh of relief once realizing that the unit tests simply were run in the wrong environment.

Listing 6-16 contains a unit test method code snippet illustrating the use of the "level = tolerable" assertion parameter.

Listing 6-16. Unit test method code snippet illustrating use of the "level = tolerable" assertion parameter

```
o
o
select *
  into table test_flights_stack
  from sflight
 where carrid eq 'AA'.
cl_abap_unit_assert=>assert_not_initial(
  act   = test_flights_stack
  msg   = 'No flights records found for testing'
  level = cl_aunit_assert=>tolerable
).
o
o
```

In the code snippet shown in Listing 6-16, table test_flights_stack is to be loaded with those records from persistence repository sflight which match the carrier identifier 'AA.' The assertion following the select statement insures conforming records had been found; if not, then it causes the message "No flights records found for testing" to be issued as a warning instead of an error.

An assertion used in the manner illustrated in Listing 6-16 is known as a *Guard Assertion*.[3] The assertion is made *prior* to calling the component under test. It guards against continuing on to the Exercise phase of the Four-Phase Test upon determining there is no point in doing so when the conditions for an effective test cannot be established, as shown in the example when no corresponding records have been retrieved from a persistence repository.

Unit tests that rely upon records retrieved from persistence repositories emanate the smell known as Resource Optimism, a variety of the smell Erratic Test, since sometimes they fail and sometimes they pass. This will be explored further in the next section.

EXERCISES

At this point, take a break from reading and shift into exercise mode. Refer to the accompanying workbook to perform the two exercises associated with workbook **Section 9: ABAP Unit Testing 107 – Diagnosing the Absence of Sufficient Test Data**.

Creating and Using Fabricated Test Data

In the previous section, we explored how to identify the lack of sufficient test data residing as records in various persistence repositories required by the code under test. In this section, we will explore how to construct unit tests such that they do not need to rely on the existence of such records. Instead, the unit test assumes the responsibility to create for itself whatever test data might be required for the code under test to execute successfully. To do so is to liberate the unit test from any dependency upon test data over which it has no control and, as a consequence, preclude it from spewing forth a foul odor reminiscent of the smell Resource Optimism.

Often such test data generation takes the form of creating an internal table of records that the code under test might otherwise expect to find in a persistence repository. Accordingly, rather than making available to the code under test an internal table of real records retrieved from a real persistence repository, the unit test simply fabricates its

---

[3]Meszaros, Gerard, *xUnit Test Patterns: Refactoring Test Code*, Addison Wesley, 2007, p. 490

own records into the internal table, assigning to those records whatever column values will cause the code under test to perform the processing tested by the unit test.

Listing 6-17 shows an example of a unit test class relying on the existence of records in the corresponding persistence repository.

Listing 6-17. Example of unit test class relying on the existence of persistence records

```
class tester definition final
                      for testing
                      risk level harmless.
  private section.
    methods adjust_flight_revenue for testing.
endclass.
class tester implementation.
  method adjust_flight_revenue.
    data test_flights_stack type standard table
                            of sflight.
    select *
      into table test_flights_stack
      from sflight
     where carrid eq 'AA'.
    perform adjust_flight_revenue changing test_flights_stack.
      o
      o
  endmethod.
endclass.
```

Notice in Listing 6-17 that method adjust_flight_revenue selects records from table sflight that match carrier identifier 'AA'. It is entirely possible that no matching records exist in this table, meaning that table test_flights_stack would be empty when the call is made to subroutine adjust_flight_revenue. Surely the test does not intend to use an empty table on this call since otherwise it could have dispensed entirely with the attempt at record retrieval and simply left the table empty. Accordingly, the test is written with the optimistic assumption that records will be found by the retrieval in method adjust_flight_revenue, but there is no guarantee that any will be found.

Listing 6-18 shows how the unit test class can be written in a way where it is not dependent on any records having been found in the persistence repository, with changes from Listing 6-17 highlighted in bold.

Listing 6-18. Listing 6-17 changed to no longer rely on the existence of persistence records

```
class tester definition final
                        for testing
                        risk level harmless.
  private section.
    methods adjust_flight_revenue for testing.
endclass.
class tester implementation.
  method adjust_flight_revenue.
    data test_flights_stack type standard table
                                of sflight.
    data test_flights_entry like line
                                of test_flights_stack.
    select *
      into table test_flights_stack
      from sflight
     where carrid eq 'AA'.
    test_flights_entry-mandt      = sy-mandt.
    test_flights_entry-fldate     = sy-datum.
    test_flights_entry-price      = 1000.
    test_flights_entry-carrid     = 'AA'.
    test_flights_entry-currency   = 'USD'.
    test_flights_entry-planetype  = '747-400'.
    test_flights_entry-seatsmax   = 385.
    do 02 times.
      add 01 to test_flights_entry-connid.
      do 05 times.
        add 01 to test_flights_entry-fldate.
        test_flights_entry-seatsocc
                            = test_flights_entry-seatsmax
```

```
                                  - sy-index * 10.
      test_flights_entry-paymentsum
                              = test_flights_entry-price
                            * test_flights_entry-seatsocc.
        append test_flights_entry
            to test_flights_stack.
      enddo.
    enddo.
    perform adjust_flight_revenue changing test_flights_stack.
      o
      o
  endmethod.
endclass.
```

Notice in Listing 6-18 that the select statement has been discarded and records otherwise expected to be retrieved are now built manually into table test_flights_stack. With this arrangement, the unit test method no longer oozes the smell Resource Optimism.

As you can see, this requires a bit more unit testing code to generate the necessary test data. When multiple unit test methods of the same unit test class require the same set of fabricated test data, then the process of creating the test data can be delegated to the static class_setup fixture method, which can create the test data once and then make it available later to whichever unit test methods might require it. Indeed, due to the new clutter of statements in the unit test method of Listing 6-18 devoted to building test records, the stench of the smell Obscure Test[4] now wafts from it. To remedy this, all the code associated with building test records, when not encapsulated into a fixture setup method, should be encapsulated into its own method and explicitly called from unit test method adjust_flight_revenue.

EXERCISES

At this point, take a break from reading and shift into exercise mode. Refer to the accompanying workbook to perform the 12 exercises associated with workbook **Section 10: ABAP Unit Testing 108 – Creating and Using Fabricated Test Data**.

---

[4]Meszaros, Gerard, *xUnit Test Patterns: Refactoring Test Code*, Addison Wesley, 2007, p. 186

Gaining Control Over References to Modifiable Global Variables Within Subroutines

The use of modifiable global variables has become a particular sore spot with ABAP programming. In some cases, these global variables are required, such as when information is to be exchanged between an ABAP program and fields on its associated screens. Unfortunately, the typical ABAP program contains a plethora of modifiable global variables, many of which easily could have been defined as local variables simply due to the fact that they are used in only a single subroutine.

For some programmers, the choice of whether to define variables locally or globally does not even occur to them after having become comfortable writing ABAP programs where all variables are defined globally. This poor habit is reinforced each time a programmer needs to create a new ABAP component and the editor itself prompts the programmer to define TOP includes and other such containers that perpetuate the indiscriminate declaration and use of global variables.

Even the book *Official ABAP Programming Guidelines* states the following regarding global variables:

Rule 6.3: Do Not Declare Global Variables

Do not declare variables in the global declaration part of a program. Variables may only be declared as attributes of classes and interfaces or locally in methods.[5]

Notice that Rule 6.3 does not mention declaring variables locally in subroutines but only in methods. This is because the same book declares that the use of subroutines in ABAP programs is obsolete:

A.1.1 Subroutines

Obsolete Construct

Subroutines that are declared with FORM-ENDFORM are obsolete.[6]

Despite subroutines having been declared obsolete, there is still a large body of ABAP code using such subroutines. Accordingly, one of the easiest ways to gain control

---

[5]Keller, Horst and Thümmel, Wolf Hagen, *Official ABAP Programming Guidelines*, Galileo Press, 2010, p. 224
[6]Ibid, p. 342

over references to modifiable global variables is for all subroutines to have signature parameters declared through which to exchange the content of the global variables required by the subroutine. This specifically means that no subroutine should contain within it a reference to a modifiable global variable. If the processing contained within a subroutine requires that it use the value held by a modifiable global variable, or in some cases even a non-modifiable global variable such as a constant, then the signature of the subroutine should be defined such that it provides the necessary formal parameters for the global variable values to be passed to or returned from the subroutine, and callers of the subroutine should provide the global variables as the corresponding actual parameters.

Listing 6-19 shows an example of a subroutine directly accessing a global variable.

Listing 6-19. Example of a subroutine directly accessing a global variable

```
data report_content type report_list.
parameters alv_list radiobutton group alv.
parameters alv_grid radiobutton group alv.
  o
  o
  perform show_report changing report_content.
  o
  o
form show_report changing report_stack type report_list.
  if alv_grid is not initial.
    perform show_alv_grid changing report_stack.
  else.
    perform show_alv_list changing report_stack.
  endif.
endform.
```

Notice in Listing 6-19 that subroutine show_report checks the value of alv_grid to determine which of two subsequent subroutines is to be called. Field alv_grid is defined as a parameter to appear on the screen as a radio button; hence, a global variable is accessed directly within subroutine show_report. Listing 6-20 shows how the subroutine show_report can be changed to accept through its signature the designation for which type of report to produce, with changes from Listing 6-19 highlighted in bold.

Listing 6-20. Listing 6-19 changed to avoid directly accessing a global variable

```
data report_content type report_list.
parameters alv_list radiobutton group alv.
parameters alv_grid radiobutton group alv.
  o
  o
  perform show_report using alv_grid
                    changing report_content.
  o
  o
form show_report using display_as_grid type xflag
                  changing report_stack type report_list.
  if display_as_grid is not initial.
    perform show_alv_grid changing report_stack.
  else.
    perform show_alv_list changing report_stack.
  endif.
endform.
```

Notice in Listing 6-20 that subroutine show_report no longer directly accesses the global variable named alv_grid but now accesses its own signature parameter to make the determination of which subsequent subroutine to call. The perform statement to subroutine show_report also was changed to specify global variable alv_grid as the field to supply the value to signature parameter display_as_grid of subroutine show_report.

To apply these changes constitutes refactoring the program. No new business processing is being introduced; instead, the subroutines are refactored to perform the same processing but now to use references to their own parameters rather than references to what otherwise might be modifiable global variables.

Note   Contrary to what has been mentioned earlier in this book about refactoring not requiring any changes to the corresponding unit tests, this type of refactoring is an exception because the unit test methods providing tests for the subroutine would need to change accordingly to provide the necessary new signature parameters on the call to the subroutine.

EXERCISES

At this point, take a break from reading and shift into exercise mode. Refer to the accompanying workbook to perform the six exercises associated with workbook **Section 11: ABAP Unit Testing 109 – Gaining Control Over References to Modifiable Global Variables Within Subroutines**.

Summary

This chapter covered the most rudimentary aspects of writing automated unit tests for ABAP components, introducing a simple unit test and then expanding upon that to describe more of the features and capabilities available through the ABAP Unit Testing Framework, including how unit tests can be written to test function modules and global classes. It further explored some of the ABAP statements and features presenting challenges to automated testing and demonstrated how the presence of automated unit tests instills the programmer with the confidence to make the necessary changes when the need arises to refactor production code, describing how to diagnose the absence of sufficient test data as well as considerations for creating fabricated test data and illustrating a way to gain control over the use of global variables in the production code. It is with this chapter that the associated exercise programs are first used as a teaching device for reinforcing the concepts presented in the book.

CHAPTER 7

Design for Testability

The previous chapter covered the basic techniques used when writing automated unit tests for ABAP programs, which included exposing some of the challenges we are likely to encounter when writing such tests. Aside from brief excursions into the considerations and techniques associated with writing unit tests for function modules and global classes, the explanations and accompanying exercise programs so far have focused on testing ABAP production components designed around the use of subroutines (FORM-ENDFORM).

In this chapter, we will explore additional ways to design ABAP components such that their procedures can be more readily subjected to automated unit tests. It is at this point that we will begin to introduce into the production path the program design features made possible by the object-oriented model, since this will enable automated unit testing coverage of ABAP components that is virtually impossible to achieve with programs designed using a purely procedural model.

Changing the Production Path to Enable Automated Testing

Often it is the case that existing production code will need to be changed to facilitate creating automated unit tests for it. Roy Osherove explains further:

> *Changing the design of your code so that it's more easily testable is a controversial issue for some developers. … [some ask] "Why should I care about testability in my design?" The question is a legitimate one. When designing software, you learn to think about what the software should accomplish and what the results will be for the end user of the system.*[1]

Osherove then proceeds to explain that a unit test represents just another user of the software and that the expectation of the software by the user known as "unit test" is that it

---

[1]Osherove, Roy, *The Art of Unit Testing*, second edition, Manning, 2014, p. 219

© James E. McDonough 2021
J. E. McDonough, *Automated Unit Testing with ABAP*, https://doi.org/10.1007/978-1-4842-6951-0_7

facilitates testability. Accordingly, this user has a beneficial effect upon the design of the software, just as the expectations of a human user would have on the functionality of the software. He goes on to state that with a testable design, writing a unit test for a procedure should be both quick and easy, resulting in one that exhibits the following characteristics:

- Executes rapidly

- Is capable of being isolated from the effects of any associated procedures

- Does not require any external configuration

- Produces a consistent and reliable pass/fail result

He sums it up by stating

These are the FICC properties: fast, isolated, configuration-free, and consistent. If it's hard to write such a test, or if it takes a long time to write it, the system isn't testable.[2]

However, designing a program so that it can be automatically unit tested provides benefits beyond just the ability to run unit tests. It also arranges the code so that it can be more easily maintained.

Suppose we are working for a company with the contract to handle ticket sales for events held at stadiums in Italy as shown in Table 7-1.

Table 7-1. *Stadiums in Italy for which ticket sales are handled*

Stadium	City
Stadio Olimpico	Rome
Stadio San Paolo	Naples
Stadio Artemio Franchi	Florence
Arena Civica	Milan
Stadio Luigi Ferraris	Genoa

---

[2]Ibid p. 220

Listing 7-1 shows an example of a simple ABAP procedure capable of producing the total count of tickets sold for events at these stadiums based on criteria qualifying both the stadiums to be included in the count and the date of the events taking place there.

Listing 7-1. Example of ABAP procedure to produce the total count of tickets sold for events

```
form report_total_tickets_sold using stadium_identifier_range
                                      event_date_range.
  data tickets_sold type sy-dbcnt.
  select count(*)
    into tickets_sold
    from zticket_sales
  where stadium_id in stadium_identifier_range
    and event_date in event_date_range.
  write / 'total number of tickets sold:', tickets_sold.
endform.
```

This example shows a procedure named report_total_tickets_sold that through its signature receives input (stadium_identifier_range and event_date_range) but returns no output and also acquires input not supplied by its caller (the select statement) and produces output not intended for its caller (the write statement).

Listing 7-2 expands upon this by providing additional code to make this an executable program, with changes highlighted in bold.

Listing 7-2. Listing 7-1 expanded to make it an executable program

```
report.
select-options stadium  for zticket_sales-stadium_id.
select-options evntdate for zticket_sales-event_date.

start-of-selection.
  perform report_total_tickets_sold using stadium
                                          evntdate.

form report_total_tickets_sold using stadium_identifier_range
                                      event_date_range.
  data tickets_sold type sy-dbcnt.
```

```
select count(*)
  into tickets_sold
  from zticket_sales
 where stadium_id in stadium_identifier_range
   and event_date in event_date_range.
 write / 'total number of tickets sold:', tickets_sold.
endform.
```

The program is now executable while remaining sufficiently simple to illustrate the different types of input and output that could appear in an ABAP program.

In its current format, it is virtually impossible to write a useful automated unit test for this program. The only component applicable to such a test is the subroutine report_total_tickets_sold. Though we could write a local class containing a unit test method calling this subroutine, there is no assertion the test can make to determine whether or not the subroutine worked correctly – it returns no information to the caller, acquires its own input that a test cannot detect, and creates a classic list report the test cannot see. In short, there is nothing this subroutine does that can be tested effectively through automation. That does not mean we need to abandon all hope of ever bringing this program under the control of automated unit tests, but only that to do so will require the production path to be refactored in a way that enables automated testing.

Categorizing Input and Output

As illustrated in the example code of Listing 7-1, a procedure will be designed to accept input and produce output. Input accepted by such a procedure can be categorized as follows:

- Content provided to the procedure by its caller

   This category of input consists of content supplied by a caller through the inbound signature parameters defined for the procedure. The content provided by these signature parameters can be used immediately by the procedure without it having to perform any processing to make that content available.

- Content acquired by the procedure during its execution

  This category of input consists of content made available to the procedure through an explicit action taken by the procedure, such as issuing an Open SQL select statement or by calling some other component capable of providing the necessary content.

- Existing content of global variables

  Global variables always are available to any procedure. The content provided by a global variable also can be used immediately by the procedure without it having to perform any processing to make that content available.

Similarly, output produced by such a procedure can be categorized as follows:

- Content returned by the procedure to its caller

  This category of output consists of content returned to a caller through the outbound signature parameters defined for the procedure.

- Content sent by the procedure to a receiver other than its caller

  This category of output consists of any content produced by the procedure but not intended for its caller, output made available by the procedure through an explicit action taken by the procedure without reference to its outbound signature parameters, such as issuing an Open SQL insert statement or through a call it makes to a designated content receiver.

- Changed content of global variables

  Global variables always are available to any procedure. The content of a global variable is always changeable by any procedure.

The input and output flowing through a procedure's signature parameters is regarded as *direct*[3] input and output, whereas input and output that does not flow through a procedure's signature parameters is regarded as *indirect*[4] input and output.

Global variables present a particularly thorny issue for procedures. While they are directly accessible by a procedure, they are also considered indirect when providing

---

[3]Meszaros, Gerard, *xUnit Test Patterns: Refactoring Test Code*, Addison Wesley, 2007, p. 792
[4]Ibid, p. 800

input to or accepting output from a procedure. Whereas the signature of a subroutine *enables* a designation for the data type of each parameter and a method of a class *requires* a data type designation for all of its signature parameters, the designation for the data types of global variables used by subroutines and methods cannot appear in their signatures, leaving the associated processing by the procedure exposed to type mismatches in those statements referencing global variables.

Accordingly, it has become widely regarded as a good programming practice to provide global variables to a subroutine or method of a class explicitly through its corresponding signature, enabling them to be treated as direct input and output. This allows defining the data type of the global variable in the signature and then supplying the global variable as the actual parameter associated with its corresponding formal parameter of the signature. We saw an example of this with Listing 6-20. By extension, it has become a good programming practice not only to provide subroutines with signatures, which is not syntactically required for subroutines, but for those signatures to designate the data type associated with the parameter, which also is not syntactically required for subroutines that do have signatures.

In order to provide an ABAP component with a comprehensive set of automated unit tests, it is desirable to have it designed such that each of its procedures references only those variables provided through its signature and only content it explicitly acquires on its own. This means we should endeavor to eliminate from each procedure any explicit references to global variables, replacing their appearance in the code of the procedure with corresponding signature parameters that can provide the necessary access to them.

Encapsulating Indirect Input and Output

The use by a procedure of direct input and output is compatible with automated unit testing, as well as the use of the indirect input and output associated with global variables. This is because a unit test method can always control both the global variables and the signature parameters used by the procedure it is testing.

The use by a procedure of indirect input and output not associated with global variables *may or may not* be compatible with automated unit testing. This is because a unit test method may or may not have control over the indirect input a procedure acquires or the indirect output a procedure produces. When the processing contained within a procedure involves indirect input or indirect output, it becomes necessary to encapsulate that activity into a called procedure that can be controlled by the unit test.

The challenge to doing this is to design the called procedure providing indirect input or accepting indirect output in such a way that enables the unit test to exert control over it while leaving the production path oblivious to the fact that the called procedure can be controlled by a unit test. Accordingly, changing the production path of the program to encapsulate indirect input and indirect output improves its *design for testability.*[5]

Let's consider the variations of called procedures available to us for encapsulating indirect input and output:

- Subroutine

    A procedure written as a subroutine easily can provide indirect input to or accept indirect output from a calling procedure. Unfortunately, it is virtually impossible to design a subroutine in such a way that a unit test method can exert control over it when it is invoked by its caller during a unit test execution. In addition, the FORM-ENDFORM construct has been rendered obsolete for many years. Accordingly, in pursuit of better design for testability, subroutines are not good candidates for encapsulating procedures called to provide indirect input or accept indirect output.

- Function module

    A procedure written as a function module also easily can provide indirect input to or accept indirect output from a calling procedure. The syntax for calling function modules effectively permits either a static call or a dynamic call to the function module based on how the name of the function module is provided on the statement. When the name of the function module to be called is a literal or the name of a defined constant, then it is regarded as a statically specified object; and when specified as a data field or parameter, it is regarded as a dynamically specified object. This means the name of the function module to be called by a procedure could be specified as a signature parameter, allowing the production path to provide the name of the function module for production purposes and the automated unit test path to provide the name of a function module to be used only during unit testing.

---

[5]Ibid, p. 7

Although the statement to call a function module procedure offers some flexibility, it has its drawbacks when applied to automated unit testing:

- A function module built solely for use during unit testing would need to be defined such that its signature matches the signature of its counterpart production path function module. Whereas this is possible, there is no static checking that could be applied to insure that both function modules have compatible signatures, leaving such coordination up to the programmer to be done manually.

- A function module can be defined only globally via the Function Builder. It is impractical to assume that a single function module could be defined as one built solely for use during unit testing and also to provide all the necessary unit testing capabilities for every procedure where it could be substituted during testing. This means that the function module repository would become polluted with the proliferation of specific function modules written to accommodate specific unit tests.

  Accordingly, in pursuit of better design for testability, function modules are not good candidates for encapsulating procedures called to provide indirect input or accept indirect output.

- Method of a class

  A procedure written as a method of a class also easily can provide indirect input to or accept indirect output from a calling procedure. The syntax for calling methods of a class provides the same flexibility found with function modules that makes it possible for them to be specified as signature parameters to the calling procedure, allowing the production path to provide the reference to the class instance to be used for production purposes and the automated unit test path to provide the reference to the class instance to be used only during unit testing. It also does not suffer the drawbacks inherent with function modules when applied to automated unit testing:

- A class built solely for use during unit testing would need to be defined such that its signature matches the signature of its counterpart production path class. This is possible when either the unit test class is a subclass of its counterpart production class or when both the production class and the counterpart unit test class implement the same interface declaring the associated methods, requiring both classes to implement all the methods defined in the interface. Either of these options will allow static checking that both classes have implemented their respective methods using the same method signatures.

- A class can be defined either globally via the Class Builder or locally to the component in which it resides. This means that classes intended to be used solely for unit testing can be defined locally to their respective components, avoiding the pollution of the class repository with the proliferation of classes written to accommodate specific unit tests as would occur with comparable function modules.

  Indeed, the preparation and use of classes in this way makes it possible to define and use classes that can be substituted for their counterpart production classes during the execution of automated unit tests. A subsequent chapter will cover this topic in more detail.

Accordingly, in pursuit of better design for testability, methods of a class make the best candidates for encapsulating procedures called to provide indirect input or accept indirect output.

Interaction Points

A unit test will require interaction with the code under test, whether it is to establish the conditions necessary for a successful test, to execute the code under test once the necessary conditions have been established, or to assert that the code under test has performed as expected. Locations in the code where the unit test method is able to interact with the code under test are known as *interaction points*.[6] Each interaction can be either *direct* or *indirect*. Each point can be either a *control point*[7] or an *observation point*.[8]

- Direct interaction points

    These are locations where a production procedure is called by a unit test method. The call is made to the procedure through its signature. Meszaros refers to this as "going in the front door."[9]

- Indirect interaction points

    These are locations where preparation is performed by a unit test prior to exercising the code under test or analysis is performed by a unit test after the code under test has been exercised. Meszaros refers to this as *Back Door Manipulation*.[10]

- Control point

    These are locations where the unit test provides some content or setting to be used by the code under test and includes the use of fixture methods. It establishes the pre-test state.

- Observation point

    These are locations where the unit test examines some content or setting provided by the code under test. It analyzes the post-test state.

Let's explore these interaction points further and see how they are used. Listing 7-3 shows the ABAP code from Listing 6-3 annotated with line numbers for subsequent reference.

Listing 7-3. Annotated code from Listing 6-3

```
01 report z_issue_message.
02   constants  valid_severities  type string value 'SIWEAX'.
03   data       severity_is_valid type abap_bool.
```

---

[6]Meszaros, Gerard, *xUnit Test Patterns: Refactoring Test Code*, Addison Wesley, 2007, p. 801
[7]Ibid, p. 791
[8]Ibid, p. 804
[9]bid, p. 40
[10]Ibid, p. 327

```
04   parameters severity           type symsgty obligatory.
05 at selection-screen.
06   perform validate_message_severity.
07   if severity_is_valid ne abap_true.
08     message e000(Ok) with 'Select a message severity from the values'
09                            valid_severities.
10   endif.
11 start-of-selection.
12   message 'Hello World!' type severity.
13 form validate_message_severity.
14   if severity ca valid_severities.
15     severity_is_valid = abap_true.
16   else
17     severity_is_valid = abap_false.
18   endif.
19 endform.
20
21 class unit_tester definition for testing risk level harmless.
22   private section.
23     methods validate_message_severity_s for testing.
24 endclass.
25 class unit_tester implementation.
26   method validate_message_severity_s.
27     severity = 'S'.
28     perform validate_message_severity.
29     call method cl_abap_unit_assert=>assert_equals
30       exporting
31         act = severity_is_valid
32         exp = abap_true
33         msg = 'Unexpected result for severity S'.
34   endmethod.
35 endclass.
```

Notice that lines 1–19 represent the production code and that lines 21–35 represent the unit test code. Notice also that there is only one procedure in the production code subject to unit testing: the subroutine validate_message_severity defined by lines 13–19.

This subroutine has no signature and is called from the production code on line 6 and from the unit test code on line 28.

Here we see that the processing of subroutine validate_message_severity inspects the content of global variable severity on line 14 and changes the content of global variable severity_is_valid on lines 15 and 17. Accordingly, it is using indirect input (global variable severity) and indirect output (global variable severity_is_valid).

Line 27 shows an example of an indirect control point as the unit test sets the value of global variable severity. The next line shows an example of a direct control point as the unit test "goes in the front door" by calling the code under test (performs subroutine validate_message_severity).

Lines 29–33 show an example of an indirect observation point as the value of global variable severity_is_valid is asserted to be equal to the expected value abap_true. The expectation at this point is that, having been called from line 28, the subroutine has performed its processing by setting global variable severity_is_valid to a value of true or false based on the value it found in global variable severity. Since the unit test already had set global variable severity to the value 'S' on line 27, the call to the subroutine on line 28 should result in global variable severity_is_valid containing the value abap_true.

Let's change the code in this listing so that subroutine validate_message_severity no longer contains any references to global variables, using the best practice mentioned earlier of providing the subroutine with signature parameters through which it can access global variables. Listing 7-4 shows the changed code, with differences highlighted in bold.

Listing 7-4. Code from Listing 7-3 changed to eliminate references to global variables within subroutine validate_message_severity

```
01 report z_issue_message.
02   constants  valid_severities  type string value 'SIWEAX'.
03   data       severity_is_valid type abap_bool.
04   parameters severity          type symsgty obligatory.
05 at selection-screen.
06   perform validate_message_severity using severity
                                       changing severity_is_valid.
07   if severity_is_valid ne abap_true.
08     message e000(0k) with 'Select a message severity from the values'
09                           valid_severities.
10   endif.
```

```
11 start-of-selection.
12   message 'Hello World!' type severity.
13 form validate_message_severity using severity
                                    type symsgty
                               changing severity_is_valid
                                    type abap_bool.
14   if severity ca valid_severities.
15     severity_is_valid = abap_true.
16   else
17     severity_is_valid = abap_false.
18   endif.
19 endform.
20
21 class unit_tester definition for testing risk level harmless.
22   private section.
23     methods validate_message_severity_s for testing.
24 endclass.
25 class unit_tester implementation.
26   method validate_message_severity_s.
27     severity = 'S'.
28     perform validate_message_severity using severity
                                    changing severity_is_valid.
29     call method cl_abap_unit_assert=>assert_equals
30       exporting
31         act = severity_is_valid
32         exp = abap_true
33         msg = 'Unexpected result for severity S'.
34   endmethod.
35 endclass.
```

Notice that all we did was to provide subroutine validate_message_severity with a signature and then change the calls to it from both the production code and the unit test code to provide the respective global variables as signature parameters. Since the names of signature parameters severity and severity_is_valid match the names of existing global variables, it means that the statements within the subroutine referring to severity and severity_is_valid now refer to the signature parameters instead of to the global variables as they had previously. This changes the categorization of its input and output from indirect to direct.

This also changes the nature of the interaction points. Setting the value of global variable severity on line 27 no longer is considered an indirect control point, nor is checking the value of global variable severity_is_valid on line 31 considered an indirect observation point. This is because now these variables have been provided as the actual parameters to the formal signature parameters defined for subroutine validate_message_severity, which now considers this direct input and output flowing through its signature. Accordingly, lines 27 and 31 no longer are considered interaction points.

Perhaps some of you are skeptical about these former indirect interaction points evaporating simply because a signature has been provided to the subroutine and global variable values are being exchanged through the signature. If so, consider that the code of unit test method validate_message_severity_s could have been written as shown in Listing 7-5, the differences with Listing 7-4 highlighted in bold.

Listing 7-5. Alternative to applying the changes to unit test method validate_message_severity_s

```
26   method validate_message_severity_s.
27     data is_the_severity_valid type abap_bool. "severity = 'S'.
28     perform validate_message_severity using 'S'
                                     changing is_the_severity_valid.
29     call method cl_abap_unit_assert=>assert_equals
30       exporting
31         act = is_the_severity_valid
32         exp = abap_true
33         msg = 'Unexpected result for severity S'.
34   endmethod.
```

Notice that now the unit test method makes no references at all to global variables, so there are no longer any points where it indirectly interacts with the code under test, but we should still expect the unit test to pass. The only interaction point remaining between unit test and code under test is the direct interaction point on line 28 where the unit test calls the code of the production path and is going in the front door of the subroutine. Whereas the unit test method is able to examine and change the values of global variables, it does not constitute an interaction point when those global variables are not used by the code under test.

Encapsulating Indirect Input Processes to Accommodate Unit Testing

This section covers the process of encapsulating the acquisition of indirect input required by a procedure into a method of a class that can be called to perform that activity for the procedure. It will require refactoring the procedure to enable it to be subjected to unit testing.

Listing 7-6 is a copy of Listing 7-2 with changes applied to show how the indirect input of subroutine report_total_tickets_sold can be encapsulated into a method of a class, with changes highlighted in bold.

Listing 7-6. Listing 7-2 with changes applied to illustrate encapsulating indirect input

```
report.
class ticket_sales_examiner definition.
  public section.
    types stadium_identifier_range type range of zticket_sales-stadium_id.
    types event_date_range         type range of zticket_sales-event_date.
    methods get_total_tickets_sold
      importing stadium_identifier type stadium_identifier_range
                event_date         type event_date_range
      exporting tickets_sold       type sy-dbcnt.
endclass.
class ticket_sales_examiner implementation.
  method get_total_tickets_sold.
    select count(*)
      into tickets_sold
      from zticket_sales
     where stadium_id in stadium_identifier
       and event_date in event_date.
  endmethod.
endclass.

data ticket_sales_examiner type ref to ticket_sales_examiner.
select-options stadium  for zticket_sales-stadium_id.
select-options evntdate for zticket_sales-event_date.
```

```
start-of-selection.
  create object ticket_sales_examiner.
  perform report_total_tickets_sold using stadium
                                          evntdate.

form report_total_tickets_sold using stadium_identifier_range
                                     event_date_range.
  data tickets_sold type sy-dbcnt.
  select count(*)
    into tickets_sold
    from zticket_sales
   where stadium_id in stadium_identifier_range
     and event_date in event_date_range.
  call method ticket_sales_examiner->get_total_tickets_sold
    exporting
      stadium_identifier = stadium_identifier_range
      event_date         = event_date_range
    importing
      tickets_sold       = tickets_sold.
  write / 'total number of tickets sold:', tickets_sold.
endform.
```

What have we done here? We've defined a new class named ticket_sales_examiner having a single method named get_total_tickets_sold. The implementation of this method has virtually the same code that had been removed from subroutine report_total_tickets_sold. The retrieval for the number of tickets sold now is encapsulated into a class that can provide that information. Accordingly, the subroutine no longer acquires this input itself but calls a method capable of doing so on its behalf. We've also defined a new global variable to hold a reference to an instance of class ticket_sales_examiner and created an instance of it in the start-of-selection event block just prior to invoking the subroutine.

Listing 7-7 shows a copy of Listing 7-6 without the stricken statements and highlighting.

Listing 7-7. A copy of Listing 7-6 without the stricken records and highlighting

```
report.
class ticket_sales_examiner definition.
  public section.
    types stadium_identifier_range type range of zticket_sales-stadium_id.
    types event_date_range         type range of zticket_sales-event_date.
    methods get_total_tickets_sold
      importing stadium_identifier type stadium_identifier_range
                event_date         type event_date_range
      exporting tickets_sold       type sy-dbcnt.
endclass.
class ticket_sales_examiner implementation.
  method get_total_tickets_sold.
    select count(*)
      into tickets_sold
      from zticket_sales
    where stadium_id in stadium_identifier
      and event_date in event_date.
  endmethod.
endclass.

data ticket_sales_examiner type ref to ticket_sales_examiner.
select-options stadium  for zticket_sales-stadium_id.
select-options evntdate for zticket_sales-event_date.

start-of-selection.
  create object ticket_sales_examiner.
  perform report_total_tickets_sold using stadium
                                          evntdate.

form report_total_tickets_sold using stadium_identifier_range
                                     event_date_range.
  data tickets_sold type sy-dbcnt.
  call method ticket_sales_examiner->get_total_tickets_sold
    exporting
      stadium_identifier = stadium_identifier_range
```

```
    event_date          = event_date_range
  importing
    tickets_sold        = tickets_sold.
 write / 'total number of tickets sold:', tickets_sold.
endform.
```

There are those who would complain that this program has had 26 lines added and 5 removed, for a net gain of 21 extra lines in a program that had only 18 lines before having made any changes, more than doubling the number of lines the program has. True, that is the case; however, software quality cannot be measured by number of lines. These changes have moved the program a step closer to being designed for testability.

Aside from the benefits this program has gained toward unit testing, it now also has a better design for its production path. The subroutine report_total_tickets_sold no longer performs a direct retrieval from a custom table, delegating this retrieval instead to a method of a class. In effect, the subroutine is no longer bound to the custom table. Now it is up to the method called by this subroutine – get_total_tickets_sold – to determine how to provide that answer. This method could determine the total count of tickets sold using a flat file or a spreadsheet or in a variety of other ways than through the customized table in use at the moment, and the subroutine making the call to it would not need to change at all. Accordingly, the program itself is more flexible and adaptable to future changes.

Again, there are some who would point out that encapsulating the code determining total ticket sales into a method of a class has only moved the location where such changes would be required if it were to become necessary to change from, say, using the customized table to using a flat file. Again, this is true, but the fact that this processing is now encapsulated into a class provides more flexible alternatives for its implementation, not the least of which is to have two classes defined, one capable of using a customized table, as it does now, and another capable of using a flat file, with both classes inheriting from a single class that can provide the definition for the methods they both implement. With this flexibility, it is even possible now to design the program such that the decision whether to use a customized table or flat file can be made *at runtime*, instantiating whichever of these two subclasses provides that service, and still the subroutine would not have to be altered in any way.

EXERCISES

At this point, take a break from reading and shift into exercise mode. Refer to the accompanying workbook to perform the 13 exercises associated with workbook **Section 12: ABAP Unit Testing 201 – Gaining Control Over Unit Test Coverage of Input.**

Encapsulating Indirect Output Processes to Accommodate Unit Testing

This section covers the process of encapsulating the handling of indirect output produced by a procedure into a method of a class that can be called to perform that activity for the procedure. This also will require refactoring the procedure to enable it to be subjected to unit testing.

Listing 7-8 is a copy of Listing 7-7 with changes applied to show how the indirect output of subroutine report_total_tickets_sold can be encapsulated into a method of a class, with changes highlighted in bold.

Listing 7-8. Listing 7-7 with changes applied to illustrate encapsulating indirect output

```
report.
class ticket_sales_examiner definition.
  public section.
    types stadium_identifier_range type range of zticket_sales-stadium_id.
    types event_date_range         type range of zticket_sales-event_date.
    methods get_total_tickets_sold
      importing stadium_identifier type stadium_identifier_range
                event_date         type event_date_range
      exporting tickets_sold       type sy-dbcnt.
endclass.
class ticket_sales_examiner implementation.
  method get_total_tickets_sold.
    select count(*)
      into tickets_sold
      from zticket_sales
```

153

```
    where stadium_id in stadium_identifier
      and event_date in event_date.
  endmethod.
endclass.

class ticket_sales_reporter definition.
  public section.
    methods show_total_tickets_sold
      importing descriptor          type string
                tickets_sold        type sy-dbcnt.
endclass.
class ticket_sales_reporter implementation.
  method show_total_tickets_sold.
    write / descriptor, tickets_sold.
  endmethod.
endclass.

data ticket_sales_examiner type ref to ticket_sales_examiner.
data ticket_sales_reporter type ref to ticket_sales_reporter.
select-options stadium  for zticket_sales-stadium_id.
select-options evntdate for zticket_sales-event_date.

start-of-selection.
  create object ticket_sales_examiner.
  create object ticket_sales_reporter.
  perform report_total_tickets_sold using stadium
                                          evntdate.

form report_total_tickets_sold using stadium_identifier_range
                                     event_date_range.
  data tickets_sold type sy-dbcnt.
  call method ticket_sales_examiner->get_total_tickets_sold
    exporting
      stadium_identifier = stadium_identifier_range
      event_date         = event_date_range
    importing
      tickets_sold       = tickets_sold.
```

```
write / 'total number of tickets sold:', tickets_sold.
call method ticket_sales_reporter->show_total_tickets_sold
  exporting
    descriptor          = 'total number of tickets sold:'
    tickets_sold        = tickets_sold.
```
endform.

What have we done here? We've defined a new class named ticket_sales_reporter having a single method named show_total_tickets_sold. The implementation of this method has virtually the same code that had been removed from subroutine report_total_tickets_sold. The presentation for the number of tickets sold now is encapsulated into a class that can provide that service. Accordingly, the subroutine no longer writes this output itself but calls a method capable of doing so on its behalf. We've also defined a new global variable to hold a reference to an instance of class ticket_sales_reporter and created an instance of it in the start-of-selection event block just prior to invoking the subroutine.

Listing 7-9 shows a copy of Listing 7-8 without the stricken statements and highlighting.

Listing 7-9. Listing 7-8 without the highlighting and stricken statements

```
report.
class ticket_sales_examiner definition.
  public section.
    types stadium_identifier_range type range of zticket_sales-stadium_id.
    types event_date_range         type range of zticket_sales-event_date.
    methods get_total_tickets_sold
      importing stadium_identifier type stadium_identifier_range
                event_date         type event_date_range
      exporting tickets_sold       type sy-dbcnt.
endclass.
class ticket_sales_examiner implementation.
  method get_total_tickets_sold.
    select count(*)
      into tickets_sold
      from zticket_sales
```

```
      where stadium_id in stadium_identifier
        and event_date in event_date.
  endmethod.
endclass.

class ticket_sales_reporter definition.
  public section.
    methods show_total_tickets_sold
      importing descriptor          type string
                tickets_sold        type sy-dbcnt.
endclass.
class ticket_sales_reporter implementation.
  method show_total_tickets_sold.
    write / descriptor, tickets_sold.
  endmethod.
endclass.

data ticket_sales_examiner type ref to ticket_sales_examiner.
data ticket_sales_reporter type ref to ticket_sales_reporter.
select-options stadium  for zticket_sales-stadium_id.
select-options evntdate for zticket_sales-event_date.

start-of-selection.
  create object ticket_sales_examiner.
  create object ticket_sales_reporter.
  perform report_total_tickets_sold using stadium
                                          evntdate.

form report_total_tickets_sold using stadium_identifier_range
                                     event_date_range.
  data tickets_sold type sy-dbcnt.
  call method ticket_sales_examiner->get_total_tickets_sold
    exporting
      stadium_identifier = stadium_identifier_range
      event_date         = event_date_range
    importing
      tickets_sold       = tickets_sold.
```

```
call method ticket_sales_reporter->show_total_tickets_sold
  exporting
    descriptor          = 'total number of tickets sold:'
    tickets_sold        = tickets_sold.
endform.
```

As we had seen with the changes to encapsulate indirect input, these changes have moved the program another step closer to being designed for testability.

Aside from the benefits this program has gained toward unit testing, it now also has a better design for its production path. The subroutine report_total_tickets_sold no longer performs a direct write to a classic list, delegating this instead to a method of a class. In effect, the subroutine is no longer bound to the use of a classic list. Now it is up to the method called by this subroutine – show_total_tickets_sold – to determine how to present this information. This method could use an ABAP MESSAGE statement, present an ALV grid using either a full-screen or popup window, call a function module capable of displaying such information, and a variety of other ways than through the classic list in use at the moment, and the subroutine making the call to it would not need to change at all. Accordingly, the program itself is more flexible and adaptable to future changes.

Despite all the changes that have been made to the production path to encapsulate the indirect input and output associated with subroutine report_total_tickets_sold, you may have noticed that the program still remains without any automated unit test to determine whether this subroutine is working correctly. This deficit will be addressed in the next chapter.

EXERCISES

At this point, take a break from reading and shift into exercise mode. Refer to the accompanying workbook to perform the six exercises associated with workbook **Section 13: ABAP Unit Testing 202 – Gaining Control Over Unit Test Coverage of Output.**

Summary

This chapter explained the concept of controlling indirect input to and indirect output from a procedure, showing how these types of input and output need to be encapsulated to insure a component is designed for testability, concluding through analysis how only object-oriented classes can provide the necessary capabilities toward this end due to the limitations inherent with function modules and subroutines as encapsulators. Interactions between the unit test and the tested procedure are described as test interaction points which can be direct or indirect as well as control or observation. Examples showed how to encapsulate both indirect input and indirect output to enable automated testing.

CHAPTER 8

Test Doubles

The previous chapter covered the considerations associated with refactoring a program to encapsulate the processes that perform the exchange of indirect input and output from the rest of its processing. This was achieved through the use of object-oriented classes that could encapsulate the respective processes. Refactoring such components into object-oriented classes as opposed to simple subroutines or function modules is done for a specific reason. It is because we will need to be able to substitute components that perform indirect input and output activities in ways that are conducive to running automated unit tests. This chapter explores this topic in more detail.

Depended-On Components

The structure of a typical program may consist of a main driving routine and multiple subroutines it calls. Each of these subroutines themselves may call other subroutines, with each subroutine performing some service required by its caller. For the purpose of illustration, Listing 8-1 shows pseudo-code for such a program.

Listing 8-1. Pseudo-code for typical program with main driving routine and multiple subroutines

```
program xyz

(global variables are defined here)

main_driving_routine
  call subroutine_01
  o
  o
```

© James E. McDonough 2021
J. E. McDonough, *Automated Unit Testing with ABAP*, https://doi.org/10.1007/978-1-4842-6951-0_8

```
   call subroutine_02
   o
   o
   call subroutine_03

subroutine_01
   call subroutine_16
   o
   o
   call subroutine_17

subroutine_02
   call subroutine_55
   o
   o
   call subroutine_72

subroutine_03
   call subroutine_95
   call subroutine_98

   o
   o
```

Notice that the main_driving_routine makes calls to subroutine_01, subroutine_02, and subroutine_03. Also notice that each one of these subroutines also makes calls to other subroutines. In each case, the subroutine that is called is considered a component on which the caller is dependent – that is, the caller is depending on the called subroutine to provide some service on its behalf. In the context of unit testing, a component on which a caller is dependent is known as a *depended-on component*,[1] abbreviated as DOC.

Notice also that none of the subroutines indicate a signature, so all information being exchanged between them is done through global variables. This would mean that each subroutine either provides indirect input to a caller or processes indirect output from a caller.

Let's suppose we wanted to provide such a program with automated unit tests. We would be challenged to write a unit test for subroutine_01 because as part of its

---

[1]Meszaros, Gerard, *xUnit Test Patterns: Refactoring Test Code*, Addison Wesley, 2007, p. 791

processing, it calls subroutine_16 and subroutine_17, its two depended-on components. The concern is that these two subroutines will perform their respective processing on behalf of subroutine_01, but during a unit test, we would want to have the unit test in control of the processing they perform. When our goal is to determine whether the processing of subroutine_01 is correct, we would want to nullify any effects to this subroutine by the components it calls. This is known as *isolating* the code under test.

Isolating the code under test will require refactoring the code so that its depended-on components can be overridden during the execution of a unit test. The first step in isolating subroutine_01 would be to provide signatures for subroutine_16 and subroutine_17 and pass to them the necessary global variables as parameters. Once that has been done, the next step would be to refactor subroutine_16 and subroutine_17 into methods of classes that can encapsulate their respective processing – for now, let's call them method_16 and method_17. Lastly, the program would be changed so that subroutine_01 has access to the instances of the new classes containing method_16 and method_17 that are to be called in place of the calls it had made to subroutine_16 and subroutine_17.

At this point, subroutine_01 would be in a state where a unit test can exert control over its called methods. The next step would be to create classes that can provide the necessary processing for method_16 and method_17 during the execution of an automated unit test, processing that would differ significantly from their production path counterparts. These types of classes are known as *test doubles*.

The Purpose of Test Doubles

A good analogy for thinking about test doubles is to consider how the motion picture industry uses what are known as stunt doubles. These are actors who have learned various ways to avoid injury when performing the dangerous activities called for in a movie. The script might describe a scene where the lead character leaps head first out of a third-floor window of an old hotel and lands in a wagon full of hay. The actor playing the lead character would not perform this leap; instead, it would be performed by a stunt double. While shooting the scene, the camera would capture the action as the lead actor runs to the window, at which point the director would yell "Cut! Send in the stunt double." Then, once the stunt double has taken the place of the lead actor, the director would yell "Lights … Camera … Action!" at which point the stunt double would perform the flying leap into the wagon of hay below that becomes part of the movie. In such cases, a stunt double usually is chosen based on their resemblance to the lead actor so that the audience remains unaware that a different person had performed the stunt.

Test doubles serve the same purpose for automated unit testing as stunt doubles do for the movie industry – specifically, test doubles substitute for actual production components when the automated unit tests are being run. Each test double replaces a called component upon which the code under test depends. It effectively becomes a surrogate for a depended-on component.

For example, let's suppose we have a simple subroutine that calculates the sales tax for each one of a set of records in an internal table supplied by the caller, where the internal table contains the jurisdiction where the sale applies and the subroutine changes each table row to include the associated sales tax. This tax calculation subroutine itself calls a subroutine which supplies the corresponding tax rate to be used. Listing 8-2 shows the ABAP code.

Listing 8-2. Example of subroutine

```
form calculate_sales_tax changing sale_items
                                    type item_table.
  field-symbols <sale_item> type item_row.
  loop at sale_items assigning <sale_item>.
    perform get_sales_tax_rate using <sale_item>-jurisdiction
                          changing <sale_item>-tax_rate.
    <sale_item>-sales_tax = <sale_item>-price * <sale_item>-tax_rate.
  endloop.
endform.
```

Notice that subroutine calculate_sales_tax calls subroutine get_sales_tax_rate. Using the prevailing sales tax rates in effect on January 1, 2020, for jurisdictions in the United States, we should expect subroutine get_sales_tax_rate to return a sales tax rate of 7.25% for California, 4.00% for New York, and zero for Alaska, a state which imposes no sales tax.

Accordingly, subroutine get_sales_tax_rate is a component on which subroutine calculate_sales_tax is dependent. As written, it would be virtually impossible during an automated unit test to substitute the processing performed by subroutine get_sales_tax_rate.

Alternative 1

As an alternative, we could refactor this subroutine such that its signature accepts a reference to the name of a function module that can provide the service of getting the associated sales tax. This way, the production path could provide the name of the function module containing the code copied from subroutine get_sales_tax_rate, and the automated unit test path could provide the name of a test double for that function module, one that can provide whatever processing might be required to satisfy the unit test. We already had concluded in the previous chapter that function modules do not make good candidates for test doubles, but let's explore this possibility anyway. Changes to the subroutine to achieve this alternative are shown in Listing 8-3, with changes from Listing 8-2 highlighted in bold.

Listing 8-3. Refactoring alternative 1: subroutine changed to accept name of function module to determine tax rate

```
form calculate_sales_tax using tax_rate_resolver
                                  type funcname
                    changing sale_items
                                    type item_table.
  field-symbols <sale_item> type item_row.
  loop at sale_items assigning <sale_item>.
    perform get_sales_tax_rate using <sale_item>-jurisdiction
                            changing <sale_item>-tax_rate.
    call function tax_rate_resolver
      exporting
        jurisdiction    = <sale_item>-jurisdiction
      importing
        sales_tax_rate = <sale_item>-tax_rate.
    <sale_item>-sales_tax = <sale_item>-price * <sale_item>-tax_rate.
  endloop.
endform.
```

Notice that depended-on subroutine get_sales_tax_rate has been replaced by a call to the name of a function module provided through the signature of the subroutine. Subroutine calculate_sales_tax no longer is dependent on subroutine get_sales_tax_rate but instead is now dependent on a function module whose name is provided by the caller.

One question that arises is this: Now that the designation of this depended-on component is being supplied through the signature of the subroutine, does it mean that its associated input shifts from being indirect input to direct input? The answer is a resounding "No!" Whereas the name of the depended-on component represents direct input to the subroutine, a value coming in "through the front door," the subroutine still must perform a specific action to acquire that input by calling that depended-on component, meaning that the input provided by the depended-on component still constitutes indirect input.

However, this does represent an example of what is known as *dependency injection*. With dependency injection, a called procedure is provided, through its signature, with the names of or references to components it is to use for its own processing. Essentially, the depended-on components called by a procedure – its dependencies – are injected into the procedure through its signature.

Using a function module in this way may be considered better than when subroutine calculate_sales_tax was dependent on subroutine get_sales_tax_rate, but it does present some exposures, as noted in the previous chapter. For one, neither the syntax checker nor the extended program check is able to determine whether this dependency is valid since it now represents a dynamic call to a function module.[2] In addition, although one function module name can be provided for the production path and a different function module name for the unit test path, both of these corresponding function modules would need to have been defined with matching parameters which, again, cannot be checked during syntax check or extended program check. Furthermore, the call cannot be checked for validity through the syntax checker; if the named function module does not exist at runtime, then class-based exception CX_SY_DYN_CALL_ILLEGAL_FUNC would be raised. In short, it leaves much up to the diligence of the programmer to insure that both the production path and the automated unit test path for this program will execute correctly.

---

[2]When the name of the function module following the CALL FUNCTION statement is a literal, the syntax checker is able to determine whether it exists prior to activating the component containing the call.

Alternative 2

Another alternative, also using the dependency injection technique, is to pass the name of a subroutine to be dynamically called, as shown in Listing 8-4, with changes from Listing 8-2 highlighted in bold.

Listing 8-4. Refactoring alternative 2: subroutine changed to accept name of some other subroutine to determine tax rate

```
form calculate_sales_tax using tax_rate_resolver
                                type formname
                      changing sale_items
                                type item_table.
  field-symbols <sale_item> type item_row.
  loop at sale_items assigning <sale_item>.
    perform (tax_rate_resolver) in program this_program_name
                               using <sale_item>-jurisdiction
                            changing <sale_item>-tax_rate.
    <sale_item>-sales_tax = <sale_item>-price * <sale_item>-tax_rate.
  endloop.
endform.
```

Here we have refactored subroutine calculate_sales_tax such that its signature accepts a reference to the name of a subroutine that can provide the service of getting the associated sales tax. This way, the production path could provide the value GET_SALES_TAX_RATE on the call to subroutine calculate_sales_tax, and the automated unit test path could provide the value of some other subroutine intended to be used only for the purpose of unit testing. Again, subroutine calculate_sales_tax no longer is dependent on subroutine get_sales_tax_ rate but instead is now dependent on a subroutine whose name is provided by the caller.

This alternative also has its exposures. Since the name of the subroutine to be called is now provided as a parameter, it constitutes a dynamic subroutine call. This means the call cannot be checked for validity through the syntax checker; if the named subroutine does not exist at runtime, then class-based exception CX_SY_DYN_CALL_ILLEGAL_ FORM would be raised. In addition, the subroutine to be used during testing would exist in this same program along with other subroutines used for the production path, meaning the program would contain code used solely for the purpose of automated unit testing, emanating the noxious odor of For Tests Only,[3] one of the more putrid variations of the smell Test Logic in Production.[4]

Alternative 3

Yet another alternative, also using the dependency injection technique, is to pass the reference to a class to be called, as shown in Listing 8-5, with changes from Listing 8-2 highlighted in bold.

Listing 8-5. Refactoring alternative 3: subroutine changed to accept interface reference. Corresponding class reference is used to determine tax rate

```
interface tax_rate_resolvable.
  methods get_tax_rate importing jurisdiction
                       type jurisdiction
                     returning value(rate)
                       type tax_rate.
endinterface.
  o
  o
class tax_rate_resolver definition.
  public section.
    interfaces tax_rate_resolvable.
    aliases get_tax_rate
        for tax_rate_resolvable~get_tax_rate.
endclass.
class tax_rate_resolver implementation.
  method get_tax_rate.
    o
    o
  endmethod.
```

---

[3]Meszaros, Gerard, *xUnit Test Patterns: Refactoring Test Code*, Addison Wesley, 2007, p. 219
[4]Ibid, p. 217

```
endclass.
    o
    o
form calculate_sales_tax using tax_rate_resolver
                                type ref to tax_rate_resolvable
                    changing sale_items
                                type item_table.
    field-symbols <sale_item> type item_row.
    loop at sale_items assigning <sale_item>.
      perform get_sales_tax_rate using <sale_item>-jurisdiction
                              changing <sale_item>-tax_rate.
      call method tax_rate_resolver->get_tax_rate
        exporting
          jurisdiction = <sale_item>-jurisdiction
        receiving
          rate         = <sale_item>-tax_rate.
      <sale_item>-sales_tax = <sale_item>-price * <sale_item>-tax_rate.
    endloop.
endform.
```

Here we have refactored subroutine calculate_sales_tax such that its signature accepts an interface reference, one to hold a reference to the instance of a class implementing that interface to provide the service of getting the associated sales tax. This way, the production path could provide on the call to subroutine calculate_sales_tax the reference to an instance of class tax_rate_resolver, one that implements interface tax_rate_resolvable, and the automated unit test path could provide the reference to the instance of some other class implementing interface tax_rate_resolvable, one for which its definition statement might even indicate FOR TESTING, to be used only for the purpose of unit testing. Again, subroutine calculate_sales_tax no longer is dependent on subroutine get_sales_tax_rate but instead is now dependent on an interface reference provided by the caller.

Though it has similarities with the alternative using a function module as shown in Listing 8-3, this alternative does not carry with it the same baggage associated with the previous alternatives using dependency injection. It can be statically checked via both the syntax checker and the extended program check. It also uses the object-oriented principle of polymorphism in accepting a reference to an interface, which necessarily would need to hold an actual reference to a class implementing that interface, enabling a reference of any class implementing this interface to be provided through dependency injection by the caller of the subroutine.

So what's the problem with this alternative? Simply this: The ABAP statement documentation for release 7.5 includes the following bullet point under the associated Notes for the USING clause of the PERFORM statement:

- "When passing an actual parameter to a USING parameter typed as a reference variable, an up cast is not possible."[5]

This bullet point is as clear as mud. To appreciate its full impact, it is necessary to understand what SAP means by an *up cast*, which is this:

If the static type of the target variable is less specific or the same as the static type of the source variable, assignment is always possible. The name up cast arises from the fact that the movement within the inheritance space is upwards. ... This includes ... passes from actual to formal parameters.[6]

Accordingly, an *up cast* on a USING clause of a PERFORM statement would imply either (1) a reference variable typed on the subroutine signature as a superclass holding an actual reference to one of its subclasses or (2) a reference variable typed on the subroutine signature as an interface holding a reference to a class implementing that interface. It seems this bullet point is indicating that such up casting during program execution is not possible.

To put into better perspective this idea of using up cast with a parameter defined by a subroutine signature, consider the following example: A class is defined named animal and has a method named speak. Another class is defined named dog, has its own method named fetch, and also inherits from class animal. An instance of class dog should be able to be used anywhere an instance of class animal is expected, but in

---

[5]https://help.sap.com/doc/abapdocu_750_index_htm/7.50/en-US/abapperform_parameters.htm

[6]https://help.sap.com/doc/abapdocu_750_index_htm/7.50/en-us/abenconversion_references.htm

such cases, the dog would be regarded simply as an animal. This is what is meant by up casting – the dog may play the part of an animal because a dog *is* an animal. Method speak of the dog may be invoked, perhaps resulting in the sound "woof" to be produced, because the animal class has a method named speak that the dog class inherits; however, the dog's method fetch cannot be invoked because the animal class provides no such method. Accordingly, a subroutine defined as

```
form visit_veterinarian using animal type ref to animal.
  o
  o
endform.
```

should be able to be called using the statement

```
perform visit_veterinarian using dog.
```

In this example, the actual parameter dog used on the call to the subroutine is being *up cast* to an animal as defined in the signature of the subroutine. Essentially, the subroutine visit_veterinarian accommodates through its signature that all dogs are animals, but not all animals are dogs.

If indeed the intention behind the bullet point noted in the preceding text is that up casting is not possible, then perhaps a better way to have suggested that restriction would be to conclusively state that such reference variables on USING clauses of PERFORM statements do not support the object-oriented principle of polymorphism. If so, this completely undermines the alternative described in Listing 8-5. But during my research, I have found that the alternative illustrated in Listing 8-5 works just fine in a release 7.4 ABAP environment. Indeed, in the counterpart documentation for that release,[7] there *is no corresponding bullet point* indicating any such restriction with reference variables on USING clauses of PERFORM statements.

Although a 7.5 environment was not available to me on which to test this, Paul Hardy has confirmed to me that indeed a 7.5 system causes syntax errors under these circumstances, which would be catastrophic to sites upon finding their programs using this feature no longer work after upgrading from 7.4 or earlier to 7.5. This is the first time I have ever heard of an instance where SAP backward compatibility is not being supported in a subsequent release – a chilling prospect.

---

[7]https://help.sap.com/doc/abapdocu_740_index_htm/7.40/en-US/abapperform_parameters.htm

Using Test Doubles

A better way is to redesign the code without perpetuating the use of subroutines so that it is capable of using a test double that can be statically checked for its relationship to the component for which it is doubling. This can be facilitated by first refactoring the code in the following way:

- Encapsulate the processing required for resolving the correct tax rate into either a base class that defines its own public methods or a class that uses an interface to provide its public method definitions.

- Encapsulate subroutine calculate_sales_tax into a class having a method whose signature accepts a reference to the base class or interface defined in the previous bullet item.

Why would it be necessary to define a base class or an interface to provide the public methods of the class resolving the correct tax rate? It is so that the method defined for the class that calculates the sales tax can accept through its signature a reference to *any class* that extends that base class or implements that interface. Once it is capable of accepting a reference to more than just a single class, then it can be called by different callers, each one sending its own version of a class instance to be used to resolve the correct tax rate. The called method then regards the reference provided through its signature simply as a class capable of providing the methods defined by the base class or interface, unaware of the actual class being used to provide that service. With such a design, it becomes possible to statically check that a test double class provides implementations for the same method declarations and their respective signatures as the class for which it is doubling.

Not only that, but a test double, when defined as a local class in the same program containing other subroutines, can be restricted for use *only during automated unit testing* by including the FOR TESTING clause in its definition. Compare this with the dynamic subroutine call scenario described in the previous section which was identified as emanating the smell Test Logic in Production. There is no way to designate a subroutine such that it is restricted only for use during unit testing, but local classes can be so designated and their use in the production path, whether intentional or accidental, would be detected and flagged as invalid by the compiler. Since the use in the production path of any local classes defined in the same program and marked as FOR

TESTING would be flagged as invalid by the compiler, their presence does not cause the program to spew forth the toxic smell of Test Logic in Production.

With this design, the production path can provide the instance of a class to resolve the sales tax rate required during normal execution, and the unit test path can provide an instance applicable to unit testing. This might sound very complicated, so let's explore this further in order to clarify it. We'll cover how this is implemented using two scenarios: the first scenario illustrates how this is implemented using the base class variation; the second illustrates the interface variation.

Test Double Using Base Class

The base class scenario consists of a single base class, also known as a superclass, defining the production path processing, and a derived class, also known as a subclass, inheriting from the base class and defining the processing to be used with the automated unit test path. Figure 8-1 shows the UML diagram of the required components with the base class scenario.

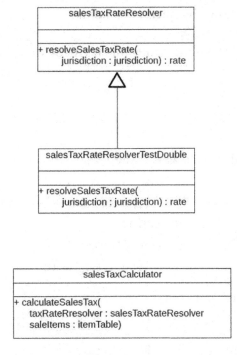

Figure 8-1. *UML diagram of the required components with the base class scenario*

This UML diagram follows the general conventions used for modeling the components of object-oriented entities interacting with each other.[8]

At the top of the UML diagram is the base class named salesTaxRateResolver providing the definition and implementation for a method named resolveSalesTaxRate, which would be implemented to provide the processing applicable to the production path.

Beneath that is the definition for a subclass named salesTaxRateResolverTestDouble. The subclass is shown to inherit from base class salesTaxRateResolver. It would redefine method resolveSalesTaxRate to provide an implementation applicable to the automated unit test path.

At the bottom of the UML diagram is a class named salesTaxCalculator. It is shown to define a public method named calculateSalesTax, the signature for which indicates that it accepts a reference to class salesTaxRateResolver and to a list of sales items of type itemTable.

Let's convert all this into ABAP code. First, as shown in Listing 8-6, is the former subroutine calculate_sales_tax as it looked in Listing 8-3 but transformed into a method of a class and invoking a different method of a different class to resolve the tax rate, with changes from Listing 8-3 shown highlighted in bold.

Listing 8-6. Subroutine calculate_sales_tax transformed into equivalent method of a class

```
(in class definition portion)

public section.
  methods calculate_sales_tax importing
                        tax_rate_resolver
                          type ref to sales_tax_rate_resolver
                      changing
                      sale_items
                        type item_table.

(in class implementation portion)
```

---

[8]For an explanation of these UML modeling conventions, refer to *Object-Oriented Design with ABAP: A Practical Approach* (James E. McDonough, Apress, 2017), Chapter 9

```
method calculate_sales_tax.
  field-symbols <sale_item> type item_row.
  loop at sale_items assigning <sale_item>.
    call method tax_rate_resolver->resolve_sales_tax_rate
      exporting
        jurisdiction   = <sale_item>-jurisdiction
      importing
        sales_tax_rate = <sale_item>-tax_rate.
    <sale_item>-sales_tax = <sale_item>-price * <sale_item>-tax_rate.
  endloop.
endmethod.
```

Next, as shown in Listing 8-7, is the definition of the base class to be used when providing the service of resolving the sales tax rate to the production path.

Listing 8-7. Base class used to resolve sales tax rate for production path

```
class sales_tax_rate_resolver definition.
  public section.
    methods resolve_sales_tax_rate
      importing
        jurisdiction type jurisdiction
      exporting
        sales_tax_rate type rate.
endclass.
class sales_tax_rate_resolver implementation.
  method resolve_sales_tax_rate.
    o
    o
    o
  endmethod.
endclass.
```

Method resolve_sales_tax_rate is shown with no specific implementation. It may require reading customized tables to find a record that matches the jurisdiction or perhaps even invoking methods of other classes to correctly resolve the sales tax rate.

Next, as shown in Listing 8-8, is the definition of the subclass to be used when providing the service of resolving the sales tax rate for the automated unit test path.

Listing 8-8. Subclass used to resolve sales tax rate for automated unit test path

```
class sales_tax_rate_resolver_tstdbl definition
                                      inheriting from
                                        sales_tax_rate_resolver
                                      for testing.
  public section.
    constants constant_sales_tax_rate type rate value '0.10'.
    methods resolve_sales_tax_rate redefinition.
endclass.
class sales_tax_rate_resolver_tstdbl implementation.
  method resolve_sales_tax_rate.
    sales_tax_rate = constant_sales_tax_rate.
  endmethod.
endclass.
```

Notice that class sales_tax_rate_resolver_tstdbl inherits from class sales_tax_rate_resolver and is marked "for testing." Notice also it indicates that it redefines method resolve_sales_tax_rate, which is shown with an implementation simply returning a constant sales tax rate to any caller.

NOTE

New class sales_tax_rate_resolver_tstdbl corresponds to the entity named salesTaxRateResolverTestDouble in the UML diagram which uses the lower camel case spelling convention for entity names. Such UML entity names do not transfer easily to ABAP names for two reasons:

1) UML names reflect the naming convention used with object-oriented languages such as Java, languages that are case-sensitive to entity names. ABAP is a case-insensitive language, meaning it does not distinguish between upper- and lowercase characters used with entity names. While it is easy to see the individual words composing an entity name using lower camel case, because each subsequent word starts with a capital letter, such names

become indecipherable and hard to read when subjected to the ABAP pretty
printer, which would convert such names into all lowercase or all uppercase
depending on the pretty printer option selected. So ABAP names usually include
underscores to separate words of an entity name, making the name longer.
Decide for yourself which of the following two names is easiest to understand –
the first uses lower camel case, and the second uses all lowercase:

- `salesTaxRateResolverTestDouble`

- `salestaxrateresolvertestdouble`

2) Entity names defined in other case-sensitive languages have virtually no
limit to their length. Comparable entity names defined in ABAP are limited
to 30 characters. Accordingly, ABAP entity names often have to use cryptic
abbreviations out of necessity, further obscuring their names. In this case, it
was necessary to reduce "test_double" down to "tstdbl" to stay within the
30-character name limit.

Let's put everything together into an ABAP report that illustrates both the
production path and the automated unit test path and how each path provides a
different instance to method calculate_sales_tax for resolving the applicable sales tax
rate, as shown in Listing 8-9.

Listing 8-9. Production path and automated unit test path illustrating the use of
a test double implemented using the base class variation

```
report zyx.

class sales_tax_rate_resolver definition.
  public section.
    methods resolve_sales_tax_rate
      importing
        jurisdiction type jurisdiction
      exporting
        sales_tax_rate type rate.
endclass.
class sales_tax_rate_resolver implementation.
  method resolve_sales_tax_rate.
```

```
      o
      o
      o
    endmethod.
  endclass.

  class sales_tax_rate_resolver_tstdbl definition
                                         inheriting from
                                           sales_tax_rate_resolver
                                         for testing.
    public section.
      constants constant_sales_tax_rate type rate value '0.10'.
      methods resolve_sales_tax_rate redefinition.
  endclass.
  class sales_tax_rate_resolver_tstdbl implementation.
   method resolve_sales_tax_rate.
      sales_tax_rate = constant_sales_tax_rate.
    endmethod.
  endclass.
  class sales_tax_calculator definition.
    public section.
      methods calculate_sales_tax importing
                                   tax_rate_resolver
                                     type ref to sales_tax_rate_resolver
                                  changing
                                    sale_items
                                      type item_table.
  endclass.
  class sales_tax_calculator implementation.
   method calculate_sales_tax.
      field-symbols <sale_item> type item_row.
      loop at sale_items assigning <sale_item>.
        call method tax_rate_resolver->resolve_sales_tax_rate
          exporting
            jurisdiction    = <sale_item>-jurisdiction
          importing
```

```
      sales_tax_rate = <sale_item>-tax_rate.
    <sale_item>-sales_tax = <sale_item>-price * <sale_item>-tax_rate.
  endloop.
  endmethod.
endclass.

start-of-selection.
  perform drive_process.

form drive_process.
  data sale_items type item_table.
  data sales_tax_calculator type ref to sales_tax_calculator.
  data sales_tax_rate_resolver type ref to sales_tax_rate_resolver.
  perform get_sale_items changing sale_items.
  create object sales_tax_rate_resolver.
  create object sales_tax_calculator.
  call method sales_tax_calculator-> calculate_sales_tax
    exporting
      tax_rate_resolver = sales_tax_rate_resolver
    changing
      sale_items        = sale_items.
  perform produce_sales_item_report using sale_items.
endform.

form get_sale_items changing sale_items type item_table.
  o
  o
endform.

form produce_sales_item_report using sale_items.
  o
  o
endform.

class sales_tax_calculator_tester definition for testing.
  private section.
    methods calculate_sales_tax_tester for testing.
    methods get_sale_items changing sale_items type item_table.
```

```
endclass.
class sales_tax_calculator_tester implementation.
  method calculate_sales_tax_tester.
    data sale_items type item_table.
    data sales_tax_calculator type ref to sales_tax_calculator.
    data sales_tax_rate_resolver type ref
                                    to sales_tax_rate_resolver_tstdbl.
    field-symbols <sale_item> type item_row.
    call method me->get_sale_items changing sale_items.
    create object sales_tax_rate_resolver.
    create object sales_tax_calculator.
    call method sales_tax_calculator-> calculate_sales_tax
      exporting
        tax_rate_resolver = sales_tax_rate_resolver
      changing
        sale_items        =  sale_items.
    loop at sale_items assigning <sale_item>.
      cl_abap_unit_assert=>assert_equals(
          act = <sale_item>-sales_tax
          exp = <sale_item>-sale_price
              * sales_tax_rate_resolver_tstdbl=>constant_sales_tax_rate
        ).
    endloop.
  endmethod.
  method get_sale_items.
    o
    o
  endmethod.
endclass.
```

Notice the following things about this code:

1. Class sales_tax_rate_resolver_tstdbl represents the test double
    for class sales_tax_rate_resolver. It defines a publicly available
    constant named constant_sales_tax_rate indicating the rate it
    will return when its method resolve_sales_tax_rate is called. This
    means that unit test method calculate_sales_tax_tester has direct

access to the rate this test double will use. Notice that the call made by unit test method calculate_sales_tax_tester to method assert_equals of class cl_abap_unit_assert is setting the expected value using this constant.

2. Subroutine drive_process defines two reference variables: one for an instance of class sales_tax_calculator and another for an instance of class sales_tax_rate_resolver. It creates instances into each of these reference variables prior to invoking method calculate_sales_tax of class sales_tax_calculator. Accordingly, when method calculate_sales_tax of class sales_tax_calculator is called by this subroutine, it is supplied with a reference to an instance of production path class sales_tax_rate_resolver.

3. Unit test method sales_tax_calculator_tester defines two local reference variables: one for an instance of class sales_tax_calculator and another for an instance of class sales_tax_rate_resolver_tstdbl, the test double inheriting from class sales_tax_rate_resolver. It creates instances into each of these reference variables prior to invoking method calculate_sales_tax of class sales_tax_calculator. Accordingly, when method calculate_sales_tax of class sales_tax_calculator is called by this unit test method, it is supplied with a reference to an instance of automated unit test path class sales_tax_rate_resolver_tstdbl.

4. The signature of method calculate_sales_tax of class sales_tax_calculator indicates that it accepts a reference to class sales_tax_rate_resolver, meaning that a reference to this class or any class inheriting from this class may be provided through this signature parameter. The validity of this reference can be statically checked by the syntax checker. This is how it becomes possible to provide it a reference to an instance of class sales_tax_rate_resolver during the production path but to provide a reference to an instance of its test double, class sales_tax_rate_resolver_tstdbl, during the automated unit test path.

5. Method calculate_sales_tax of class sales_tax_calculator is completely unaware that there is either a production path or an automated unit test path. It behaves no differently for either of these executions. It is oblivious to the fact that it has been directed to make a call to method resolve_sales_tax_rate using an instance of class sales_tax_rate_resolver during execution of the production path but make a call to the same method using an instance of class sales_tax_rate_resolver_tstdbl during execution of the automated unit test path. It simply is provided through its signature the component on which it depends. Accordingly, it has no way to know when or whether it is being tested.

6. The code base has now become more flexible and maintainable due simply to the changes to accommodate unit testing. How so? The answer is that it now becomes possible for the production path of this component to be changed quickly and easily to specify a different class to provide the tax rate resolution service. When the code was composed of one subroutine calling another, as shown in Listing 8-2, it would require a change to the calling subroutine to change the name of the called one.

    With the design shown in Listing 8-9, the business process encapsulated in calling method sales_tax_calculator no longer needs to change simply to accommodate a change to the way the sales tax rate is resolved. Instead, it simply is provided with a reference to a different instance of a class that can perform this service.

    This may seem insignificant at first, but it means that the production path of the program now has the flexibility to decide *at runtime* which instance of a class will provide this tax rate resolution service.

Test Double Using Interface

The interface scenario consists of two classes implementing the same interface. The interface defines the methods to be implemented by both of the classes, and each class would need to implement those methods according to the role it plays. One class would implement those methods to provide the applicable processing for the production path, and the other, the test double, would implement those methods the way they would be applicable to the automated unit test path. Figure 8-2 shows the UML diagram of the required components with the interface scenario.

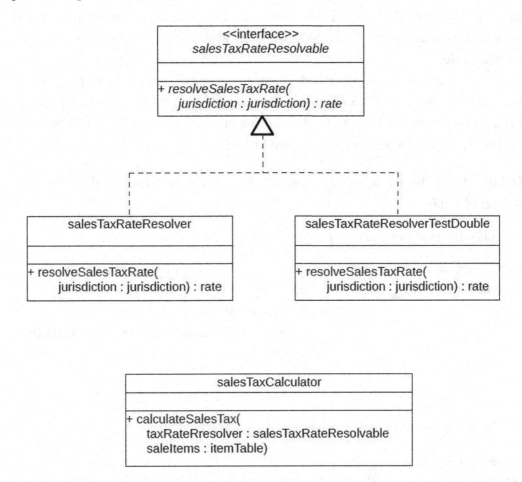

Figure 8-2. *UML diagram of the required components with the interface scenario*

At the top of the UML diagram is an interface named salesTaxRateResolvable providing the definition for a method named resolveSalesTaxRate.

Beneath that are definitions for two classes: salesTaxRateResolver and salesTaxRateResolverTestDouble. Each of these two classes is shown to implement interface salesTaxRateResolvable, which means that each class needs to provide its own implementation for method resolveSalesTaxRate defined by this interface. The implementation of method resolveSalesTaxRate in class salesTaxRateResolver would provide the processing applicable to the production path, whereas the implementation of this same method in class salesTaxRateResolverTestDouble would provide the processing applicable to the automated unit test path.

At the bottom of the UML diagram is a class named salesTaxCalculator. It is shown to define a public method named calculateSalesTax, the signature for which indicates that it accepts a reference to interface salesTaxRateResolvable and to a list of sales items of type itemTable.

Let's convert all this into ABAP code. First, as shown in Listing 8-10, is the former subroutine calculate_sales_tax as it looked in Listing 8-3 but transformed into a method of a class and invoking a different method of a different class to resolve the tax rate, with changes from Listing 8-3 shown highlighted in bold.

Listing 8-10. Subroutine calculate_sales_tax transformed into equivalent method of a class

(in class definition portion)

```
public section.
  methods calculate_sales_tax importing
                             tax_rate_resolver
                                 type ref to sales_tax_rate_resolvable
                             changing
                             sale_items
                                 type item_table.
```

(in class implementation portion)

```
method calculate_sales_tax.
  field-symbols <sale_item> type item_row.
  loop at sale_items assigning <sale_item>.
    call method tax_rate_resolver->resolve_sales_tax_rate
      exporting
```

```
      jurisdiction    = <sale_item>-jurisdiction
    importing
      sales_tax_rate = <sale_item>-tax_rate.
    <sale_item>-sales_tax = <sale_item>-price * <sale_item>-tax_rate.
  endloop.
endmethod.
```

The highlighting indicates how this new class differs from its subroutine counterpart, but we had seen a similar transformation to a class by this subroutine in the base class scenario shown by Listing 8-6. The only difference between Listing 8-6 and Listing 8-10 is the type used with the importing parameter defined for method calculate_sales_tax: in Listing 8-6 it is defined as type ref to sales_tax_rate_resolver, a class, but in Listing 8-10 it is defined as type ref to sales_tax_rate_resolvable, an interface.

Next, as shown in Listing 8-11, is the definition of the interface and the production path class providing the service of resolving the sales tax rate.

Listing 8-11. Interface and the production path class providing the service of resolving the sales tax rate

```
interface sales_tax_rate_resolvable.
  methods resolve_sales_tax_rate
    importing
      jurisdiction type jurisdiction
    exporting
      sales_tax_rate type rate.
endinterface.

class sales_tax_rate_resolver definition.
  public section.
    interfaces sales_tax_rate_resolvable.
    aliases resolve_sales_tax_rate
        for sales_tax_rate_resolvable~resolve_sales_tax_rate.
endclass.
class sales_tax_rate_resolver implementation.
  method resolve_sales_tax_rate.
```

```
    o
    o
    o
  endmethod.
endclass.
```

Next, as shown in Listing 8-12, is the definition of the automated unit test path class providing the service of resolving the sales tax rate.

Listing 8-12. Automated unit test path class providing the service of resolving the sales tax rate

```
class sales_tax_rate_resolver_tstdbl definition
                                   for testing.
  public section.
    constants constant_sales_tax_rate type rate value '0.10'.
    interfaces sales_tax_rate_resolvable.
    aliases resolve_sales_tax_rate
        for sales_tax_rate_resolvable~resolve_sales_tax_rate.
endclass.
class sales_tax_rate_resolver_tstdbl implementation.
  method resolve_sales_tax_rate.
    sales_tax_rate = constant_sales_tax_rate.
  endmethod.
endclass.
```

The implementations shown for method resolve_sales_tax_rate in class sales_tax_rate_resolver, shown in Listing 8-11, and in class sales_tax_rate_resolver_tstdbl, shown in Listing 8-12, are identical to their respective counterparts in Listing 8-7 and Listing 8-8.

Let's put everything together into an ABAP component that illustrates both the production path and the automated unit test path and how each path provides a different instance to method calculate_sales_tax for resolving the applicable sales tax rate, as shown in Listing 8-13.

Listing 8-13. Production path and automated unit test path illustrating the use of a test double implemented using the interface variation

```
report zyx.

interface sales_tax_rate_resolvable.
  methods resolve_sales_tax_rate
    importing
      jurisdiction type jurisdiction
    exporting
      sales_tax_rate type rate.
endinterface.

class sales_tax_rate_resolver definition.
  public section.
    interfaces sales_tax_rate_resolvable.
    aliases resolve_sales_tax_rate
        for sales_tax_rate_resolvable~resolve_sales_tax_rate.
endclass.
class sales_tax_rate_resolver implementation.
  method resolve_sales_tax_rate.
    o
    o
    o
  endmethod.
endclass.

class sales_tax_rate_resolver_tstdbl definition
                                    for testing.
  public section.
    constants constant_sales_tax_rate type rate value '0.10'.
    interfaces sales_tax_rate_resolvable.
    aliases resolve_sales_tax_rate
        for sales_tax_rate_resolvable~resolve_sales_tax_rate.
endclass.
class sales_tax_rate_resolver_tstdbl implementation.
  method resolve_sales_tax_rate.
```

```
      sales_tax_rate = constant_sales_tax_rate.
    endmethod.
  endclass.
  class sales_tax_calculator definition.
    public section.
      methods calculate_sales_tax importing
                                       tax_rate_resolver
                                         type ref to sales_tax_rate_resolvable
                                     changing
                                       sale_items
                                         type item_table.
  endclass
  class sales_tax_calculator implementation.
    method calculate_sales_tax.
      field-symbols <sale_item> type item_row.
      loop at sale_items assigning <sale_item>.
        call method tax_rate_resolver->resolve_sales_tax_rate
          exporting
            jurisdiction   = <sale_item>-jurisdiction
          importing
            sales_tax_rate = <sale_item>-tax_rate.
        <sale_item>-sales_tax = <sale_item>-price * <sale_item>-tax_rate.
      endloop.
    endmethod.
  endclass.

  start-of-selection.
    perform drive_process.

  form drive_process.
    data sale_items type item_table.
    data sales_tax_calculator type ref to sales_tax_calculator.
    data sales_tax_rate_resolvable type ref to sales_tax_rate_resolvable.
    perform get_sale_items changing sale_items.
    create object sales_tax_rate_resolvable
            type sales_tax_rate_resolver.
```

```
    create object sales_tax_calculator.
    call method sales_tax_calculator-> calculate_sales_tax
      exporting
        tax_rate_resolver = sales_tax_rate_resolvable
      changing
        sale_items        =  sale_items.
    perform produce_sales_item_report using sale_items.
endform.
form get_sale_items changing sale_items type item_table.
    o
    o
endform.

form produce_sales_item_report using sale_items.
    o
    o
endform.

class sales_tax_calculator_tester definition for testing.
  private section.
    methods calculate_sales_tax_tester for testing.
    methods get_sale_items changing sale_items type item_table.
endclass.
class sales_tax_calculator_tester implementation.
  method calculate_sales_tax_tester.
    data sale_items type item_table.
    data sales_tax_calculator type ref to sales_tax_calculator.
    data sales_tax_rate_resolvable type ref to sales_tax_rate_resolvable.
    field-symbols <sale_item> type item_row.
    call method me->get_sale_items changing sale_items.
    create object sales_tax_rate_resolvable
            type sales_tax_rate_resolver_tstdbl.
    create object sales_tax_calculator.
    call method sales_tax_calculator-> calculate_sales_tax
      exporting
        tax_rate_resolver = sales_tax_rate_resolvable
```

```
    changing
      sale_items           =  sale_items.
  loop at sale_items assigning <sale_item>.
    cl_abap_unit_assert=>assert_equals(
        act = <sale_item>-sales_tax
        exp = <sale_item>-sale_price
            * sales_tax_rate_resolver_tstdbl=>constant_sales_tax_rate
      ).
  endloop.
 endmethod.
 method get_sale_items.
   o
   o
 endmethod.
endclass.
```

Notice the following things about this code:

1. Class sales_tax_rate_resolver_tstdbl represents the test double
    for class sales_tax_rate_resolver. It defines a publicly available
    constant named constant_sales_tax_rate indicating the rate it
    will return when its method resolve_sales_tax_rate is called. This
    means that unit test method calculate_sales_tax_tester has direct
    access to the rate this test double will use. Notice that the call
    made by unit test method calculate_sales_tax_tester to method
    assert_equals of class cl_abap_unit_assert is setting the expected
    value using this constant. This is identical to what we saw with the
    base class variation.

2. Subroutine drive_process creates into its local variable sales_tax_
    collector an instance of class sales_tax_calculator. It also creates
    into its local variable defined as reference to interface sales_tax_
    rate_resolvable an instance of production path class sales_tax_
    rate_resolver. Accordingly, when method calculate_sales_tax of
    class sales_tax_calculator is called by this subroutine, it is supplied
    with a reference to an instance of production path class sales_tax_
    rate_resolver.

3. Unit test method sales_tax_calculator_tester creates into its local variable sales_tax_collector an instance of class sales_tax_calculator, the same as is done by subroutine drive_process. It also creates into its local variable defined as reference to interface sales_tax_rate_resolvable not an instance of production path class sales_tax_rate_resolver but an instance of automated unit test path class sales_tax_rate_resolver_tstdbl. Accordingly, when method calculate_sales_tax of class sales_tax_calculator is called by this unit test method, it is supplied with a reference to an instance of automated unit test path class sales_tax_rate_resolver_tstdbl.

4. The signature of method calculate_sales_tax of class sales_tax_calculator indicates that it accepts a reference to interface sales_tax_rate_resolvable, meaning that a reference to any class implementing this interface may be provided through this signature parameter. The validity of this reference can be statically checked by the syntax checker. This is how it becomes possible to provide a reference to an instance of class sales_tax_rate_resolver during the production path but to provide a reference to an instance of its test double, class sales_tax_rate_resolver_tstdbl, during the automated unit test path.

5. Method calculate_sales_tax of class sales_tax_calculator is completely unaware that there is either a production path or an automated unit test path. It behaves no differently for either of these executions. It is oblivious to the fact that it has been directed to make a call to method resolve_sales_tax_rate using an instance of class sales_tax_rate_resolver during execution of the production path but make a call to the same method using an instance of class sales_tax_rate_resolver_tstdbl during execution of the automated unit test path. It simply is provided through its signature the component on which it depends. Accordingly, it has no way to know when or whether it is being tested. This also is identical to what we saw with the base class variation.

Categories of Test Doubles

Test doubles are categorized by the specific purpose they serve. The general categories are these: input test doubles and output test doubles. That is, test doubles generally provide the service of supplying input to or accepting output from a component being tested. Indeed, the kind of input and output associated with test doubles is known as *indirect* input and output. The distinction is important because it implies that the code under test is making its own request to acquire input for its own use or is making its own request to send output to a component capable of accepting it. It distinguishes *indirect* input and output from the *direct* input and output exchanged through the signature of the component under test.

Gerard Meszaros has defined the following terms to describe the specific types of test doubles[9]:

- Dummy object

  A dummy object test double represents an object that is defined but not intended to be used in any meaningful way. Often it represents an object instantiated for the purpose of satisfying the need to specify a type-compatible non-optional parameter defined for a method signature. Meszaros notes in his explanation of a dummy object that it is not the same as a null object, because a null object *is used* to provide do-nothing behavior, whereas a dummy object is not intended to be used at all. Accordingly, it represents neither input nor output test double.

- Test stub

  A test stub is an object intended to provide indirect input to a component under test when the component under test invokes its methods. It enables forcing the code under test to traverse a specific path based on the input received from the test stub. One variation of test stub is known as a *Responder*[10] which is capable of providing either valid or invalid input through the call signature. Another variation is known as a *Saboteur*[11] which is capable of throwing exceptions for the purpose of testing whether the caller is capable of handling them appropriately.

---

[9]Meszaros, Gerard, *xUnit Test Patterns: Refactoring Test Code*, Addison Wesley, 2007, p. 133
[10]Ibid, p. 524
[11]Ibid, p. 524

- Test spy

    A test spy is an object intended to accept indirect output from a component under test when the component under test invokes its methods. It is intended to record the *indirect output* sent to it by the code under test. Once the code under test has completed its processing, the test spy can be queried to determine whether it had received the expected output from the code under test. Often the test spy will contain its own unique methods to be invoked where it will perform its own automated unit testing assertions upon the output it had or had not received from the code under test.

- **Mock object**

    A mock object is an object intended to accept indirect output from a component under test when the component under test invokes its methods. It is intended to record the *sequence* of calls made to its methods. Once the code under test has completed its processing, the mock object can be queried to determine whether it had received from the code under test the calls to its methods the expected number of times and in the expected sequence. Usually it will contain its own unique methods to be invoked where it will perform its own automated unit testing assertions upon the sequence of method calls, but it differs from the test spy in that it is not validating output received but instead the sequence and number of calls made to its methods.

    There are three variations of the mock object: strict, lenient, and very lenient. A strict mock object will pass the unit test only when the calls to its methods were made in the correct sequence and for the expected number of times and there were no calls to any of its methods not expected to be called. A lenient mock object will allow the test to pass so long as its methods expected to be called were called the expected number of times, regardless of their sequence. A very lenient mock object will allow the test to pass so long as its methods expected to be called were called the expected number of times, regardless of their sequence and despite unexpected calls made to its other methods.

- Fake object

  A fake object is an object intended to provide indirect input to
  or accept indirect output from a component under test when
  the component under test invokes its methods. Typically it is
  used to replace the functionality of a real indirect input or output
  component but using a simpler implementation. Often it is used
  to substitute for a depended-on component that runs too slowly
  for the purposes of unit testing or one that is not available in
  the testing environment. Its purpose is not so much to facilitate
  providing input or accepting output enabling test validation as it
  is to provide the automated unit test a lightweight component to
  replace one that is not practical for use with the test.

Using Test Doubles for Indirect Input

In this section, we will explore further the use of test doubles to supply indirect input.
We finished the previous chapter with a program in which we had encapsulated both the
indirect input and indirect output associated with a subroutine for reporting total ticket
sales, as shown in Listing 7-9.

Listing 8-14 is a copy of Listing 7-9 but with a unit test added to test its subroutine,
with changes highlighted in bold.

Listing 8-14. Ticket sales program with unit test

```
report.
class ticket_sales_examiner definition.
  public section.
    types stadium_identifier_range type range of zticket_sales-stadium_id.
    types event_date_range        type range of zticket_sales-event_date.
    methods get_total_tickets_sold
      importing stadium_identifier type stadium_identifier_range
                event_date         type event_date_range
      exporting tickets_sold       type sy-dbcnt.
endclass.
```

```
class ticket_sales_examiner implementation.
  method get_total_tickets_sold.
    select count(*)
      into tickets_sold
      from zticket_sales
    where stadium_id in stadium_identifier
      and event_date in event_date.
  endmethod.
endclass.

class ticket_sales_reporter definition.
  public section.
    methods show_total_tickets_sold
      importing descriptor        type string
               tickets_sold      type sy-dbcnt.
endclass.
class ticket_sales_reporter implementation.
  method show_total_tickets_sold.
    write / descriptor, tickets_sold.
  endmethod.
endclass.

data ticket_sales_examiner type ref to ticket_sales_examiner.
data ticket_sales_reporter type ref to ticket_sales_reporter.
select-options stadium  for zticket_sales-stadium_id.
select-options evntdate for zticket_sales-event_date.

start-of-selection.
  create object ticket_sales_examiner.
  create object ticket_sales_reporter.
  perform report_total_tickets_sold using stadium
                                          evntdate.

form report_total_tickets_sold using stadium_identifier_range
                                     event_date_range.
  data tickets_sold type sy-dbcnt.
```

```
  call method ticket_sales_examiner->get_total_tickets_sold
    exporting
      stadium_identifier = stadium_identifier_range
      event_date         = event_date_range
    importing
      tickets_sold       = tickets_sold.
  call method ticket_sales_reporter->show_total_tickets_sold
    exporting
      descriptor         = 'total number of tickets sold:'
      tickets_sold       = tickets_sold.
endform.
```

```
class tester definition for testing risk level harmless.
  private section.
    methods report_total_tickets_sold for testing.
endclass.
class tester implementation.
  method report_total_tickets_sold.
    data stadium    type ticket_sales_examiner->stadium_identifier_range.
    data event_date_type ticket_sales_examiner->event_date_range.
    create object ticket_sales_examiner.
    create object ticket_sales_reporter.
    perform report_total_tickets_sold using stadium
                                            event_date.
  endmethod.
endclass.
```

The implementation for unit test method report_total_tickets_sold contains the bare minimum necessary to call subroutine report_total_tickets_sold without causing a runtime exception. It is not much of a test because it has no assertion to determine whether the called subroutine worked as expected. If we were to run this unit test as it is currently defined, we should find that the unit test would be interrupted during its execution to present the "Internal Session for Isolated Test Class Execution" screen upon encountering the write statement in the encapsulated indirect output processing of method show_total_tickets_sold of the instance of class ticket_sales_reporter. This would require the programmer to press a key to allow the unit test to continue on to its completion, an issue to be addressed later.

For now, give some consideration to how we could test subroutine report_total_tickets_sold. What type of test could we write that would offer convincing evidence that it worked properly? It accepts two direct input parameters which it passes along on the call to method get_total_tickets_sold, providing the subroutine with indirect input. Then it passes the value returned from that method along on the call to method show_total_tickets_sold, the receiver of the indirect output produced by the subroutine. How could a unit test invoking this subroutine assert that the number of tickets sold provided by the indirect input was correctly passed on to the receiver of the indirect output?

At this point, we want to focus on the encapsulated indirect input provided by method get_total_tickets_sold of the instance of class ticket_sales_examiner. When the automated unit test is executed, we want to provide a test double for this class so that the unit test can exert control over the subroutine, insuring that the subroutine receives a value for number of tickets sold determined by the unit test itself. Since the subroutine relies on a global variable to provide the reference for the class that produces this indirect input, it is a simple matter for the unit test to preemptively set that global variable with a reference to a test double. So first we will need to define a test double. Listing 8-15 shows how we would create one using a base class.

Listing 8-15. Indirect input test double for use with the ticket sales program

```
class ticket_sales_examiner_tstdbl definition
                                inheriting from ticket_sales_examiner.
  public section.
    constants constant_tickets_sold type sy-dbcnt value 591.
    methods get_total_tickets_sold redefinition.
endclass.
class ticket_sales_examiner_tstdbl implementation.
  method get_total_tickets_sold.
    tickets_sold = constant_tickets_sold.
  endmethod.
endclass.
```

The new test double class is named ticket_sales_examiner_tstdbl and indicates that it inherits from class ticket_sales_examiner. Notice that it redefines method get_total_tickets_sold defined by its superclass. Notice also that its implementation of this redefined method is to set the number of tickets sold to a constant defined in its public section.

Listing 8-16 shows how this would be incorporated into the program and made available by the unit test for use by the subroutine, with changes from Listing 8-14 highlighted in bold.

Listing 8-16. Indirect input test double incorporated into the ticket sales program and made available by the unit test for use by the subroutine

```
report.
class ticket_sales_examiner definition.
  public section.
    types stadium_identifier_range type range of zticket_sales-stadium_id.
    types event_date_range        type range of zticket_sales-event_date.
    methods get_total_tickets_sold
      importing stadium_identifier type stadium_identifier_range
                event_date         type event_date_range
      exporting tickets_sold       type sy-dbcnt.
endclass.
class ticket_sales_examiner implementation.
  method get_total_tickets_sold.
    select count(*)
      into tickets_sold
      from zticket_sales
     where stadium_id in stadium_identifier
       and event_date in event_date.
  endmethod.
endclass.

class ticket_sales_examiner_tstdbl definition
                                  inheriting from ticket_sales_examiner.
  public section.
    constants constant_tickets_sold type sy-dbcnt value 591.
    methods get_total_tickets_sold redefinition.
endclass.
class ticket_sales_examiner_tstdbl implementation.
  method get_total_tickets_sold.
    tickets_sold = constant_tickets_sold.
  endmethod.
endclass.
```

```
class ticket_sales_reporter definition.
  public section.
    methods show_total_tickets_sold
      importing descriptor        type string
                tickets_sold      type sy-dbcnt.
endclass.
class ticket_sales_reporter implementation.
  method show_total_tickets_sold.
    write / descriptor, tickets_sold.
  endmethod.
endclass.

data ticket_sales_examiner type ref to ticket_sales_examiner.
data ticket_sales_reporter type ref to ticket_sales_reporter.
select-options stadium  for zticket_sales-stadium_id.
select-options evntdate for zticket_sales-event_date.

start-of-selection.
  create object ticket_sales_examiner.
  create object ticket_sales_reporter.
  perform report_total_tickets_sold using stadium
                                          evntdate.

form report_total_tickets_sold using stadium_identifier_range
                                     event_date_range.
  data tickets_sold type sy-dbcnt.
  call method ticket_sales_examiner->get_total_tickets_sold
    exporting
      stadium_identifier = stadium_identifier_range
      event_date         = event_date_range
    importing
      tickets_sold       = tickets_sold.
  call method ticket_sales_reporter->show_total_tickets_sold
    exporting
      descriptor         = 'total number of tickets sold:'
      tickets_sold       = tickets_sold.
endform.
```

```
class tester definition for testing risk level harmless.
  private section.
    methods report_total_tickets_sold for testing.
endclass.
class tester implementation.
  method report_total_tickets_sold.
    data stadium    type ticket_sales_examiner->stadium_identifier_range.
    data event_date_type ticket_sales_examiner->event_date_range.
    create object ticket_sales_examiner type ticket_sales_examiner_tstdbl.
    create object ticket_sales_reporter.
    perform report_total_tickets_sold using stadium
                                            event_date.
  endmethod.
endclass.
```

Notice that the unit test method was changed to include the type of ticket_sales_ examiner object to create. Now when this unit test method is executed, it will create into global variable ticket_sales_examiner an instance of test double ticket_sales_examiner_ tstdbl and then call subroutine report_total_tickets_sold, so that when the subroutine invokes method get_total_tickets_sold through global variable ticket_sales_examiner, it will be invoking a method of class ticket_sales_examiner_tstdbl. The method of this test double has been implemented always to return the value assigned to its constant named constant_tickets_sold, shown in the preceding code as having the value 591.

Accordingly, when subroutine report_total_tickets_sold is invoked through the automated unit test path, it will receive the value 591 as its indirect input from the call to method get_total_tickets_sold. This is how the unit test has exerted control over the subroutine – it has insured that the subroutine receives its indirect input through a test double. More to the point, the indirect input received by the subroutine from the test double – the value 591 for total ticket sales – also is a value directly available to the unit test through a public constant defined by the test double. This means that the unit test not only has controlled how the subroutine receives its indirect input but also is aware of what the indirect input value is. Meanwhile, the production path of this program remains unaffected, and the subroutine gets whatever value of total ticket sales is supplied to it by the instance of class ticket_sales_examiner instantiated during the start-of-selection event block.

This illustrates an example of the use of *Back Door Manipulation*.[12] The unit test method has gone through the back door to set the value of global variable ticket_sales_ examiner used by the subroutine prior to calling it because there is no way to provide this to the subroutine via its signature – the front door.

Even though the unit test defined by Listing 8-16 still does not yet make any assertions on the behavior of subroutine report_total_tickets_sold, the program has moved a step closer to being designed for testability.

EXERCISES

At this point, take a break from reading and shift into exercise mode. Refer to the accompanying workbook to perform the nine exercises associated with workbook **Section 14: ABAP Unit Testing 301 – Introducing a Test Double for Input**.

Using Test Doubles for Indirect Output

In this section, we will explore further the use of test doubles to supply indirect output. We finished the preceding section with the ticket sales program changed to provide both an indirect input test double and a unit test method to invoke its subroutine, as shown in Listing 8-16.

At this point, we want to focus on the encapsulated indirect output received by method show_total_tickets_sold of the instance of class ticket_sales_reporter. When executed as is, the unit test would be interrupted to present the "Internal Session for Isolated Test Class Execution" screen upon encountering the write statement in the encapsulated indirect output processing of method show_total_tickets_sold of the instance of class ticket_sales_reporter. To prevent this, we want to provide a test double for this class so that the unit test can exert control over the subroutine, insuring that the subroutine sends the number of tickets sold to a receiver determined by the unit test itself, one that will not contain a write statement to interrupt its execution. Since the subroutine relies on a global variable to provide the reference for the class that receives this indirect output, it is a simple matter for the unit test to preemptively set that global variable with a reference to a test double. So first we will need to define a test double. Listing 8-17 shows how we would create one using a base class.

---

[12]Meszaros, Gerard, *xUnit Test Patterns: Refactoring Test Code*, Addison Wesley, 2007, p. 327

Listing 8-17. Indirect output test double for use with the ticket sales program

```
class ticket_sales_reporter_tstdbl definition
                                    inheriting from ticket_sales_reporter.
  public section.
    methods show_total_tickets_sold redefinition.
endclass.
class ticket_sales_reporter_tstdbl implementation.
  method show_total_tickets_sold.
  endmethod.
endclass.
```

The new test double class is named ticket_sales_reporter_tstdbl and indicates that it inherits from class ticket_sales_reporter. Notice that it redefines method show_total_tickets_sold defined by its superclass. Notice also that its implementation of this redefined method is to do nothing, meaning it will accept the method parameters but will ignore them.

Listing 8-18 shows how this would be incorporated into the program shown by Listing 8-17 and made available by the unit test for use by the subroutine, with changes highlighted in bold.

Listing 8-18. Indirect output test double incorporated into the ticket sales program and made available by the unit test for use by the subroutine

```
report.
class ticket_sales_examiner definition.
  public section.
    types stadium_identifier_range type range of zticket_sales-stadium_id.
    types event_date_range         type range of zticket_sales-event_date.
    methods get_total_tickets_sold
      importing stadium_identifier type stadium_identifier_range
                event_date         type event_date_range
      exporting tickets_sold       type sy-dbcnt.
endclass.
class ticket_sales_examiner implementation.
  method get_total_tickets_sold.
    select count(*)
```

```
       into tickets_sold
       from zticket_sales
     where stadium_id in stadium_identifier
         and event_date in event_date.
   endmethod.
endclass.

class ticket_sales_examiner_tstdbl definition
                                 inheriting from ticket_sales_examiner.
  public section.
    constants constant_tickets_sold type sy-dbcnt value 591.
    methods get_total_tickets_sold redefinition.
endclass.
class ticket_sales_examiner_tstdbl implementation.
  method get_total_tickets_sold.
    tickets_sold = constant_tickets_sold.
  endmethod.
endclass.

class ticket_sales_reporter definition.
  public section.
    methods show_total_tickets_sold
      importing descriptor        type string
                tickets_sold      type sy-dbcnt.
endclass.
class ticket_sales_reporter implementation.
  method show_total_tickets_sold.
    write / descriptor, tickets_sold.
  endmethod.
endclass.

class ticket_sales_reporter_tstdbl definition
                                 inheriting from ticket_sales_reporter.
  public section.
    methods show_total_tickets_sold redefinition.
endclass.
class ticket_sales_reporter_tstdbl implementation.
```

```
  method show_total_tickets_sold.
  endmethod.
endclass.

data ticket_sales_examiner type ref to ticket_sales_examiner.
data ticket_sales_reporter type ref to ticket_sales_reporter.
select-options stadium  for zticket_sales-stadium_id.
select-options evntdate for zticket_sales-event_date.

start-of-selection.
  create object ticket_sales_examiner.
  create object ticket_sales_reporter.
  perform report_total_tickets_sold using stadium
                                          evntdate.

form report_total_tickets_sold using stadium_identifier_range
                                     event_date_range.
  data tickets_sold type sy-dbcnt.
  call method ticket_sales_examiner->get_total_tickets_sold
    exporting
      stadium_identifier = stadium_identifier_range
      event_date         = event_date_range
    importing
      tickets_sold       = tickets_sold.
  call method ticket_sales_reporter->show_total_tickets_sold
    exporting
      descriptor         = 'total number of tickets sold:'
      tickets_sold       = tickets_sold.
endform.

class tester definition for testing risk level harmless.
  private section.
    methods report_total_tickets_sold for testing.
endclass.
class tester implementation.
  method report_total_tickets_sold.
    data stadium    type ticket_sales_examiner->stadium_identifier_range.
```

```
  data event_date_type ticket_sales_examiner->event_date_range.
  create object ticket_sales_examiner type ticket_sales_examiner_tstdbl.
  create object ticket_sales_reporter type ticket_sales_reporter_tstdbl.
  perform report_total_tickets_sold using stadium
                                      event_date.
endmethod.
endclass.
```

Notice that the unit test method was changed to include the type of ticket_sales_ reporter object to create. Now when this unit test method is executed, it will create into global variable ticket_sales_reporter an instance of test double ticket_sales_reporter_ tstdbl and then call subroutine report_total_tickets_sold, so that when the subroutine invokes method show_total_tickets_sold through global variable ticket_sales_reporter, it will be invoking a method of class ticket_sales_reporter_tstdbl. The method of this test double has been implemented always to ignore anything it receives from its caller.

Accordingly, when subroutine report_total_tickets_sold is invoked through the automated unit test path, it will send the value 591 as its indirect output on the call to method show_total_tickets_sold, which will be ignored by this receiver, but more importantly, will not cause the test execution to be interrupted by the presentation of the "Internal Session for Isolated Test Class Execution" screen. This is how the unit test has exerted control over the subroutine – it has insured that the subroutine sends its indirect output to a test double. Meanwhile, the production path of this program remains unaffected, and the subroutine sends its total ticket sales output to the receiver supplied to it by the instance of class ticket_sales_reporter instantiated during the start-of-selection event block.

This certainly is an improvement since the programmer no longer would need to press a key to enable the unit test to run to completion, but it still does not represent a satisfactory test for subroutine report_total_tickets_sold – it makes no assertion about the behavior of the subroutine. So what does the subroutine do that we could possibly test? Let's summarize what this subroutine does: it acquires as indirect input the value of total number of tickets sold and then produces as indirect output a report of the total number of tickets sold. Both its indirect input and indirect output have been encapsulated into classes to provide these capabilities. In addition, each of these classes has its own test double for use during the unit test path. As such, we could write a unit test asserting that the total number of tickets sold provided to the subroutine by the indirect input test double also is received by the indirect output test double.

At this point, the unit test is aware that 591 is the number the subroutine will be provided by its indirect input test double for total number of tickets sold, but currently it has no way to check that its indirect output test double receives this value. So let's enhance the indirect output test double to be able to capture and record the value it receives from its last caller. Listing 8-19 shows how we might do that, with changes from Listing 8-17 highlighted in bold.

Listing 8-19. Indirect output test double enhanced to capture and record parameter value sent by last caller

```
class ticket_sales_reporter_tstdbl definition
                                    inheriting from ticket_sales_reporter.
  public section.
    methods show_total_tickets_sold redefinition.
    methods get_last_caller_tickets_sold
      exporting
        tickets_sold type sy-dbcnt.
  private section.
    last_caller_tickets_sold type sy-dbcnt.
endclass.
class ticket_sales_reporter_tstdbl implementation.
  method show_total_tickets_sold.
    last_caller_tickets_sold = tickets_sold.
  endmethod.
  method get_last_caller_tickets_sold.
    tickets_sold = last_caller_tickets_sold.
  endmethod.
endclass.
```

Notice we now have declared a private attribute to record the parameter tickets_sold sent by the most recent caller. The implementation of its method show_total_tickets_ sold also has been changed to capture this value. In addition, a public method has been declared through which a caller may retrieve the value of the new private attribute.

Listing 8-20 shows the enhanced test double incorporated into the program shown by Listing 8-18 and used by the unit test to retrieve the value of its attribute last_caller_ tickets_sold, with changes to the unit test method highlighted in bold.

Listing 8-20. Enhanced indirect output test double incorporated into the ticket sales program and made available by the unit test for use by the subroutine

```
report.
class ticket_sales_examiner definition.
  public section.
    types stadium_identifier_range type range of zticket_sales-stadium_id.
    types event_date_range        type range of zticket_sales-event_date.
    methods get_total_tickets_sold
      importing stadium_identifier type stadium_identifier_range
                event_date         type event_date_range
      exporting tickets_sold       type sy-dbcnt.
endclass.
class ticket_sales_examiner implementation.
  method get_total_tickets_sold.
    select count(*)
      into tickets_sold
      from zticket_sales
    where stadium_id in stadium_identifier
      and event_date in event_date.
  endmethod.
endclass.

class ticket_sales_examiner_tstdbl definition
                                  inheriting from ticket_sales_examiner.
  public section.
    constants constant_tickets_sold type sy-dbcnt value 591.
    methods get_total_tickets_sold redefinition.
endclass.
class ticket_sales_examiner_tstdbl implementation.
  method get_total_tickets_sold.
    tickets_sold = constant_tickets_sold.
  endmethod.
endclass.

class ticket_sales_reporter definition.
  public section.
```

```
    methods show_total_tickets_sold
       importing descriptor          type string
                 tickets_sold        type sy-dbcnt.
endclass.
class ticket_sales_reporter implementation.
  method show_total_tickets_sold.
    write / descriptor, tickets_sold.
  endmethod.
endclass.

class ticket_sales_reporter_tstdbl definition
                                   inheriting from ticket_sales_reporter.
  public section.
    methods show_total_tickets_sold redefinition.
    methods get_last_caller_tickets_sold
      exporting
        tickets_sold type sy-dbcnt.
  private section.
    last_caller_tickets_sold type sy-dbcnt.
endclass.
class ticket_sales_reporter_tstdbl implementation.
  method show_total_tickets_sold.
    last_caller_tickets_sold = tickets_sold.
  endmethod.
  method get_last_caller_tickets_sold.
    tickets_sold = last_caller_tickets_sold.
  endmethod.
endclass.

data ticket_sales_examiner type ref to ticket_sales_examiner.
data ticket_sales_reporter type ref to ticket_sales_reporter.
select-options stadium  for zticket_sales-stadium_id.
select-options evntdate for zticket_sales-event_date.

start-of-selection.
  create object ticket_sales_examiner.
  create object ticket_sales_reporter.
```

```
   perform report_total_tickets_sold using stadium
                                       evntdate.

form report_total_tickets_sold using stadium_identifier_range
                                     event_date_range.
   data tickets_sold type sy-dbcnt.
   call method ticket_sales_examiner->get_total_tickets_sold
     exporting
       stadium_identifier = stadium_identifier_range
       event_date         = event_date_range
     importing
       tickets_sold       = tickets_sold.
   call method ticket_sales_reporter->show_total_tickets_sold
     exporting
       descriptor         = 'total number of tickets sold:'
       tickets_sold       = tickets_sold.
endform.

class tester definition for testing risk level harmless.
   private section.
     methods report_total_tickets_sold for testing.
endclass.
class tester implementation.
   method report_total_tickets_sold.
     data stadium    type ticket_sales_examiner->stadium_identifier_range.
     data event_date_type ticket_sales_examiner->event_date_range.
     data ticket_sales_reporter_tstdbl type ref
                                      to ticket_sales_reporter_tstdbl.
     data last_caller_tickets_sold type sy-dbcnt.
     create object ticket_sales_examiner type ticket_sales_examiner_tstdbl.
     create object ticket_sales_reporter type ticket_sales_reporter_tstdbl.
     perform report_total_tickets_sold using stadium
                                       event_date.
     try.
       ticket_sales_reporter_tstdbl ?= ticket_sales_reporter.
       ticket_sales_reporter_tstdbl->get_last_caller_tickets_sold(
```

```
        importing
          tickets_sold = last_caller_tickets_sold
        ).
    catch cx_sy_move_cast_error.
      cl_abap_unit_assert=>fail(
        msg = 'specializing cast has failed'
        ).
    endtry.
  endmethod.
endclass.
```

Notice that the unit test method now explicitly declares its own local reference variable defined as an instance of class ticket_sales_reporter_tstdbl and has included a try-endtry block to move into this new reference variable the reference to the instance of the test double from the corresponding global variable. This is necessary because method get_last_caller_tickets_sold cannot be referenced through a reference variable defined as type ref to ticket_sales_reporter, which is the way global variable ticket_sales_reporter defines it. Assuming the assignment does not fail, then the unit test calls method get_last_caller_tickets_sold and saves the answer in the new local variable declared to hold this value.

Now we are able to assert that the behavior of subroutine report_total_tickets_sold is correct. The unit test path makes available to the execution of the subroutine the test double ticket_sales_examiner_tstdbl, which means it knows that this test double will supply the subroutine with its public constant named constant_tickets_sold as the value for the total tickets sold. It also makes available to the execution of the subroutine the test double ticket_sales_reporter_tstdbl, which means it knows that this test double will capture and record the value of the total tickets sold when method show_total_tickets_sold of the test double is invoked and that this value can be retrieved by calling test double method get_last_caller_tickets_sold. So the assertion we can write for this unit test is that the value retrieved from the call to get_last_caller_tickets_sold of class ticket_sales_reporter_tstdbl is the same value as the constant named constant_tickets_sold of class ticket_sales_examiner_tstdbl, as shown in Listing 8-21 which shows how the unit test method in Listing 8-20 would be changed to include the assertion, with changes from its counterpart in Listing 8-20 highlighted in bold.

Listing 8-21. Assertion applied to unit test method of ticket sales program

```
method report_total_tickets_sold.
  data stadium     type ticket_sales_examiner->stadium_identifier_range.
  data event_date_type ticket_sales_examiner->event_date_range.
  data ticket_sales_reporter_tstdbl type ref
                                    to ticket_sales_reporter_tstdbl.
  data last_caller_tickets_sold type sy-dbcnt.
  create object ticket_sales_examiner type ticket_sales_examiner_tstdbl.
  create object ticket_sales_reporter type ticket_sales_reporter_tstdbl.
  perform report_total_tickets_sold using stadium
                                    event_date.
  try.
    ticket_sales_reporter_tstdbl ?= ticket_sales_reporter.
    ticket_sales_reporter_tstdbl->get_last_caller_tickets_sold(
      importing
        tickets_sold = last_caller_tickets_sold
      ).
  catch cx_sy_move_cast_error.
    cl_abap_unit_assert=>fail(
      msg = 'specializing cast has failed'
      ).
  endtry.
  cl_abap_unit_assert=>assert_equals(
    act = last_caller_tickets_sold
    exp = ticket_sales_examiner_tstdbl=>constant_tickets_sold
    ).
endmethod.
```

This unit test now asserts that the processing of subroutine report_total_tickets_sold is correct. Test double ticket_sales_reporter_tstdbl now represents an example of a test spy – not only does it receive indirect output from a caller but it captures and records that output for later interrogation.

EXERCISES

At this point, take a break from reading and shift into exercise mode. Refer to the accompanying workbook to perform the 14 exercises associated with workbook **Section 15: ABAP Unit Testing 302 – Introducing a Test Double for Output.**

Summary

Test doubles used in testing software are analogous to stunt doubles used in the motion picture industry – in both cases, a surrogate takes the place of the primary performer. The concept of "depended-on components" was presented, and it was illustrated how test doubles may be defined either through class inheritance or through the use of interfaces. Test doubles fall into one of five categories:

- Dummy object – An object satisfying syntax requirements but not intended to be used

- Test stub – An object supplying indirect input to a caller during a unit test

- Test spy – An object collecting indirect output from a caller during a unit test

- Mock object – An object recording and verifying the sequence of calls made to it during a unit test

- Fake object – An object taking the place of a slower or nonexistent entity

Examples showed how to define test doubles through inheritance and to use them in an automated unit testing scenario to provide indirect input to and accept indirect output from a tested procedure, enabling a unit test to be defined capable of confirming that the indirect input provided to the caller was reflected in the indirect output it produced.

CHAPTER 9

Service Locator

Previous chapters explored how to encapsulate indirect input and output into classes providing those services and elaborated on the usefulness of test doubles capable of simulating those services during a unit test. This chapter introduces the service locator as a way to manage those services.

Purpose of a Service Locator

A service locator is a design feature implemented into a program for the purpose of providing a central registry for the various entities providing services to the program. It can be thought of simply as a list of services, each service having an associated entity assigned to provide that particular service. What makes it so useful is that the services are established at program runtime, enabling the program to determine *during execution* the specific entities it prefers to provide each of the respective services. Implicit with a service locator is that during execution there is only one entity designated to provide a particular service.

Here is a simple example of a service locator. Every year, my municipality sends to me a calendar for the upcoming year showing the dates on which various activities are to occur, such as holidays when municipal offices will be closed, meetings scheduled for the planning board, recycling pickup dates, and other information of interest to all residents. One of the calendar pages is titled *Easy Access Municipal Service Directory*; and it includes, among other things, a chart listing the phone numbers associated with some of the municipal services that can be requested by any resident, as shown in the example service directory in Figure 9-1.

© James E. McDonough 2021
J. E. McDonough, *Automated Unit Testing with ABAP*, https://doi.org/10.1007/978-1-4842-6951-0_9

Service	Phone number
Emergency – Fire, Police, Rescue	**911**
Police, non-emergency	123-456-7800
Municipal offices	123-456-7819
Animal control	123-456-7828
Recreation	123-456-7837
Public works	123-456-7846
Fire safety bureau	123-456-7855

Figure 9-1. *Example of a municipal service directory*

From this, a resident is able simply to look up the desired service and dial the corresponding phone number to request it, such as dialing 123-456-7828 to request animal control to attend to a stray dog roaming the neighborhood. The resident placing the call has no idea who will answer the phone, nor should they care – they simply know that by dialing the listed number, they will be connected to the person who performs or is in charge of that service.

The following year, there may be new services provided, with corresponding phone numbers for residents to call, or perhaps one or more of the phone numbers for the current list of services will be changed. Regardless, the resident simply performs a lookup in this chart of the desired service and dials the associated number, secure in the knowledge that they will be put in contact with the correct person to provide the service.

Using a Service Locator

This same concept applies to software through the service locator.[1] Meszaros refers to this feature also by the terms Dependency Lookup, Object Factory, Component Broker, and Component Registry. There are variations for how a service locator can be defined, but all of them simply provide to a software component access to an instance of a class that can provide the desired service.

---

[1]Meszaros, Gerard, *xUnit Test Patterns: Refactoring Test Code*, Addison Wesley, 2007, p. 686

The ticket sales program used with the previous two chapters included classes to facilitate examining and reporting ticket sales. These are two independent services that can be provided for the program. Figure 9-2 shows how they can be represented in a service directory.

Service	Provider of service
Examination of ticket sales	Reference to instance of ticket_sales_examiner
Reporting of ticket sales	Reference to instance of ticket_sales_reporter

Figure 9-2. Example of services associated with ticket sales program

With this arrangement, the program would refer to this service directory any time it needs to obtain the instance of the class assigned to provide the service required.

Listing 9-1 shows a simple example of defining a class named service_locator for providing the indirect input and output services required by the ticket sales program shown in Listing 8-19.

Listing 9-1. Service locator class for ticket sales program

```
class service_locator definition create private.
  public section.
    class-methods get_service_locator
                    returning value(instance)
                      type ref to service_locator.
    methods      get_ticket_sales_examiner
                    returning value(instance)
                      type ref to ticket_sales_examiner.
    methods      get_ticket_sales_reporter
                    returning value(instance)
                      type ref to ticket_sales_reporter.
    methods      set_ticket_sales_examiner
                    importing ticket_sales_examiner
                      type ref to ticket_sales_examiner.
    methods      set_ticket_sales_reporter
                    importing ticket_sales_reporter
                      type ref to ticket_sales_reporter.
```

```
  private section.
    class-data service_locator type ref to service_locator.
    data ticket_sales_examiner type ref to ticket_sales_examiner.
    data ticket_sales_reporter type ref to ticket_sales_reporter.
endclass.
class service_locator implementation.
  method get_service_locator.
    if service_locator is not bound.
      create object service_locator.
    endif.
    instance = service_locator.
  endmethod.
  method get_ticket_sales_examiner.
    instance = ticket_sales_examiner.
  endmethod.
  method get_ticket_sales_reporter.
    instance = ticket_sales_reporter.
  endmethod.
  method set_ticket_sales_examiner.
    me->ticket_sales_examiner = ticket_sales_examiner.
  endmethod.
  method set_ticket_sales_reporter.
    me->ticket_sales_reporter = ticket_sales_reporter.
  endmethod.
endclass.
```

Notice that class service_locator is defined as a singleton class by virtue of (a) the "create private" clause on its definition statement, meaning that only class service_locator is able to create instances of this class, and (b) the implementation of static method get_service_locator, which will create an instance of class service_locator into its private static attribute service_locator only once, upon the first call to it. Notice also that the class has a private attribute defined to hold a reference to an instance of class ticket_sales_examiner and another to hold a reference to an instance of class ticket_sales_reporter. Finally, notice that the class defines getter and setter methods to provide external entities ways to register or request the instance providing a particular service.

One of the peripheral benefits with the use of a service locator is that a program using it does not need to declare global variables to hold references to instances managed by the service locator. Listing 9-2 shows how the production path of the ticket sales program shown in Listing 8-19 would be affected by the introduction of a service locator, with changes highlighted in bold.

Listing 9-2. Production path of ticket sales program showing use of service locator class

```
o
o
o
data ticket_sales_examiner type ref to ticket_sales_examiner.
data ticket_sales_reporter type ref to ticket_sales_reporter.
select-options stadium  for zticket_sales-stadium_id.
select-options evntdate for zticket_sales-event_date.

start-of-selection.
  create object ticket_sales_examiner.
  create object ticket_sales_reporter.
  perform create_services.
  perform report_total_tickets_sold using stadium
                                          evntdate.

form create_services.
  data service_locator type ref to service_locator.
  data ticket_sales_examiner type ref to ticket_sales_examiner.
  data ticket_sales_reporter type ref to ticket_sales_reporter.
  service_locator = service_locator=>get_instance( ).
  create object ticket_sales_examiner.
  service_locator->set_ticket_sales_examiner(
    ticket_sales_examiner ).
  create object ticket_sales_reporter.
  service_locator->set_ticket_sales_reporter(
    ticket_sales_reporter ).
endform.
```

```
form report_total_tickets_sold using stadium_identifier_range
                                     event_date_range.
  data service_locator type ref to service_locator.
  data ticket_sales_examiner type ref to ticket_sales_examiner.
  data ticket_sales_reporter type ref to ticket_sales_reporter.
  data tickets_sold type sy-dbcnt.
  service_locator = service_locator=>get_instance( ).
  ticket_sales_examiner = service_locator->get_ticket_sales_examiner( ).
  ticket_sales_reporter = service_locator->get_ticket_sales_reporter( ).
  call method ticket_sales_examiner->get_total_tickets_sold
    exporting
      stadium_identifier = stadium_identifier_range
      event_date         = event_date_range
    importing
      tickets_sold       = tickets_sold.
  call method ticket_sales_reporter->show_total_tickets_sold
    exporting
      descriptor         = 'total number of tickets sold:'
      tickets_sold       = tickets_sold.
endform.
o
o
o
```

Notice that the global variables have been eliminated and now a new subroutine named create_services performs the processing for creating instances of classes ticket_sales_examiner and ticket_sales_reporter and then registering them with the service locator. Notice also that subroutine report_total_tickets_sold has been modified to retrieve from the service locator the instances of classes ticket_sales_examiner and ticket_sales_reporter it calls.

Although two global variables have been eliminated, it is hard to justify the additional complexity introduced into the program by the extra code required to compensate for their removal. Notice that existing subroutine report_total_tickets_sold now consists of three local variables and the processing to fill them with references to instances of classes. Many would say this program is worse than it was when it had global variables, and I would agree. A better design would be one where the service locator makes its services available through public read-only attributes. Listing 9-3 shows an alternative definition for the service locator class, with lines highlighted in bold showing where it differs from Listing 9-1.

Listing 9-3. Alternative definition for service locator class for ticket sales program

```
class service_locator definition create private.
  public section.
    class-methods class_constructor.
    class-methods get_service_locator
                    returning value(instance)
                      type ref to service_locator.
    methods       get_ticket_sales_examiner
                    returning value(instance)
                      type ref to ticket_sales_examiner.
    methods       get_ticket_sales_reporter
                    returning value(instance)
                      type ref to ticket_sales_reporter.
    methods       set_ticket_sales_examiner
                    importing ticket_sales_examiner
                      type ref to ticket_sales_examiner.
    methods       set_ticket_sales_reporter
                    importing ticket_sales_reporter
                      type ref to ticket_sales_reporter.
  private section.
    class-data singleton type ref to service_locator read-only.
    data ticket_sales_examiner type ref to ticket_sales_examiner
                                                      read-only.
    data ticket_sales_reporter type ref to ticket_sales_reporter
                                                      read-only.
endclass.
class service_locator implementation.
  method class_constructor.
    create instance singleton.
  endmethod.
```

```
method get_service_locator.
  if service_locator is not bound.
    create object service_locator.
  endif.
  instance = service_locator.
endmethod.
method get_ticket_sales_examiner.
  instance = ticket_sales_examiner.
endmethod.
method get_ticket_sales_reporter.
  instance = ticket_sales_reporter.
endmethod.
method set_ticket_sales_examiner.
  me->ticket_sales_examiner = ticket_sales_examiner.
endmethod.
method set_ticket_sales_reporter.
  me->ticket_sales_reporter = ticket_sales_reporter.
endmethod.
endclass.
```

It is still a singleton class; and its former attribute named service locator, holding the reference to the singleton instance, has been renamed as singleton. Notice that the method to request an instance of this class has been eliminated because the reference to the singleton instance has been elevated from private to public visibility, making this attribute directly available to external entities. In addition, notice that the getter methods to request instances of the classes providing the ticket_sales_examiner and ticket_sales_reporter services have been eliminated because these respective instance attributes also have been elevated from private to public visibility, obviating the need for getter methods. Notice also that the former private attributes, all now public, include the "read-only" qualifier, meaning their values, while accessible to any entity, can be changed only by the class in which they are defined. Listing 9-4 shows this class declaration without the highlighting and stricken lines.

Listing 9-4. Same as Listing 9-3 but without the associated highlighting and stricken lines

```
class service_locator definition create private.
  public section.
    class-methods class_constructor.
    methods        set_ticket_sales_examiner
                     importing ticket_sales_examiner
                       type ref to ticket_sales_examiner.
    methods        set_ticket_sales_reporter
                     importing ticket_sales_reporter
                       type ref to ticket_sales_reporter.
    class-data singleton type ref to service_locator read-only.
    data ticket_sales_examiner type ref to ticket_sales_examiner
                                                        read-only.
    data ticket_sales_reporter type ref to ticket_sales_reporter
                                                        read-only.
endclass.
class service_locator implementation.
  method class_constructor.
    create instance singleton.
  endmethod.
  method set_ticket_sales_examiner.
    me->ticket_sales_examiner = ticket_sales_examiner.
  endmethod.
  method set_ticket_sales_reporter.
    me->ticket_sales_reporter = ticket_sales_reporter.
  endmethod.
endclass.
```

Notice how much simpler the class has become just by making its attributes publicly accessible. Listing 9-5 shows how subroutines create_services and report_total_tickets_sold described by Listing 9-2 would be affected, with changes highlighted in bold.

Listing 9-5. Effect on Listing 9-2 subroutines by using service locator shown in Listing 9-4

```
form create_services.
  data service_locator type ref to service_locator.
  data ticket_sales_examiner type ref to ticket_sales_examiner.
  data ticket_sales_reporter type ref to ticket_sales_reporter.
  service_locator = service_locator=>get_instance( ).
  create object ticket_sales_examiner.
  service_locator=>singleton->set_ticket_sales_examiner(
    ticket_sales_examiner ).
  create object ticket_sales_reporter.
  service_locator=>singleton->set_ticket_sales_reporter(
    ticket_sales_reporter ).
endform.

form report_total_tickets_sold using stadium_identifier_range
                                     event_date_range.
  data service_locator type ref to service_locator.
  data ticket_sales_examiner type ref to ticket_sales_examiner.
  data ticket_sales_reporter type ref to ticket_sales_reporter.
  data tickets_sold type sy-dbcnt.
  service_locator = service_locator=>get_instance( ).
  ticket_sales_examiner = service_locator->get_ticket_sales_examiner( ).
  ticket_sales_reporter = service_locator->get_ticket_sales_reporter( ).
  call method ticket_sales_examiner->get_total_tickets_sold
  service_locator=>singleton->ticket_sales_examiner->get_total_tickets_sold
    exporting
      stadium_identifier = stadium_identifier_range
      event_date         = event_date_range
    importing
      tickets_sold       = tickets_sold.
  call method ticket_sales_reporter->show_total_tickets_sold
 service_locator=>singleton->ticket_sales_reporter->show_total_tickets_sold
    exporting
      descriptor         = 'total number of tickets sold:'
```

```
    tickets_sold        = tickets_sold.
endform.
```

As can be seen in Listing 9-5, the effect upon subroutine report_total_ticket_sales has been to remove all the extra lines of processing that it would have required, as shown in Listing 9-2, with the implementation of a service locator class as it is shown in Listing 9-1. Listing 9-6 shows the full ticket sales program using the merged code from Listing 8-19 and Listing 8-20 along with the changes to use the service locator shown in Listing 9-4, with changes highlighted in bold.

Listing 9-6. Full ticket sales program using service locator shown in Listing 9-4

```
report.
class ticket_sales_examiner definition.
  public section.
    types stadium_identifier_range type range of zticket_sales-stadium_id.
    types event_date_range         type range of zticket_sales-event_date.
    methods get_total_tickets_sold
      importing stadium_identifier type stadium_identifier_range
                event_date         type event_date_range
      exporting tickets_sold       type sy-dbcnt.
endclass.
class ticket_sales_examiner implementation.
  method get_total_tickets_sold.
    select count(*)
      into tickets_sold
      from zticket_sales
    where stadium_id in stadium_identifier
      and event_date in event_date.
  endmethod.
endclass.

class ticket_sales_examiner_tstdbl definition
                                  inheriting from ticket_sales_examiner.
  public section.
    constants constant_tickets_sold type sy-dbcnt value 591.
    methods get_total_tickets_sold redefinition.
```

```
endclass.
class ticket_sales_examiner_tstdbl implementation.
  method get_total_tickets_sold.
    tickets_sold = constant_tickets_sold.
  endmethod.
endclass.

class ticket_sales_reporter definition.
  public section.
    methods show_total_tickets_sold
      importing descriptor         type string
               tickets_sold        type sy-dbcnt.
endclass.
class ticket_sales_reporter implementation.
  method show_total_tickets_sold.
    write / descriptor, tickets_sold.
  endmethod.
endclass.

class ticket_sales_reporter_tstdbl definition
                                  inheriting from ticket_sales_reporter.
  public section.
    methods show_total_tickets_sold redefinition.
    methods get_last_caller_tickets_sold
      exporting
        tickets_sold type sy-dbcnt.
  private section.
    last_caller_tickets_sold type sy-dbcnt.
endclass.
class ticket_sales_reporter_tstdbl implementation.
  method show_total_tickets_sold.
    last_caller_tickets_sold = tickets_sold.
  endmethod.
  method get_last_caller_tickets_sold.
    tickets_sold = last_caller_tickets_sold.
  endmethod.
endclass.
```

```
class service_locator definition create private.
  public section.
    class-methods class_constructor.
    methods         set_ticket_sales_examiner
                       importing ticket_sales_examiner
                         type ref to ticket_sales_examiner.
    methods         set_ticket_sales_reporter
                       importing ticket_sales_reporter
                         type ref to ticket_sales_reporter.
    class-data singleton type ref to service_locator read-only.
    data ticket_sales_examiner type ref to ticket_sales_examiner
                                                        read-only.
    data ticket_sales_reporter type ref to ticket_sales_reporter
                                                        read-only.
endclass.
class service_locator implementation.
  method class_constructor.
    create instance singleton.
  endmethod.
  method set_ticket_sales_examiner.
    me->ticket_sales_examiner = ticket_sales_examiner.
  endmethod.
  method set_ticket_sales_reporter.
    me->ticket_sales_reporter = ticket_sales_reporter.
  endmethod.
endclass.

data ticket_sales_examiner type ref to ticket_sales_examiner.
data ticket_sales_reporter type ref to ticket_sales_reporter.
select-options stadium  for zticket_sales-stadium_id.
select-options evntdate for zticket_sales-event_date.
start-of-selection.
  create object ticket_sales_examiner.
  create object ticket_sales_reporter.
  perform create_services.
```

223

```
    perform report_total_tickets_sold using stadium
                                             evntdate.
```

form create_services.
  data ticket_sales_examiner type ref to ticket_sales_examiner.
  data ticket_sales_reporter type ref to ticket_sales_reporter.
  create object ticket_sales_examiner.
  service_locator=>singleton->set_ticket_sales_examiner(
    ticket_sales_examiner).
  create object ticket_sales_reporter.
  service_locator=>singleton->set_ticket_sales_reporter(
    ticket_sales_reporter).
endform.

```
form report_total_tickets_sold using stadium_identifier_range
                                    event_date_range.
    data tickets_sold type sy-dbcnt.
    call method
```
ticket_sales_examiner->get_total_tickets_sold
  service_locator=>singleton->ticket_sales_examiner->get_total_tickets_sold
```
      exporting
        stadium_identifier = stadium_identifier_range
        event_date         = event_date_range
      importing
        tickets_sold       = tickets_sold.
    call method
```
ticket_sales_reporter->show_total_tickets_sold
 service_locator=>singleton->ticket_sales_reporter->show_total_tickets_sold
```
      exporting
        descriptor         = 'total number of tickets sold:'
        tickets_sold       = tickets_sold.
endform.
class tester definition for testing risk level harmless.
  private section.
    methods report_total_tickets_sold for testing.
endclass.
class tester implementation.
  method report_total_tickets_sold.
```

```
data stadium    type ticket_sales_examiner->stadium_identifier_range.
data event_date_type ticket_sales_examiner->event_date_range.
data ticket_sales_reporter_tstdbl type ref
                                to ticket_sales_reporter_tstdbl.
data last_caller_tickets_sold type sy-dbcnt.
data ticket_sales_examiner type ticket_sales_examiner.
data ticket_sales_reporter type ticket_sales_reporter.
create object ticket_sales_examiner type ticket_sales_examiner_tstdbl.
create object ticket_sales_reporter type ticket_sales_reporter_tstdbl.
service_locator=>singleton->set_ticket_sales_examiner(
  ticket_sales_examiner ).
service_locator=>singleton->set_ticket_sales_reporter(
  ticket_sales_reporter ).
perform report_total_tickets_sold using stadium
                                event_date.
try.
  ticket_sales_reporter_tstdbl ?= ticket_sales_reporter.
    service_locator=>singleton->ticket_sales_reporter.
  ticket_sales_reporter_tstdbl->get_last_caller_tickets_sold(
    importing
      tickets_sold = last_caller_tickets_sold
    ).
catch cx_sy_move_cast_error.
  cl_abap_unit_assert=>fail(
    msg = 'specializing cast has failed'
    ).
endtry.
cl_abap_unit_assert=>assert_equals(
  act = last_caller_tickets_sold
  exp = ticket_sales_examiner_tstdbl=>constant_tickets_sold
  ).
  endmethod.
endclass.
```

Notice that with the removal of the global variables defining ticket_sales_examiner and ticket_sales_reporter, it was necessary to change the unit test method to define these as local variables into which corresponding instances could be created before requesting the service locator to register them.

There is plenty of information available on the Internet further describing the "service locator" design pattern, along with its adherents and critics providing the pros and cons for using it with software components. The Wikipedia page (`https://en.wikipedia.org/wiki/Service_locator_pattern`) suggests that some scholars consider it to be an anti-pattern (a pattern to be avoided) which " ... obscures dependencies and makes software harder to test," but indeed I have found it to be particularly helpful for facilitating automated unit testing, as I think you might agree after completing the associated exercises.

EXERCISES

At this point, take a break from reading and shift into exercise mode. Refer to the accompanying workbook to perform the seven exercises associated with workbook **Section 16: ABAP Unit Testing 401 – Introducing a Service Locator.**

Using a Service Factory

One variation of a service locator serves simply as a list of the services required during the execution of an ABAP program, as previously described. Another variation has the service locator explicitly instantiating the objects to be used for the services it manages. When a service locator is not designed to instantiate the objects providing the services it manages, then it is often accompanied by a service factory.

A service factory creates the instances of the services managed by the service locator. It is itself a class encapsulating the tasks associated with creating the various services to be used by the program. Once it instantiates an object, it will call the service locator to have the object registered as the designated service.

Listing 9-7 shows how we might define a service factory for creating the services managed by the ticket sales program, which essentially encapsulates the processing currently performed by the subroutine create_services of the ticket sales program.

Listing 9-7. Service factory for use with the ticket sales program

```
class service_factory definition create private.
  public section.
    class-data singleton type ref to service_factory read-only.
    class-methods class_constructor.
    methods create_ticket_sales_examiner.
    methods create_ticket_sales_reporter.
endclass.
class service_factory implementation.
  method class_constructor.
    create instance singleton.
  endmethod.
  method create_ticket_sales_examiner.
    data ticket_sales_examiner type ref to ticket_sales_examiner.
    create object ticket_sales_examiner.
    service_locator=>singleton->set_ticket_sales_examiner(
        ticket_sales_examiner ).
  endmethod.
  method create_ticket_sales_reporter.
    data ticket_sales_reporter type ref to ticket_sales_reporter.
    create object ticket_sales_reporter.
    service_locator=>singleton->set_ticket_sales_reporter(
        ticket_sales_reporter ).
  endmethod.
endclass.
```

This eliminates the need for the subroutine create_services to exist. Listing 9-8 shows how the start-of-selection event block and create_services subroutine shown in Listing 9-6 would be changed to use the service factory, with changes highlighted in bold.

Listing 9-8. Effects upon ticket sales program start-of-selection event block and subroutine create_services to use service factory

```
start-of-selection.
  perform create_services.
  service_factory=>singleton->create_ticket_sales_examiner( ).
  service_factory=>singleton->create_ticket_sales_reporter( ).
  perform report_total_tickets_sold using stadium
                                          evntdate.

form create_services.
  data ticket_sales_examiner type ref to ticket_sales_examiner.
  data ticket_sales_reporter type ref to ticket_sales_reporter.
  create object ticket_sales_examiner.
  service_locator=>singleton->set_ticket_sales_examiner(
    ticket_sales_examiner ).
  create object ticket_sales_reporter.
  service_locator=>singleton->set_ticket_sales_reporter(
    ticket_sales_reporter ).
endform.
```

When there are many services to be managed by the service locator, then the service factory usually will contain a method by which all the services can be created with a single call. Listing 9-9 shows how we might change the service factory to provide such a capability, with changes from Listing 9-7 highlighted in bold.

Listing 9-9. Service factory with a single method capable of creating all services

```
class service_factory definition create private.
  public section.
    class-data singleton type ref to service_factory read-only.
    class-methods class_constructor.
    methods create_all_services.
    methods create_ticket_sales_examiner.
    methods create_ticket_sales_reporter.
endclass.
class service_factory implementation.
  method class_constructor.
```

```
    create instance singleton.
  endmethod.
  method create_all_services.
    create_ticket_sales_examiner( ).
    create_ticket_sales_reporter( ).
  endmethod.
  method create_ticket_sales_examiner.
    data ticket_sales_examiner type ref to ticket_sales_examiner.
    create object ticket_sales_examiner.
    service_locator=>singleton->set_ticket_sales_examiner(
        ticket_sales_examiner ).
  endmethod.
  method create_ticket_sales_reporter.
    data ticket_sales_reporter type ref to ticket_sales_reporter.
    create object ticket_sales_reporter.
    service_locator=>singleton->set_ticket_sales_reporter(
        ticket_sales_reporter ).
  endmethod.
endclass.
```

Organizing Local Components

Due to the nature of the ABAP compiler, I have found that when most or all of the classes have been defined locally, then it becomes advantageous to have the service locator and the service factory defined as two separate components. This is because the compiler needs to have already parsed the definitions of the classes referenced by subsequent classes and subroutines, and it increases clutter to have to specify a preemptive class definition deferral statement for each class referenced before the compiler encounters its definition.

Indeed, with more complex programs, I have found that the use of a service locator will impose the following demands upon the design of the program:

- Attributes of the service locator holding the references to the objects providing the services it manages should be defined as references to interfaces and not to classes.

- Classes providing services managed by a service locator should specify an interface to define all of its public methods.

- The sequence of the classes and interfaces should be in the following order:

    1. All interfaces

    2. The service locator class

    3. All classes providing a service managed by the service locator

    4. The service factory

    5. Any component calling a method of the service factory

The preceding first two bullets call for accessing class instances through an interface reference variable and not through a reference variable defined as the concrete classes they are. This alone has beneficial consequences on the design of the components since it conforms with the advice given by object-oriented scholars who suggest this as a good way of keeping the code flexible:

- "Program to an interface, not an implementation."[2]

- "**Dependency Inversion Principle** – Depend upon abstractions. Do not depend upon concretions."[3]

Notice in the sequence shown in the preceding list that the service locator, whose attributes holding references to service objects all are defined as references to interfaces, should appear after the definitions of all the interfaces. Notice also that all of the classes providing services managed by the service locator should be defined after the service locator. This means that any of these classes can define a service managed by the service locator and can obtain the services provided by any of the other classes defining a service managed by the service locator irrespective of the sequence in which they are defined. This is because through the service locator there is no direct reference between these classes – each instance of a class providing a service is accessed through an interface reference. Notice also that the service factory, the one instantiating and registering services with the service locator, is positioned to insure that (a) it has been preceded by all the class definitions that could possibly be used to provide an instance

---

[2]Erich Gamma, Richard Helm, Ralph Johnson, and John Vlissides, *Design Patterns: Elements of Reusable Object-Oriented Software*, Addison-Wesley, 1994, p. 18

[3]See `http://butunclebob.com/ArticleS.UncleBob.PrinciplesOfOod`

of a service it creates to be managed by the service locator and (b) it is followed by any component that would call one of its methods.

Let's see this with an example. Listing 9-10 is a copy of Listing 9-6 changed to reflect how to define and arrange the components in sequence described in the preceding list, with changes highlighted in bold.

Listing 9-10. Ticket sales program using service factory

```
report.
interface ticket_sales_examinable.
   types stadium_identifier_range type range of zticket_sales-stadium_id.
   types event_date_range          type range of zticket_sales-event_date.
   methods get_total_tickets_sold
      importing stadium_identifier type stadium_identifier_range
                event_date         type event_date_range
      exporting tickets_sold       type sy-dbcnt.
endinterface.

interface ticket_sales_reportable.
   methods show_total_tickets_sold
      importing descriptor         type string
                tickets_sold       type sy-dbcnt.
endinterface.

class service_locator definition create private.
  public section.
    class-methods class_constructor.
    methods        set_ticket_sales_examiner
                     importing ticket_sales_examiner
                       type ref to ticket_sales_examinable.
    methods        set_ticket_sales_reporter
                     importing ticket_sales_reporter
                       type ref to ticket_sales_reportable.
    class-data singleton type ref to service_locator read-only.
    data ticket_sales_examiner type ref to ticket_sales_examinable
                                                         read-only.
    data ticket_sales_reporter type ref to ticket_sales_reportable
                                                         read-only.
```

```
endclass.
class service_locator implementation.
  method class_constructor.
    create instance singleton.
  endmethod.
  method set_ticket_sales_examiner.
    me->ticket_sales_examiner = ticket_sales_examiner.
  endmethod.
  method set_ticket_sales_reporter.
    me->ticket_sales_reporter = ticket_sales_reporter.
  endmethod.
endclass.

class ticket_sales_examiner definition.
  public section.
    types stadium_identifier_range type range of zticket_sales-stadium_id.
    types event_date_range         type range of zticket_sales-event_date.
    methods get_total_tickets_sold
      importing stadium_identifier type stadium_identifier_range
                event_date         type event_date_range
      exporting tickets_sold       type sy-dbcnt.
    interfaces ticket_sales_examinable.
    aliases get_total_tickets_sold
              for ticket_sales_examinable~get_total_tickets_sold.
endclass.
class ticket_sales_examiner implementation.
  method get_total_tickets_sold.
    select count(*)
      into tickets_sold
      from zticket_sales
     where stadium_id in stadium_identifier
       and event_date in event_date.
  endmethod.
endclass.
```

```
class ticket_sales_examiner_tstdbl definition
                                inheriting from ticket_sales_examiner.
  public section.
    constants constant_tickets_sold type sy-dbcnt value 591.
    methods get_total_tickets_sold redefinition.
    interfaces ticket_sales_examinable.
    aliases get_total_tickets_sold
              for ticket_sales_examinable~get_total_tickets_sold.
endclass.
class ticket_sales_examiner_tstdbl implementation.
  method get_total_tickets_sold.
    tickets_sold = constant_tickets_sold.
  endmethod.
endclass.

class ticket_sales_reporter definition.
  public section.
    methods show_total_tickets_sold
      importing descriptor          type string
                tickets_sold        type sy-dbcnt.
    interfaces ticket_sales_reportable.
    aliases show_total_tickets_sold
              for ticket_sales_reportable->get_total_tickets_sold.
endclass.
class ticket_sales_reporter implementation.
  method show_total_tickets_sold.
    write / descriptor, tickets_sold.
  endmethod.
endclass.

class ticket_sales_reporter_tstdbl definition
                                inheriting from ticket_sales_reporter.
  public section.
    methods show_total_tickets_sold redefinition.
    interfaces ticket_sales_reportable.
    aliases show_total_tickets_sold
```

233

```
              for ticket_sales_reportable->get_total_tickets_sold.
    methods get_last_caller_tickets_sold
      exporting
        tickets_sold type sy-dbcnt.
  private section.
    last_caller_tickets_sold type sy-dbcnt.
endclass.
class ticket_sales_reporter_tstdbl implementation.
  method show_total_tickets_sold.
    last_caller_tickets_sold = tickets_sold.
  endmethod.
  method get_last_caller_tickets_sold.
    tickets_sold = last_caller_tickets_sold.
  endmethod.
endclass.

class service_factory definition create private.
  public section.
    class-data singleton type ref to service_factory read-only.
    class-methods class_constructor.
    methods create_all_services.
    methods create_ticket_sales_examiner.
    methods create_ticket_sales_reporter.
endclass.
class service_factory implementation.
  method class_constructor.
    create instance singleton.
  endmethod.
  method create_all_services.
    create_ticket_sales_examiner( ).
    create_ticket_sales_reporter( ).
  endmethod.
  method create_ticket_sales_examiner.
    data ticket_sales_examiner type ref to ticket_sales_examinable.
    create object ticket_sales_examiner type ticket_sales_examiner.
    service_locator=>singleton->set_ticket_sales_examiner(
```

```
        ticket_sales_examiner ).
    endmethod.
    method create_ticket_sales_reporter.
      data ticket_sales_reporter type ref to ticket_sales_reportable.
      create object ticket_sales_reporter type ticket_sales_reporter.
      service_locator=>singleton->set_ticket_sales_reporter(
          ticket_sales_reporter ).
    endmethod.
endclass.

select-options stadium  for zticket_sales-stadium_id.
select-options evntdate for zticket_sales-event_date.

start-of-selection.
    perform create_services.
    service_factory=>singleton->create_all_services( ).
    perform report_total_tickets_sold using stadium
                                            evntdate.

form create_services.
    data ticket_sales_examiner type ref to ticket_sales_examiner.
    data ticket_sales_reporter type ref to ticket_sales_reporter.
    create object ticket_sales_examiner.
    service_locator=>singleton->set_ticket_sales_examiner(
      ticket_sales_examiner ).
    create object ticket_sales_reporter.
    service_locator=>singleton->set_ticket_sales_reporter(
      ticket_sales_reporter ).
endform.

form report_total_tickets_sold using stadium_identifier_range
                                     event_date_range.
    data tickets_sold type sy-dbcnt.
    call method
    service_locator=>singleton->ticket_sales_examiner->get_total_tickets_sold
      exporting
        stadium_identifier = stadium_identifier_range
```

```
      event_date          = event_date_range
    importing
      tickets_sold        = tickets_sold.
  call method
 service_locator=>singleton->ticket_sales_reporter->show_total_tickets_sold
    exporting
      descriptor          = 'total number of tickets sold:'
      tickets_sold        = tickets_sold.
endform.

class tester definition for testing risk level harmless.
  private section.
    methods report_total_tickets_sold for testing.
endclass.
class tester implementation.
  method report_total_tickets_sold.
    data stadium     type ticket_sales_examinable=>stadium_identifier_range.
    data event_date_type ticket_sales_examinable=>event_date_range.
    data ticket_sales_reporter_tstdbl type ref
                                        to ticket_sales_reporter_tstdbl.
    data last_caller_tickets_sold type sy-dbcnt.
    data ticket_sales_examiner type ticket_sales_examinable.
    data ticket_sales_reporter type ticket_sales_reportable.
    create object ticket_sales_examiner type ticket_sales_examiner_tstdbl.
    create object ticket_sales_reporter type ticket_sales_reporter_tstdbl.
    service_locator=>singleton->set_ticket_sales_examiner(
      ticket_sales_examiner ).
    service_locator=>singleton->set_ticket_sales_reporter(
      ticket_sales_reporter ).
    perform report_total_tickets_sold using stadium
                                            event_date.

    try.
      ticket_sales_reporter_tstdbl ?=
        service_locator=>singleton->ticket_sales_reporter.
      ticket_sales_reporter_tstdbl->get_last_caller_tickets_sold(
        importing
```

```
        tickets_sold = last_caller_tickets_sold
      ).
    catch cx_sy_move_cast_error.
      cl_abap_unit_assert=>fail(
        msg = 'specializing cast has failed'
        ).
    endtry.
    cl_abap_unit_assert=>assert_equals(
      act = last_caller_tickets_sold
      exp = ticket_sales_examiner_tstdbl=>constant_tickets_sold
      ).
  endmethod.
endclass.
```

Notice first that there are two new interfaces appearing at the top of the listing: ticket_sales_examinable and ticket_sales_reportable. Interface ticket_sales_examinable is defined using the very same public types and methods removed from class ticket_sales_examiner. Likewise, interface ticket_sales_reportable is defined using the very same public method removed from class ticket_sales_reporter. The respective classes from which code was moved into an interface have been replaced with interfaces and aliases statements indicating the interface now defining its public section.

Notice also that test double classes ticket_sales_examiner_tstdbl and ticket_sales_reporter_tstdbl have been changed to no longer inherit from a superclass and also have their public declarations of redefined inherited methods replaced with the same interfaces and aliases statements appearing now in their former superclasses. In addition, notice that subroutine create_services has been removed and that the start-of-selection event block has been changed from calling subroutine create_services to calling method create_all_services of the service factory. Finally, notice that local variables ticket_sales_examiner and ticket_sales_reporter defined for unit test method report_total_tickets_sold have been changed from references to their respective classes to references to their respective interfaces.

Listing 9-11 shows the same code as Listing 9-10 but without the highlighting and stricken code.

Listing 9-11. Listing 9-10 without the highlighting and stricken code

```
report.
interface ticket_sales_examinable.
    types stadium_identifier_range type range of zticket_sales-stadium_id.
    types event_date_range         type range of zticket_sales-event_date.
    methods get_total_tickets_sold
      importing stadium_identifier type stadium_identifier_range
                event_date         type event_date_range
      exporting tickets_sold       type sy-dbcnt.
endinterface.

interface ticket_sales_reportable.
    methods show_total_tickets_sold
      importing descriptor          type string
                tickets_sold        type sy-dbcnt.
endinterface.

class service_locator definition create private.
  public section.
    class-methods class_constructor.
    methods       set_ticket_sales_examiner
                    importing ticket_sales_examiner
                      type ref to ticket_sales_examinable.
    methods       set_ticket_sales_reporter
                    importing ticket_sales_reporter
                      type ref to ticket_sales_reportable.
    class-data singleton type ref to service_locator read-only.
    data ticket_sales_examiner type ref to ticket_sales_examinable
                                                        read-only.
    data ticket_sales_reporter type ref to ticket_sales_reportable
                                                        read-only.
endclass.
class service_locator implementation.
```

```
  method class_constructor.
    create instance singleton.
  endmethod.
  method set_ticket_sales_examiner.
    me->ticket_sales_examiner = ticket_sales_examiner.
  endmethod.
  method set_ticket_sales_reporter.
    me->ticket_sales_reporter = ticket_sales_reporter.
  endmethod.
endclass.

class ticket_sales_examiner definition.
  public section.
    interfaces ticket_sales_examinable.
    aliases get_total_tickets_sold
            for ticket_sales_examinable~get_total_tickets_sold.
endclass.
class ticket_sales_examiner implementation.
  method get_total_tickets_sold.
    select count(*)
      into tickets_sold
      from zticket_sales
     where stadium_id in stadium_identifier
       and event_date in event_date.
  endmethod.
endclass.

class ticket_sales_examiner_tstdbl definition.
  public section.
    constants constant_tickets_sold type sy-dbcnt value 591.
    interfaces ticket_sales_examinable.
    aliases get_total_tickets_sold
            for ticket_sales_examinable~get_total_tickets_sold.
endclass.
class ticket_sales_examiner_tstdbl implementation.
  method get_total_tickets_sold.
```

```abap
      tickets_sold = constant_tickets_sold.
    endmethod.
endclass.

class ticket_sales_reporter definition.
  public section.
    interfaces ticket_sales_reportable.
    aliases show_total_tickets_sold
              for ticket_sales_reportable->get_total_tickets_sold.
endclass.
class ticket_sales_reporter implementation.
  method show_total_tickets_sold.
    write / descriptor, tickets_sold.
  endmethod.
endclass.

class ticket_sales_reporter_tstdbl definition.
  public section.
    interfaces ticket_sales_reportable.
    aliases show_total_tickets_sold
              for ticket_sales_reportable->get_total_tickets_sold.
    methods get_last_caller_tickets_sold
      exporting
        tickets_sold type sy-dbcnt.
  private section.
    last_caller_tickets_sold type sy-dbcnt.
endclass.
class ticket_sales_reporter_tstdbl implementation.
  method show_total_tickets_sold.
    last_caller_tickets_sold = tickets_sold.
  endmethod.
  method get_last_caller_tickets_sold.
    tickets_sold = last_caller_tickets_sold.
  endmethod.
endclass.

class service_factory definition create private.
```

```
  public section.
    class-data singleton type ref to service_factory read-only.
    class-methods class_constructor.
    methods create_all_services.
    methods create_ticket_sales_examiner.
    methods create_ticket_sales_reporter.
endclass.
class service_factory implementation.
  method class_constructor.
    create instance singleton.
  endmethod.
  method create_all_services.
    create_ticket_sales_examiner( ).
    create_ticket_sales_reporter( ).
  endmethod.
  method create_ticket_sales_examiner.
    data ticket_sales_examiner type ref to ticket_sales_examinable.
    create object ticket_sales_examiner type ticket_sales_examiner.
    service_locator=>singleton->set_ticket_sales_examiner(
        ticket_sales_examiner ).
  endmethod.
  method create_ticket_sales_reporter.
    data ticket_sales_reporter type ref to ticket_sales_reportable.
    create object ticket_sales_reporter type ticket_sales_reporter.
    service_locator=>singleton->set_ticket_sales_reporter(
        ticket_sales_reporter ).
  endmethod.
endclass.

select-options stadium  for zticket_sales-stadium_id.
select-options evntdate for zticket_sales-event_date.

start-of-selection.
  service_factory=>singleton->create_all_services( ).
  perform report_total_tickets_sold using stadium
                                          evntdate.
```

```
form report_total_tickets_sold using stadium_identifier_range
                                      event_date_range.
  data tickets_sold type sy-dbcnt.
  call method
  service_locator=>singleton->ticket_sales_examiner->get_total_tickets_sold
    exporting
      stadium_identifier = stadium_identifier_range
      event_date         = event_date_range
    importing
      tickets_sold       = tickets_sold.
  call method
 service_locator=>singleton->ticket_sales_reporter->show_total_tickets_sold
    exporting
      descriptor         = 'total number of tickets sold:'
      tickets_sold       = tickets_sold.
endform.

class tester definition for testing risk level harmless.
  private section.
    methods report_total_tickets_sold for testing.
endclass.
class tester implementation.
  method report_total_tickets_sold.
    data stadium    type ticket_sales_examinable=>stadium_identifier_range.
    data event_date_type ticket_sales_examinable=>event_date_range.
    data ticket_sales_reporter_tstdbl type ref
                                  to ticket_sales_reporter_tstdbl.
    data last_caller_tickets_sold type sy-dbcnt.
    data ticket_sales_examiner type ticket_sales_examinable.
    data ticket_sales_reporter type ticket_sales_reportable.
    create object ticket_sales_examiner type ticket_sales_examiner_tstdbl.
    create object ticket_sales_reporter type ticket_sales_reporter_tstdbl.
    service_locator=>singleton->set_ticket_sales_examiner(
      ticket_sales_examiner ).
    service_locator=>singleton->set_ticket_sales_reporter(
      ticket_sales_reporter ).
```

```
  perform report_total_tickets_sold using stadium
                                          event_date.
  try.
    ticket_sales_reporter_tstdbl ?=
      service_locator=>singleton->ticket_sales_reporter.
    ticket_sales_reporter_tstdbl->get_last_caller_tickets_sold(
      importing
        tickets_sold = last_caller_tickets_sold
      ).
  catch cx_sy_move_cast_error.
    cl_abap_unit_assert=>fail(
      msg = 'specializing cast has failed'
      ).
  endtry.
  cl_abap_unit_assert=>assert_equals(
    act = last_caller_tickets_sold
    exp = ticket_sales_examiner_tstdbl=>constant_tickets_sold
    ).
  endmethod.
endclass.
```

Now that it is easier to read, notice that these local components have been organized as previously recommended:

- Attributes of the service locator holding the references to the objects providing the services for ticket_sales_examiner and ticket_sales_ reporter have been defined as references to interfaces ticket_sales_ examinable and ticket_sales_reportable, respectively.

- Classes ticket_sales_examiner and ticket_sales_reporter specify interfaces ticket_sales_examiner and ticket_sales_reporter, respectively, to define all of their public methods; classes ticket_ sales_examiner_tstdbl and ticket_sales_reporter_tstdbl have been similarly changed to specify interfaces ticket_sales_examinable and ticket_sales_reportable, respectively.

- The classes and interfaces appear in the following order:

  1. Interfaces ticket_sales_examinable and ticket_sales_
     reportable appear first.

  2. The service locator class appears next.

  3. Classes ticket_sales_examiner, ticket_sales_examiner_tstdbl,
     ticket_sales_reporter, and ticket_sales_reporter_tstdbl, all of
     which provide services manageable by the service locator,
     appear next.

  4. The service factory appears after all the classes it uses to
     create services, specifically, ticket_sales_examiner and ticket_
     sales_reporter.

  5. The service factory is followed by components calling its
     methods, specifically, the start-of-selection classic event block.

To make it easier to visualize the sequence of these entities, Listing 9-12 shows a
condensed version of Listing 9-11.

Listing 9-12. Condensed version of Listing 9-11

```
interface ticket_sales_examinable.
interface ticket_sales_reportable.

class service_locator definition create private.

class ticket_sales_examiner definition.
class ticket_sales_examiner_tstdbl definition.
class ticket_sales_reporter definition.
class ticket_sales_reporter_tstdbl definition.

class service_factory definition create private.

select-options stadium  for zticket_sales-stadium_id.
select-options evntdate for zticket_sales-event_date.

start-of-selection.
  service_factory=>singleton->create_all_services( ).
  perform report_total_tickets_sold using stadium
                                          evntdate.
```

```
form report_total_tickets_sold using stadium_identifier_range
                                      event_date_range.

class tester definition for testing risk level harmless.
    o
    o
  method report_total_tickets_sold.
    o
    o
    service_locator=>singleton->set_ticket_sales_examiner(
      ticket_sales_examiner ).
    service_locator=>singleton->set_ticket_sales_reporter(
      ticket_sales_reporter ).
    o
    o
endclass.
```

In the condensed Listing 9-12, it is easy to see that all the interfaces appear first, followed by the service locator, followed by those classes defining services managed by the service locator, followed by the service factory, followed by the components calling methods of the service factory. Notice that since method create_all_services of the service factory is called during the start-of-selection classic ABAP event block, the start-of-selection block appears after the definition of the service factory class.

Notice also that the unit test class does not make use of the service factory; instead, it instantiates its own services and makes direct calls to the service locator to register them. Accordingly, the definitions for test classes ticket_sales_examiner_tstdbl and ticket_sales_reportable_tstdbl need not appear directly following their respective production classes as shown, but simply need to follow the service locator and precede the unit test class that instantiates them.

Before leaving this section, there is one more improvement that can be made to unit test class tester. Its sole method report_total_tickets_sold has changed significantly since it was first introduced in Listing 8-13 to the way it now appears in Listing 9-11. The component being tested by this method is subroutine report_total_tickets_sold, but the statement to perform that subroutine is buried between the code establishing the conditions necessary for running the test and the code asserting the test results. With a few simple changes to this unit test class, it could be made easier to understand exactly what is being tested by its method, as shown in Listing 9-13 with changes from its version in Listing 9-11 highlighted in bold.

Listing 9-13. Modified version of unit test class tester to enable better visibility to the purpose of the test

```
class tester definition for testing risk level harmless.
  private section.
    methods setup.
    methods report_total_tickets_sold for testing.
    methods validate_test_results.
endclass.
class tester implementation.
  method setup. report_total_tickets_sold.
    data stadium     type ticket_sales_examinable=>stadium_identifier_range.
    data event_date_type ticket_sales_examinable=>event_date_range.
    data ticket_sales_reporter_tstdbl type ref
                                        to ticket_sales_reporter_tstdbl.
    data last_caller_tickets_sold type sy-dbcnt.
    data ticket_sales_examiner type ticket_sales_examinable.
    data ticket_sales_reporter type ticket_sales_reportable.
    create object ticket_sales_examiner type ticket_sales_examiner_tstdbl.
    create object ticket_sales_reporter type ticket_sales_reporter_tstdbl.
    service_locator=>singleton->set_ticket_sales_examiner(
      ticket_sales_examiner ).
    service_locator=>singleton->set_ticket_sales_reporter(
      ticket_sales_reporter ).
  endmethod.
  method report_total_tickets_sold.
    data stadium     type ticket_sales_examinable=>stadium_identifier_range.
    data event_date_type ticket_sales_examinable=>event_date_range.
    perform report_total_tickets_sold using stadium
                                        event_date.

    validate_test_results( ).
  endmethod.
  method validate_test_results.
    data ticket_sales_reporter_tstdbl type ref
                                        to ticket_sales_reporter_tstdbl.
    data last_caller_tickets_sold type sy-dbcnt.
```

```
    try.
      ticket_sales_reporter_tstdbl ?=
        service_locator=>singleton->ticket_sales_reporter.
      ticket_sales_reporter_tstdbl->get_last_caller_tickets_sold(
        importing
          tickets_sold = last_caller_tickets_sold
        ).
    catch cx_sy_move_cast_error.
      cl_abap_unit_assert=>fail(
        msg = 'specializing cast has failed'
        ).
    endtry.
    cl_abap_unit_assert=>assert_equals(
      act = last_caller_tickets_sold
      exp = ticket_sales_examiner_tstdbl=>constant_tickets_sold
      ).
  endmethod.
endclass.
```

Notice there are now two new methods: setup and validate_test_results. The statements establishing the conditions necessary for running the test, formerly located in method report_total_tickets_sold, now appear in the setup method, a method automatically called by the test runner prior to calling any method marked "for testing." Also notice that the statements validating the results produced by calling the subroutine have been removed from method report_total_tickets_sold and now appear in method validate_test_results, which is called by method report_total_tickets_sold.

Listing 9-14 is a copy of Listing 9-13 without the highlighting and stricken lines.

Listing 9-14. Listing 9-13 without highlighting and stricken lines

```
class tester definition for testing risk level harmless.
  private section.
    methods setup.
    methods report_total_tickets_sold for testing.
    methods validate_test_results.
endclass.
class tester implementation.
```

```
method setup.
  data ticket_sales_examiner type ticket_sales_examinable.
  data ticket_sales_reporter type ticket_sales_reportable.
  create object ticket_sales_examiner type ticket_sales_examiner_tstdbl.
  create object ticket_sales_reporter type ticket_sales_reporter_tstdbl.
  service_locator=>singleton->set_ticket_sales_examiner(
    ticket_sales_examiner ).
  service_locator=>singleton->set_ticket_sales_reporter(
    ticket_sales_reporter ).
endmethod.
method report_total_tickets_sold.
  data stadium    type ticket_sales_examinable=>stadium_identifier_range.
  data event_date type ticket_sales_examinable=>event_date_range.
  perform report_total_tickets_sold using stadium
                                           event_date.
  validate_test_results( ).
endmethod.
method validate_test_results.
  data ticket_sales_reporter_tstdbl type ref
                                    to ticket_sales_reporter_tstdbl.
  data last_caller_tickets_sold type sy-dbcnt.
  try.
    ticket_sales_reporter_tstdbl ?=
      service_locator=>singleton->ticket_sales_reporter.
    ticket_sales_reporter_tstdbl->get_last_caller_tickets_sold(
      importing
        tickets_sold = last_caller_tickets_sold
      ).
  catch cx_sy_move_cast_error.
    cl_abap_unit_assert=>fail(
      msg = 'specializing cast has failed'
      ).
  endtry.
  cl_abap_unit_assert=>assert_equals(
    act = last_caller_tickets_sold
```

```
      exp = ticket_sales_examiner_tstdbl=>constant_tickets_sold
      ).
  endmethod.
endclass.
```

With unit test method report_total_tickets_sold reduced down to only four lines, it becomes abundantly clear that subroutine report_total_tickets_sold is the component being tested and that it is being called with empty values.

EXERCISES

At this point, take a break from reading and shift into exercise mode. Refer to the accompanying workbook to perform the eight exercises associated with workbook **Section 17: ABAP Unit Testing 402 – Introducing a Service Factory.**

Summary

A service locator is a centralized services management facility for the services required by a software component. It assumes the responsibility to make each service it manages available through a corresponding designated entity registered to provide the corresponding service. Its use improves the design for testability of production components. A service factory is a complementary component collaborating with the service locator, creating and registering the services managed by the service locator. Examples illustrated the use of interfaces to define the public methods of the classes providing the services managed by the service locator, with interfaces being preferred over inheritance when the services being managed are defined by local classes.

CHAPTER 10

Leveraging the Service Locator

The previous chapter introduced the service locator and described how it could handle the various services required by the program as well as facilitate the use of test doubles during unit testing. At this point, the examples of services managed by the service locator were provided by local classes. It also is capable of managing program services and their respective unit testing doubles for global classes and function modules.

Also at this point, there remain some unresolved issues with the ability to run clean unattended unit tests. In this chapter, we will explore how the service locator can be leveraged to handle these outstanding issues as well as to manage services supplied by function modules and global classes.

Issues Requiring Leverage

The Chapter 5 section titled "Challenges Presented by the MESSAGE Statement" and Chapter 6 section titled "Exploring the Effects of the MESSAGE Statement" covered unit testing results attributable to the MESSAGE Statement, but we still have no viable solution for the unit test failures certain to be triggered upon encountering an ABAP MESSAGE statement with a severity of error, abort, or exit. This remains the only identified impediment to running successful unit tests.

© James E. McDonough 2021
J. E. McDonough, *Automated Unit Testing with ABAP*, https://doi.org/10.1007/978-1-4842-6951-0_10

The Chapter 5 section titled "Challenges to Effectively Testing ABAP Code" told of the effects on unit tests attributable to ALV reports and classic list statements. We subsequently found that we could encapsulate the reception of this type of indirect output into classes capable of providing reports formatted using either classic list statements or ALV, with test doubles defined for these classes used to enable automated unit tests to run to completion unattended. Although this seems to be a reasonable solution for handling output presented by both ALV and classic list statements, it is practical only with ALV.

With ALV there is an associated internal table containing the content to be displayed in the report, and a specific function module or class method must be called to present it. This makes it easy to identify the two lines of code where the internal table is contributing content to the report and the request is being made to present it.

In contrast, classic list processing statements could be scattered throughout a program, each one contributing some new full or partial row to be presented in a report that for executable programs has no associated statement to indicate it is to be presented. A unit test encountering any one of these classic list statements would require manual intervention to enable the test to run to completion. Accordingly, the disjointed nature of constructing classic list output and the lack of complete control over the presentation of the resulting report present challenges with devising a way to avoid encountering these statements during a unit test.

The following topics are presented in the sequence of what might loosely be considered the relative amount of time required to complete the respective implementation, from least time to most:

- Managing global classes

- Managing function modules

- Managing message statements

- Managing list processing statements

Using the Service Locator to Manage Global Classes

Having the service locator manage a global class requires simply that the attribute
holding the reference to the instance providing the service be defined as a reference
to either a global class or a global interface. When defined as a reference to a global
class, then the attribute may hold a reference to an instance of that class or of any class
inheriting directly or indirectly from it, including local classes. When defined as a
reference to an interface, then the attribute may hold a reference to any global or local
class implementing that interface.

Suppose it had been determined that the local classes defined in the ticket sales
program to represent ticket sales examiner and ticket sales reporter and their respective
local interfaces were applicable to other similar programs and therefor migrated
to the global class repository. Adhering to the naming conventions associated with
global classes would require that the classes be renamed from ticket_sales_examiner
and ticket_sales_reporter to zcl_ticket_sales_examiner and zcl_ticket_sales_reporter,
respectively, and the interfaces be renamed from ticket_sales_examinable and
ticket_sales_reportable to zif_ticket_sales_examinable and zif_ticket_sales_reportable,
respectively.

Listing 10-1 shows the service locator class copied from Listing 9-11 and changed to
reflect these two classes and two interfaces now defined as global entities, with changes
highlighted in bold.

Listing 10-1. Service locator class from Listing 9-11 changed to reflect local
classes migrated to global class repository

```
class service_locator definition create private.
  public section.
    class-methods class_constructor.
    methods      set_ticket_sales_examiner
                   importing ticket_sales_examiner
                     type ref to zif_ticket_sales_examinable.
    methods      set_ticket_sales_reporter
                   importing ticket_sales_reporter
                     type ref to zif_ticket_sales_reportable.
    class-data singleton type ref to service_locator read-only.
```

```
    data ticket_sales_examiner type ref to zif_ticket_sales_examinable
                                                     read-only.
    data ticket_sales_reporter type ref to zif_ticket_sales_reportable
                                                     read-only.
endclass.
class service_locator implementation.
  method class_constructor.
    create instance singleton.
  endmethod.
  method set_ticket_sales_examiner.
    me->ticket_sales_examiner = ticket_sales_examiner.
  endmethod.
  method set_ticket_sales_reporter.
    me->ticket_sales_reporter = ticket_sales_reporter.
  endmethod.
endclass.
```

Notice the only changes made were to apply the prefix "zif_" to the names of the former local interfaces on the type clauses of the two methods statements and the two data statements. The entity creating these objects and calling the setter methods of the service locator would need a corresponding change to instantiate an object compatible with these respective global class definitions.

Listing 10-2 includes only the two methods from the service factory copied from Listing 9-11 that create instances of objects to be managed by the service locator and shows how those methods would change when interfaces ticket_sales_examinable and ticket_sales_reportable are migrated to the global class repository, with changes highlighted in bold.

Listing 10-2. Service factory class methods changed to reflect local classes migrated to global class repository

```
  method create_ticket_sales_examiner.
    data ticket_sales_examiner type ref to zif_ticket_sales_examinable.
    create object ticket_sales_examiner type ticket_sales_examiner.
    service_locator=>singleton->set_ticket_sales_examiner(
      ticket_sales_examiner ).
  endmethod.
```

```
method create_ticket_sales_reporter.
  data ticket_sales_reporter type ref to zif_ticket_sales_reportable.
  create object ticket_sales_reporter type ticket_sales_reporter.
  service_locator=>singleton->set_ticket_sales_reporter(
     ticket_sales_reporter ).
endmethod.
```

Notice the only difference is that the type assigned to the local variable defined within each method is changed to indicate the global interface prefix each interface now has.

EXERCISES

At this point, take a break from reading and shift into exercise mode. Refer to the accompanying workbook to perform the six exercises associated with workbook **Section 18: ABAP Unit Testing 501 – Gaining Control Over Global Class Dependencies.**

Using the Service Locator to Manage Function Modules

The ability of the service locator to manage a function module is only slightly more involved than its ability to manage a reference to an instance of a class. Unlike instances of classes, function modules need not be instantiated before they can be used. Accordingly, a service locator attribute defined to manage the function module assigned to perform a service cannot be defined as a reference variable as it can be for instances of classes. Instead, the attribute would simply be defined to hold the name of the corresponding function module. An attribute defined as type funcname would do this nicely. Once the service locator attribute has been set with the name of the function module to provide the associated service, a call to that function module can be made using the name found in the corresponding attribute.

We'll see this through an example shortly. First, let's identify a situation where two different function modules might be defined to have the same signatures and provide similar services such that they are interchangeable. A good example of this comes from the very first exercise program, which when executed prompts the user to decide whether the resulting report is to be presented as an ALV list or an ALV grid.

Listing 10-3 shows the code of a subroutine that determines the function module to be used to display an ALV report based on whether or not the caller is indicating to render the report as a grid.

Listing 10-3. Subroutine defined to determine name of ALV display function module via service locator

```
form set_alv_function_module_name using alv_style_grid
                                          type xflag
                     changing alv_display_function_module
                                          type funcname.
   constants alv_list_function_module type funcname
                              value 'REUSE_ALV_LIST_DISPLAY'.
   constants alv_grid_function_module type funcname
                              value 'REUSE_ALV_GRID_DISPLAY'.
   if alv_style_grid is initial.
     alv_display_function_module = alv_list_function_module.
   else.
     alv_display_function_module = alv_grid_function_module.
   endif.
endform.
```

Indeed, we might characterize this subroutine as a rudimentary version of a service locator since its purpose is to determine the name of a function module to provide the ALV reporting service. Listing 10-4 shows the code for a portion of a procedure to render an ALV report after first calling the subroutine shown in Listing 10-3 to determine the name of the function module to be used.

Listing 10-4. Portion of subroutine defined to determine name of ALV display function module

```
   o
   o
   perform set_alv_function_module_name
         using alv_style_grid
       changing alv_display_function_module.
   call function alv_display_function_module
```

```
    exporting
      is_layout   = alv_layout
      it_fieldcat = alv_fieldcatalog
    tables
      t_outtab    = report_content
    exceptions
      others      = 0.
  o
  o
```

Notice that the first statement calls a subroutine to identify the name of the ALV function module capable of producing the ALV report in the desired format and the next statement calls that function module. Notice also that the CALL FUNCTION statement is using the dynamic variation of the syntax by specifying a variable to supply the name of the function module to be called. The function module called will be either REUSE_ALV_LIST_DISPLAY or REUSE_ALV_GRID_DISPLAY depending on the value returned into variable alv_display_function_module by subroutine set_alv_function_module_name.

Listing 10-5 is a copy of the service locator class from Listing 9-11 modified to show how an ALV reporting function module would be managed by the service locator, with changes highlighted in bold.

Listing 10-5. Listing 9-11 showing how an ALV reporting function module would be managed by the service locator

```
class service_locator definition create private.
  public section.
    class-methods class_constructor.
    methods        set_ticket_sales_examiner
                     importing ticket_sales_examiner
                       type ref to ticket_sales_examinable.
    methods        set_ticket_sales_reporter
                     importing ticket_sales_reporter
                       type ref to ticket_sales_reportable.
    methods        set_alv_report_function_module
                     importing alv_function_module_name
                       type funcname.
    class-data singleton type ref to service_locator read-only.
```

257

```
      data ticket_sales_examiner type ref to ticket_sales_examinable
                                                     read-only.
      data ticket_sales_reporter type ref to ticket_sales_reportable
                                                     read-only.
    data alv_function_module_name type funcname read-only.
endclass.
class service_locator implementation.
  method class_constructor.
    create instance singleton.
  endmethod.
  method set_ticket_sales_examiner.
    me->ticket_sales_examiner = ticket_sales_examiner.
  endmethod.
  method set_ticket_sales_reporter.
    me->ticket_sales_reporter = ticket_sales_reporter.
  endmethod.
  method set_alv_report_function_module.
    me->alv_function_module_name = alv_function_module_name.
  endmethod.
endclass.
```

Notice that a new public read-only attribute named alv_function_module_name was defined. Notice also that a new setter method was defined named set_alv_report_function_module which accepts a value of type funcname, and its implementation, similar to the other setter methods that already had been defined for the service locator, is to set the new public attribute to the name of the function module the caller sends.

Now that the service locator is capable of managing the name of the function module to provide rendering of ALV reports, the program using it would need to call its setter method to assign the corresponding function module to be used when presenting ALV reports.

Listing 10-6 is a copy of Listing 10-3 and modified to show how the subroutine would be changed to enable the service locator to manage the name of the function module to present ALV reports, with changes highlighted in bold.

Listing 10-6. Subroutine defined to determine name of ALV display function module and register it with the service locator

```
form set_alv_function_module_name using alv_style_grid
                                        type xflag
                      changing alv_display_function_module
                              type funcname.
    constants alv_list_function_module type funcname
                                value 'REUSE_ALV_LIST_DISPLAY'.
    constants alv_grid_function_module type funcname
                                value 'REUSE_ALV_GRID_DISPLAY'.
    if alv_style_grid is initial.
      alv_display_function_module = alv_list_function_module.
      service_locator=>singleton->set_alv_report_function_module(
        alv_list_function_module ).
    else.
      alv_display_function_module = alv_grid_function_module.
      service_locator=>singleton->set_alv_report_function_module(
        alv_grid_function_module ).
    endif.
endform.
```

Notice that the signature of the subroutine no longer includes a changing parameter through which to pass a value back to the caller. Notice also that it calls the setter method set_alv_report_function_module of the service locator class to register the appropriate function module to be used for ALV reporting.

Listing 10-7 is a copy of Listing 10-6 without the highlighting and stricken lines.

Listing 10-7. Listing 10-6 without highlighting and stricken lines

```
form set_alv_function_module_name using alv_style_grid
                                          type xflag.
    constants alv_list_function_module type funcname
                                value 'REUSE_ALV_LIST_DISPLAY'.
    constants alv_grid_function_module type funcname
                                value 'REUSE_ALV_GRID_DISPLAY'.
    if alv_style_grid is initial.
```

```
      service_locator=>singleton->set_alv_report_function_module(
        alv_list_function_module ).
    else.
      service_locator=>singleton->set_alv_report_function_module(
        alv_grid_function_module ).
    endif.
endform.
```

Listing 10-8 is a copy of Listing 10-4, the code for a portion of a procedure to render an ALV report after first calling the subroutine shown in Listing 10-3 to determine the name of the function module to be used, showing how it would change once the service locator is managing the name of the ALV reporting function module, with changes highlighted in bold.

Listing 10-8. Portion of subroutine defined to determine name of ALV display function module

```
    o
    o
    perform set_alv_function_module_name
            using alv_style_grid
        changing alv_display_function_module.
    call function alv_display_function_module
                  service_locator=>singleton->alv_function_module_name
      exporting
        is_layout   = alv_layout
        it_fieldcat = alv_fieldcatalog
      tables
        t_outtab    = report_content
      exceptions
        others      = 0.
    o
    o
```

Notice that this procedure no longer provides a signature parameter specifying a variable into which subroutine set_alv_function_module_name will return the name of a function module. Notice also that it is calling the function module through the public attribute alv_function_module_name of the singleton instance of class service_locator.

The Chapter 7 section titled "Encapsulating Indirect Input and Output" lists the reasons why function modules do not make good candidates for encapsulating processing intended to be overridden by a unit test. When function modules already exist, a better approach would be to define a class that can encapsulate a call to the function module and then to define a test double for that class. However, as shown by the example of interchangeable function modules REUSE_ALV_LIST_DISPLAY and REUSE_ALV_GRID_DISPLAY, there may be situations where it makes sense for a new function module to be defined as a test double for an existing one. When that is the case, the service locator can manage the production version of the function module and its associated test double using the process described in the preceding text.

EXERCISES

At this point, take a break from reading and shift into exercise mode. Refer to the accompanying workbook to perform the five exercises associated with workbook **Section 19: ABAP Unit Testing 502 – Gaining Control Over Function Module Dependencies.**

Using the Service Locator to Manage MESSAGE Statements

The Chapter 5 section titled "Challenges Presented by the MESSAGE Statement" described how the severity of a message issued via the MESSAGE statement could affect the control flow of the program, specifically noting that messages of severities error, abort, and exit will cause procedures in which they are issued to be discontinued immediately. It also raised the issue that encountering an ABAP MESSAGE statement of severity error, abort, or exit during a unit test will cause an unconditional failure of the unit test. This section addresses both of these issues.

Handling MESSAGE Statements Triggering Unconditional Unit Test Failures

Listing 10-9 shows a file name validation subroutine using message statements to alert the user to problems found with values specified for parameters appearing on an initial selection screen.

Listing 10-9. Subroutine providing selection screen validation

```
form validate_file_name using unix_file_name
                              type localfile
                        pc_file_name
                              type localfile.
  if unix_file_name is initial and pc_file_name is initial.
    message e000(0k) with 'Must specify either unix file name'
                          'or PC file name'.
  endif.
  if unix_file_name is not initial and pc_file_name is not initial.
    message e000(0k) with 'May specify either unix file name'
                          'or PC file name, not both'.
  endif.
endform.
```

In this case, the selection screen has two parameters for file names: one for the name of a unix file and another for the name of a PC file. We can see from the message statements that these are mutually exclusive parameters, but one needs to have been supplied with a corresponding file name. Error messages are issued when the user leaves both parameters blank or specifies non-blank values for both.

Listing 10-10 shows a unit test for testing subroutine validate_file_name shown in Listing 10-9.

Listing 10-10. Unit test class for testing subroutine validate_file_name

```
class validate_file_name_tester definition
                              for testing
                              risk level harmless.
  private section.
```

```
    methods validate_no_file_specified for testing.
    methods validate_2_files_specified for testing.
endclass.
class validate_file_name_tester implementation.
  method validate_no_file_specified.
    clear sy-msgty.
    perform validate_file_name using space
                                     space.
    cl_abap_unit_assert=>assert_equals(
      act = sy-msgty
      exp = 'E'
      ).
  endmethod.
  method validate_2_files_specified.
    clear sy-msgty.
    perform validate_file_name using '\'
                                     '/'.
    cl_abap_unit_assert=>assert_equals(
      act = sy-msgty
      exp = 'E'
      ).
  endmethod.
endclass.
```

Notice that each method clears system field sy-msgty, then calls subroutine validate_file_name using parameter values certain to cause the subroutine to identify an invalid combination of values, and then asserts that field sy-msgty has been set to indicate a message severity of error. Both unit tests would pass if not for the fact that the test runner unconditionally fails unit tests with class-based exception CX_AUNIT_UNCAUGHT_MESSAGE when a message statement of severity error is encountered during their execution.

The Chapter 6 section titled "Exploring the Effects of the MESSAGE Statement" provided some analysis and investigation about intercepting the class-based exception CX_AUNIT_UNCAUGHT_MESSAGE thrown during a unit test when an ABAP MESSAGE statement of severity error or abort is encountered, through which it was concluded that a unit test was not able to intercept it. Accordingly, the MESSAGE statement presents a predicament with writing unit tests for procedures where an ABAP MESSAGE statement of severity error, abort, or exit could be encountered.

Since the message text accompanying the MESSAGE statement simply represents indirect output – output produced by a procedure but not intended to be returned to its caller through its signature parameters – one way to resolve this predicament is to encapsulate issuing such messages into a callable procedure representing a service manageable by the service locator and, as a result, one over which a unit test can exert control. To do so will involve the following changes to the production path of the program:

- Define a class having a public method that can be called to issue a message.

- Change the service locator to be able to manage the service provided by this class.

- Replace each explicit MESSAGE statement in the program with a call to the corresponding service managed by the service locator.

There are further considerations to be taken into account. For one, the ABAP MESSAGE statement has a few variations with its syntax, as illustrated with the following examples of error message statements:

1. `message e001.`

2. `message e001(zyx).`

3. `message id 'zyx' type 'E' num 001.`

4. `message 'Error has been detected' type 'E'.`

The first three examples of message statements shown in the preceding list are functionally equivalent, with example #1 relying on the class of messages having been established through the MESSAGE-ID clause of a corresponding report, program, or function-pool statement. In addition, all three of these may have optional WITH clauses to indicate accompanying text to be inserted into placeholders of the message. Example #4 is a message with no associated message class.

Another consideration is that a message statement can be accompanied by the optional clauses DISPLAY LIKE, RAISING, and INTO. We can ignore accommodating messages with the INTO clause because there would be no associated indirect output resulting from it.

Based on all of this, we would want to define a class that can handle the variations of MESSAGE statements found throughout our program. Listing 10-11 shows an interface defining methods to do this.

Listing 10-11. Interface defining methods to be implemented by a class encapsulating the issuance of MESSAGE statements

```
interface message_dispatchable.
    types message_type    type symsgty.
    types message_id      type symsgid.
    types message_number  type symsgno.
    types message_text    type symsgv.
    constants status_message      type message_type value 'S'.
    constants information_message type message_type value 'I'.
    constants warning_message     type message_type value 'W'.
    constants error_message       type message_type value 'E'.
    constants abort_message       type message_type value 'A'.
    constants exit_message        type message_type value 'X'.
    methods issue_identified_message
            importing
              message_severity
                type message_type default status_message
              message_display_severity
                type message_type optional
              id
                type message_id
              number
                type message_number
              text_01
                type message_text optional
              text_02
                type message_text optional
              text_03
                type message_text optional
              text_04
                type message_text optional.
```

```
    methods issue_unidentified_message
              importing
                message_severity
                  type message_type default status_message
                message_display_severity
                  type message_type optional
                text
                  type clike.
endinterface.
```

Notice this interface defines two methods: method issue_identified_message defines a method signature compatible with the preceding MESSAGE statement examples #2 and #3; method issue_unidentified_message defines a method signature compatible with the preceding MESSAGE statement example #4.

Listing 10-12 shows the production path class implementing the methods of interface message_dispatchable and encapsulating the issuance of MESSAGE statements.

Listing 10-12. Production class encapsulating the issuance of MESSAGE statements

```
class messenger definition.
  public section.
    interfaces message_dispatchable.
    aliases issue_identified_message
              for message_dispatchable~issue_identified_message.
    aliases issue_unidentified_message
              for message_dispatchable~issue_unidentified_message.
endclass.
class messenger implementation.
  method issue_identified_message.
    data message_display_type type message_dispatchable=>message_type.
    message_display_type = message_display_severity.
    if message_display_type is initial.
      message_display_type = message_severity.
    endif.
    message id      id
```

```
            type    message_severity
            number  number
            display like message_display_type
            with    text_01 text_02 text_03 text_04.
              .
  endmethod.
  method issue_unidentified_message.
    data message_display_type type message_dispatchable=>message_type.
    message_display_type = message_display_severity.
    if message_display_type is initial.
      message_display_type = message_severity.
    endif.
    message text type message_severity
                display like message_display_type.
  endmethod.
endclass.
```

Notice that the entire public section of this class is provided by the interface message_dispatchable it implements. Notice also that each method ends with a message statement using the parameters sent by the caller.

Now that we have the class to provide the messenger service, the service locator can be modified to manage it.

Listing 10-13 is a copy of the service locator from Listing 10-5 changed to accommodate a messenger service as a reference to an interface, with changes highlighted in bold.

Listing 10-13. Service locator from Listing 10-5 changed to accommodate managing a messenger service

```
class service_locator definition create private.
  public section.
    class-methods class_constructor.
    methods      set_ticket_sales_examiner
                    importing ticket_sales_examiner
                      type ref to ticket_sales_examinable.
    methods      set_ticket_sales_reporter
                    importing ticket_sales_reporter
```

```
                    type ref to ticket_sales_reportable.
    methods         set_alv_report_function_module
                      importing alv_function_module_name
                        type funcname.
    methods         set_message_dispatcher
                      importing message_dispatcher
                        type ref to message_dispatchable.
    class-data singleton type ref to service_locator read-only.
    data ticket_sales_examiner type ref to ticket_sales_examinable
                                              read-only.
    data ticket_sales_reporter type ref to ticket_sales_reportable
                                              read-only.
    data alv_function_module_name type funcname read-only.
    data message_dispatcher type ref to message_dispatchable read-only.
endclass.
class service_locator implementation.
  method class_constructor.
    create instance singleton.
  endmethod.
  method set_ticket_sales_examiner.
    me->ticket_sales_examiner = ticket_sales_examiner.
  endmethod.
  method set_ticket_sales_reporter.
    me->ticket_sales_reporter = ticket_sales_reporter.
  endmethod.
  method set_alv_report_function_module.
    me->alv_function_module_name = alv_function_module_name.
  endmethod.
  method set_message_dispatcher.
    me->message_dispatcher = message_dispatcher.
  endmethod.
endclass.
```

Notice that there is now a new public read-only attribute named message_dispatcher and a corresponding public setter method for it.

Listing 10-14 shows a subroutine for creating an instance of class messenger and registering it with the service locator as the message_dispatcher service.

Listing 10-14. Subroutine creating message dispatch service and registering it with the service locator

```
form create_message_dispatcher.
  data messenger type ref to message_dispatchable.
  create object messenger type messenger.
  service_locator=>singleton->set_message_dispatcher( messenger ).
endform.
```

The subroutine shown in Listing 10-14 would be called at some point during the initial execution of the program to register the message dispatcher to be used for issuing messages with production path executions. With components defined as shown in Listings 10-11, 10-12, 10-13, and 10-14, it becomes possible to replace an ABAP MESSAGE statement with a call through the public attribute of the service locator providing the service.

Listing 10-15 shows how the subroutine in Listing 10-9 would be changed to do this, with changes highlighted in bold.

Listing 10-15. Screen validation subroutine with message statements replaced with equivalent calls to a service managed by the service locator

```
form validate_file_name using unix_file_name
                                type localfile
                              pc_file_name
                                type localfile.
  if unix_file_name is initial and pc_file_name is initial.
    message e000(ok) with 'Must specify either unix file name'
                          'or PC file name'.
    service_locator=>singleton->message_dispatcher->issue_identified_message(
        exporting
          message_severity = 'E'
          id               = 'OK'
          number           = 000
```

```
        text_01          = 'Must specify either unix file name'
        text_02          = 'or PC file name'
    ).
endif.
if unix_file_name is not initial and pc_file_name is not initial.
    message e000(Ok) with 'May specify either unix file name'
                        'or PC file name, not both'.
service_locator=>singleton->message_dispatcher->issue_identified_message(
    exporting
        message_severity = 'E'
        id               = 'OK'
        number           = 000
        text_01          = 'May specify either unix file name'
        text_02          = 'or PC file name, not both'
    ).
endif.
endform.
```

Notice that each explicit message statement has been replaced with a call to a method of a service managed by the service locator. The call requires specifying parameters to achieve the same result, parameters not necessary with its associated message statement, but each parameter value has been extracted directly from the message statement being replaced.

Listing 10-16 is a copy of Listing 10-15 without the highlighting and stricken lines.

Listing 10-16. Listing 10-15 without the highlighting and stricken lines

```
form validate_file_name using unix_file_name
                              type localfile
                            pc_file_name
                              type localfile.
  if unix_file_name is initial and pc_file_name is initial.
  service_locator=>singleton->message_dispatcher->issue_identified_message(
      exporting
        message_severity = 'E'
        id               = 'OK'
        number           = 000
```

```
            text_01           = 'Must specify either unix file name'
            text_02           = 'or PC file name'
        ).
    endif.
    if unix_file_name is not initial and pc_file_name is not initial.
    service_locator=>singleton->message_dispatcher->issue_identified_message(
        exporting
          message_severity = 'E'
          id               = 'OK'
          number           = 000
          text_01          = 'May specify either unix file name'
          text_02          = 'or PC file name, not both'
        ).
    endif.
endform.
```

At this point, we would undertake the task of replacing all the MESSAGE statements in the program with corresponding calls to the message_dispatch service managed by the service locator. Once that has been completed, the program can be considered designed for testability. This is because a unit test would now be able to register with the service locator an instance of a test double implementing the message_dispatchable interface, one that *does not* use the MESSAGE statement, guaranteeing no more unconditional unit test failures due to encountering a MESSAGE statement with a severity of error, abort, or exit.

Listing 10-17 shows such a test double.

Listing 10-17. Test double for class messenger

```
class messenger_test_double definition for testing.
  public section.
    interfaces message_dispatchable.
    aliases issue_identified_message
            for message_dispatchable~issue_identified_message.
    aliases issue_unidentified_message
            for message_dispatchable~issue_unidentified_message.
endclass.
class messenger_test_double implementation.
```

```
method issue_identified_message.
  sy-msgty = message_severity.
  sy-msgid = id.
  sy-msgno = number.
  sy-msgv1 = text_01.
  sy-msgv2 = text_02.
  sy-msgv3 = text_03.
  sy-msgv4 = text_04.
endmethod.
method issue_unidentified_message.
  data: begin of message_content
      ,    text_01 type message_dispatchable=>message_text
      ,    text_02 type message_dispatchable=>message_text
      ,    text_03 type message_dispatchable=>message_text
      ,    text_04 type message_dispatchable=>message_text
      , end    of message_content
      .
  sy-msgty = message_severity.
  sy-msgid = '00'
  sy-msgno = 000.
  message_content = text.
  sy-msgv1 = message_content-text_01.
  sy-msgv2 = message_content-text_02.
  sy-msgv3 = message_content-text_03.
  sy-msgv4 = message_content-text_04.
endmethod.
endclass.
```

Notice that the implementations for both methods cause the respective system variables changed by the MESSAGE statement to be set with the values they would receive if the corresponding MESSAGE statement had been issued by the method. This makes it possible to write a unit test class for testing subroutine validate_file_name that can pass. Listing 10-18 shows how the unit test from Listing 10-10 would be adjusted to do this, with changes highlighted in bold.

Listing 10-18. Adjusted unit test class for testing subroutine validate_file_name

```
class validate_file_name_tester definition
                                 for testing
                                 risk level harmless.
  private section.
    methods setup.
    methods validate_no_file_specified for testing.
    methods validate_2_files_specified for testing.
endclass.
class validate_file_name_tester implementation.
  method setup.
    data messenger type ref to message_dispatchable.
    create object messenger type messenger_test_double.
    service_locator=>singleton->set_message_dispatcher( messenger ).
  endmethod.
  method validate_no_file_specified.
    clear sy-msgty.
    perform validate_file_name using space
                                    space.
    cl_abap_unit_assert=>assert_equals(
      act = sy-msgty
      exp = 'E'
      ).
  endmethod.
  method validate_2_files_specified.
    clear sy-msgty.
    perform validate_file_name using '\'
                                    '/'.
    cl_abap_unit_assert=>assert_equals(
      act = sy-msgty
      exp = 'E'
      ).
  endmethod.
endclass.
```

Notice that this unit test class has a setup method which will create an instance of class messenger_test_double and then register that instance with the service locator as the instance to be used to provide the message dispatch service. The setup method is automatically called prior to executing either of the methods defined as "for testing."

Executing this program normally and specifying values for both a unix file name and a PC file name on the initial selection screen would result in the error message "May specify either unix file name or PC file name, not both" appearing to the user. Assuming this message is issued during the at selection-screen classic ABAP event block, it enables the user to correct the problem and try again. Executing the automated unit tests of this program as shown in the preceding text would indicate passing tests for test methods validate_no_file_specified and validate_2_files_specified, despite both of these test methods calling the very same subroutine that causes error messages to be issued by the production path.

Handling Unit Test Failures Arising from MESSAGE Statement Control Flow

Now that the service locator is capable of handling MESSAGE statements as a service and offering a way to specify a test double for a procedure that would issue messages, an automated unit test also would need to account for the program flow control that could be expected when a message of severity error, abort, or exit is encountered.

Suppose the screen validation subroutine of Listing 10-9 had additional parameter validations to perform, as shown in Listing 10-19, with changes highlighted in bold.

Listing 10-19. Subroutine from Listing 10-9 with additional selection screen validation

```
form validate_file_name using unix_file_name
                              type localfile
                            pc_file_name
                              type localfile.
  if unix_file_name is initial and pc_file_name is initial.
    message e000(0k) with 'Must specify either unix file name'
                      'or PC file name'.
  endif.
  if unix_file_name is not initial and pc_file_name is not initial.
```

```
    message e000(0k) with 'May specify either unix file name'
                         'or PC file name, not both'.
  endif.
  if unix_file_name ca '\'.
    message w000(0k) with 'Value "\" appears in unix file name'.
  endif.
  if pc_file_name ca '/'.
    message w000(0k) with 'Value "/" appears in PC file name'.
  endif.
endform.
```

Notice that now there are warning messages issued when a specified unix or PC file name contains a value typically found with the other type of file. During a production run, neither of these two new conditions for checking file name characters would be encountered if either of the preceding two conditions had been met. Instead, program flow would be interrupted, and the subroutine would be exited immediately with the issuance of the associated error message.

Listing 10-20 indicates how the subroutine appearing in Listing 10-19 would be changed to use the service locator described by Listing 10-13, with changes highlighted in bold.

Listing 10-20. Subroutine from Listing 10-19 changed to use service locator to issue messages

```
form validate_file_name using unix_file_name
                                type localfile
                              pc_file_name
                                type localfile.
  if unix_file_name is initial and pc_file_name is initial.
    message e000(0k) with 'Must specify either unix file name'
                         'or PC file name'.
    service_locator=>singleton->message_dispatcher->issue_identified_message(
        exporting
          message_severity = 'E'
          id               = 'OK'
          number           = 000
```

```
        text_01              = 'Must specify either unix file name'
        text_02              = 'or PC file name'
    ).
  endif.
  if unix_file_name is not initial and pc_file_name is not initial.
    message e000(0k) with 'May specify either unix file name'
                          'or PC file name, not both'.
  service_locator=>singleton->message_dispatcher->issue_identified_message(
      exporting
        message_severity = 'E'
        id               = 'OK'
        number           = 000
        text_01          = 'May specify either unix file name'
        text_02          = 'or PC file name, not both'
    ).
  endif.
  if unix_file_name ca '\'.
    message w000(0k) with 'Value "\" appears in unix file name'.
  service_locator=>singleton->message_dispatcher->issue_identified_message(
      exporting
        message_severity = 'W'
        id               = 'OK'
        number           = 000
        text_01          = 'Value "\" appears in unix file name'
    ).
  endif.
  if pc_file_name ca '/'.
    message w000(0k) with 'Value "/" appears in PC file name'.
  service_locator=>singleton->message_dispatcher->issue_identified_message(
      exporting
        message_severity = 'W'
        id               = 'OK'
        number           = 000
        text_01          = 'Value "/" appears in PC file name'
    ).
  endif.
endform.
```

Notice that each MESSAGE statement has been replaced with a corresponding call to the service locator. This is similar to the changes illustrated by Listing 10-15 which showed how Listing 10-9 would change for the same reason.

Listing 10-21 shows the merged content of Listing 10-20 without the highlighting and stricken lines and with the corresponding unit test for this subroutine from Listing 10-18.

Listing 10-21. Merged content of subroutine from Listing 10-20 without highlighting and stricken lines and with unit test from Listing 10-18

```
form validate_file_name using unix_file_name
                              type localfile
                         pc_file_name
                              type localfile.
  if unix_file_name is initial and pc_file_name is initial.
  service_locator=>singleton->message_dispatcher->issue_identified_message(
      exporting
        message_severity = 'E'
        id               = 'OK'
        number           = 000
        text_01          = 'Must specify either unix file name'
        text_02          = 'or PC file name'
      ).
  endif.
  if unix_file_name is not initial and pc_file_name is not initial.
  service_locator=>singleton->message_dispatcher->issue_identified_message(
      exporting
        message_severity = 'E'
        id               = 'OK'
        number           = 000
        text_01          = 'May specify either unix file name'
        text_02          = 'or PC file name, not both'
      ).
  endif.
  if unix_file_name ca '\'.
  service_locator=>singleton->message_dispatcher->issue_identified_message(
      exporting
```

```
          message_severity = 'W'
          id               = 'OK'
          number           = 000
          text_01          = 'Value "\" appears in unix file name'
        ).
    endif.
    if pc_file_name ca '/'.
    service_locator=>singleton->message_dispatcher->issue_identified_message(
        exporting
          message_severity = 'W'
          id               = 'OK'
          number           = 000
          text_01          = 'Value "/" appears in PC file name'
        ).
    endif.
endform.

class validate_file_name_tester definition
                                 for testing
                                 risk level harmless.
  private section.
    methods setup.
    methods validate_no_file_specified for testing.
    methods validate_2_files_specified for testing.
endclass.
class validate_file_name_tester implementation.
  method setup.
    data messenger type ref to message_dispatchable.
    create object messenger type messenger_test_double.
    service_locator=>singleton->set_message_dispatcher( messenger ).
  endmethod.
  method validate_no_file_specified.
    clear sy-msgty.
    perform validate_file_name using space
                                     space.
    cl_abap_unit_assert=>assert_equals(
```

```
    act = sy-msgty
    exp = 'E'
    ).
  endmethod.
  method validate_2_files_specified.
    clear sy-msgty.
    perform validate_file_name using '\'
                                     '/'.
    cl_abap_unit_assert=>assert_equals(
      act = sy-msgty
      exp = 'E'
      ).
  endmethod.
endclass.
```

If this unit test were to be executed as written, unit test method validate_no_file_specified would pass, but unit test method validate_2_files_specified would fail. How could that be?! This is the same unit test that would have passed when the subroutine consisted of only the first two conditions! The answer is that an error message issued by subroutine validate_file_name would interrupt the flow of control only when run in its production mode.

When executed during a unit test where the error message statement is not encountered (and as a consequence does not have a chance to cause an unconditional failure of the unit test), the flow of control in the subroutine continues through to the end of it. This means the two conditions issuing warning messages will be executed even when it determines one of the preceding error conditions is true. Since unit test method validate_2_files_specified specifies a unix file value of '\' and a PC file value of '/' on the call to the subroutine, the last three of the four conditions in subroutine validate_file_name are met. Accordingly, based on the processing performed by test double messenger_test_double to set system variable sy-msgty with the message severity of the most recent call made to it, only the message severity associated with the final condition of subroutine validate_file_name will be the one to reflect the value to be found in sy-msgty when control returns to the unit test method. Unit test method validate_2_files_specified fails because it is asserting that sy-msgty contains 'E,' but the final condition of the subroutine it called caused this value to be set to 'W.'

So what are the options available to rectifying this problem?

One is to recognize that subroutine validate_file_name is doing more than its name implies. It contains conditions checking not only that the selected file name is *valid* but also alerting the user to the possibility that the file name might be *unintended*. This violates the Single Responsibility Principle,[1] which states that procedures should do only one thing. Accordingly, the conditions checking for an unintended file name could be split out into a separate subroutine, named appropriately, that could be called after this subroutine for the production path and called by separate and distinct unit tests for the unit test path. Though this solution is attractive on its merits of improving code clarity, it may be more than we are willing to undertake after already having implemented all the new changes simply to prevent unit tests from unconditional failures for having encountered MESSAGE statements of severity error, abort, or exit.

Another option is to include a simple RETURN statement immediately following calls to the service locator to handle messages of types error, abort, and exit. This would mimic during a unit test the behavior arising when messages with these severity values are encountered through the production path. The production path would never encounter the RETURN statement, but it would prevent unit test method validate_2_files_specified described in Listing 10-21 from failing. This option is even worse than the previous solution. The first of its problems is that the severity of a message provided on a service locator call to the message dispatcher may be provided by a variable, so there would need to be conditional logic checking the variable value to determine whether the RETURN statement should be executed to mimic for a unit test the flow control interruption resulting from the production path. The more disturbing problem is that it means production procedures would contain logic that is applicable only to the execution of an automated unit test. This is never a good idea!

A better option is to enhance class messenger_test_double so that it can record all the messages that might be issued during the execution of a procedure and then assert in the unit test that the procedure issued the expected messages.

Listing 10-22 is a copy of Listing 10-17 indicating how class messenger_test_double would be changed to record the content of messages issued through its method issue_identified_message, with changes highlighted in bold.

---

[1] See http://butunclebob.com/ArticleS.UncleBob.PrinciplesOfOod

Listing 10-22.   Class messenger_test_double enhanced with capability to record messages issued through method issue_identified_message

```
class messenger_test_double definition for testing.
  public section.
    interfaces message_dispatchable.
    aliases issue_identified_message
            for message_dispatchable~issue_identified_message.
    aliases issue_unidentified_message
            for message_dispatchable~issue_unidentified_message.
    types: begin of identified_message_row
        ,    type          type message_dispatchable=>message_type
        ,    display_type  type message_dispatchable=>message_type
        ,    id            type message_dispatchable=>message_id
        ,    number        type message_dispatchable=>message_number
        ,    text_01       type message_dispatchable=>message_text
        ,    text_02       type message_dispatchable=>message_text
        ,    text_03       type message_dispatchable=>message_text
        ,    text_04       type message_dispatchable=>message_text
        , end    of identified_message_row
        , identified_message_list
                    type standard table
                      of identified_message_row
        .

    data identified_message_stack
                    type identified_message_list
                        read-only.
endclass.
class messenger_test_double implementation.
  method issue_identified_message.
    data identified_message_entry like line
                              of identified_message_stack.
    identified_message_entry-type = message_severity.
    if message_display_severity is not initial.
      identified_message_entry-display_type = message_display_severity.
    else.
```

281

```abap
      identified_message_entry-display_type = message_severity.
    endif.
    identified_message_entry-id = id.
    identified_message_entry-number = number.
    identified_message_entry-text_01 = text_01.
    identified_message_entry-text_02 = text_02.
    identified_message_entry-text_03 = text_03.
    identified_message_entry-text_04 = text_04.
    append identified_message_entry to identified_message_stack.
    sy-msgty = message_severity.
    sy-msgid = id.
    sy-msgno = number.
    sy-msgv1 = text_01.
    sy-msgv2 = text_02.
    sy-msgv3 = text_03.
    sy-msgv4 = text_04.
  endmethod.
  method issue_unidentified_message.
    data: begin of message_content
        ,    text_01 type message_dispatchable=>message_text
        ,    text_02 type message_dispatchable=>message_text
        ,    text_03 type message_dispatchable=>message_text
        ,    text_04 type message_dispatchable=>message_text
        , end    of message_content
        .
    sy-msgty = message_severity.
    sy-msgid = '00'
    sy-msgno = 000.
    message_content = text.
    sy-msgv1 = message_content-text_01.
    sy-msgv2 = message_content-text_02.
    sy-msgv3 = message_content-text_03.
    sy-msgv4 = message_content-text_04.
  endmethod.
endclass.
```

Notice the new public read-only attribute identified_message_stack defined as an internal table to record all message content flowing through method issue_identified_ message. Notice also that method issue_identified_message has extra code to capture the respective values of the signature parameters in a new row appended to the new public attribute. These changes transform class messenger_test_double into a test spy.

Listing 10-23 shows how the unit test method validate_2_files_specified defined in Listing 10-21 could be changed to assert that the value it uses on the call to subroutine validate_file_name causes three messages to be recorded by the test double, with changes highlighted in bold.

Listing 10-23. Unit test method validate_2_files_specified changed to inspect the messages recorded by test spy messenger_test_double

```
method validate_2_files_specified.
  data messenger_test_double type ref to messenger_test_double.
  data identified_message_entry like line
        of messenger_test_double->identified_message_stack.
  data error_message_count type int4.
  data warning_message_count type int4.
  clear sy-msgty.
  perform validate_file_name using '\'
                                    '/'.
  try.
    messenger_test_double ?=
      service_locator=>singleton->message_dispatchable.
  catch cx_sy_move_cast_error.
    cl_abap_unit_assert=>fail(
      msg = 'specializing cast has failed'
      ).
  endtry.
  cl_abap_unit_assert=>assert_equals(
    act = sy-msgty
    exp = 'E'
    ).
  loop at messenger_test_double->identified_message_stack
    into                         identified_message_entry.
```

```
      case identified_message_entry-type.
        when 'E'.
          add 01 to error_message_count.
        when 'W'.
          add 01 to warning_message_count.
      endcase.
    endloop.
    cl_abap_unit_assert=>assert_equals(
      act = error_message_count
      exp = 01
      msg = 'Unexpected count of error messages'
      ).
    cl_abap_unit_assert=>assert_equals(
      act = warning_message_count
      exp = 02
      msg = 'Unexpected count of warning messages'
      ).
  endmethod.
```

Notice that now this unit test method defines four new variables and no longer clears sy-msgty prior to calling the subroutine. Notice also that after calling the subroutine, it has a try-endtry block where it performs a specializing cast to move the service locator instance providing the message dispatch service into a reference field defined specifically as one of type messenger_test_double. This enables the unit test to have access to the new attribute of class messenger_test_double holding the rows of message parameter values resulting from the calls to its method issue_identified_message.

Finally, notice that the former assertion statement has been discarded, replaced with a loop through the rows in internal table identified_message_stack of class messenger_test_double counting the number of messages of type error and of type warning and then performing assertions on those numbers. Since there will be no implicit control flow interruption in subroutine validate_file_name when called by unit test validate_2_files_specified, we should expect that there will be three calls to the messenger test double: one with an error message and two with warning messages.

Although not shown in this example, for consistency, we would want to apply the same relative changes to method issue_unidentified_message of class messenger_test_double.

There remains a small issue to be discovered with unit test method validate_2_files_ specified shown in Listing 10-23, one that relates to reporting of failures. Can you find it in Listing 10-23? Listing 10-24 is a copy of Listing 10-23 without the highlighting and stricken lines but with two slight changes highlighted in bold.

Listing 10-24. Unit test method validate_2_files_specified changed to cause failures with both assertions

```
method validate_2_files_specified.
  data messenger_test_double type ref to messenger_test_double.
  data identified_message_entry like line
        of messenger_test_double->identified_message_stack.
  data error_message_count type int4.
  data warning_message_count type int4.
  perform validate_file_name using '\'
                                    '/'.
  try.
    messenger_test_double ?=
      service_locator=>singleton->message_dispatchable.
  catch cx_sy_move_cast_error.
    cl_abap_unit_assert=>fail(
      msg = 'specializing cast has failed'
      ).
  endtry.
  loop at messenger_test_double->identified_message_stack
    into                          identified_message_entry.
    case identified_message_entry-type.
      when 'E'.
        add 01 to error_message_count.
      when 'W'.
        add 01 to warning_message_count.
    endcase.
  endloop.
  cl_abap_unit_assert=>assert_equals(
    act = error_message_count
    exp = 02 " 01
```

```
      msg = 'Unexpected count of error messages'
      ).
  cl_abap_unit_assert=>assert_equals(
    act = warning_message_count
    exp = 01 " 02
    msg = 'Unexpected count of warning messages'
    ).
  endmethod.
```

Notice that both calls to method assert_equals of class cl_abap_unit_assert have had the values of the exp parameter changed to a value guaranteed to cause an assertion failure. The small problem is that when this unit test is executed and these failures await, the ABAP Unit Result Display report will show only that one of these failures has been triggered. This is because all assertion methods of class cl_abap_unit_assert have a default value of "method" for their quit parameter, meaning that unless explicitly stated otherwise, the first assertion failure caused by a call to a method of class cl_abap_unit_assert will cause the unit test method in which it occurs to be immediately discontinued.

In the example in Listing 10-24, we should expect the ABAP Unit Result Display report to show that unit test method validate_2_files_specified fails and is accompanied by only one failure message: "Unexpected count of error messages." The assertion against the number of warning messages is never performed because the unit test method is exited immediately upon the assertion failure against the number of error messages. In its current state, the unit test would diagnose this error message count failure; then after correcting this and rerunning the unit test, we would be presented with the assertion failure diagnosing the incorrect number of warning messages. In such cases, it would be to our advantage for the unit test method to diagnose both failures. To do this would require that we supply the quit parameter with the value "no" for the first assertion so that its failure does not prevent the unit test from also testing the second assertion, as shown in Listing 10-25 with changes highlighted in bold.

Listing 10-25. Unit test method changed to allow both assertion failures to be diagnosed in a single unit test run

```
method validate_2_files_specified.
  data messenger_test_double type ref to messenger_test_double.
  data identified_message_entry like line
        of messenger_test_double->identified_message_stack.
```

```abap
data error_message_count type int4.
data warning_message_count type int4.
perform validate_file_name using '\'
                                  '/'.

try.
  messenger_test_double ?=
    service_locator=>singleton->message_dispatchable.
catch cx_sy_move_cast_error.
  cl_abap_unit_assert=>fail(
    msg = 'specializing cast has failed'
    ).
endtry.
loop at messenger_test_double->identified_message_stack
   into                        identified_message_entry.
  case identified_message_entry-type.
    when 'E'.
      add 01 to error_message_count.
    when 'W'.
      add 01 to warning_message_count.
  endcase.
endloop.
cl_abap_unit_assert=>assert_equals(
  act = error_message_count
  exp = 02 " 01
  msg = 'Unexpected count of error messages'
  quit = cl_aunit_assert=>no
  ).
cl_abap_unit_assert=>assert_equals(
  act = warning_message_count
  exp = 01 " 02
  msg = 'Unexpected count of warning messages'
  ).
endmethod.
```

Now, even though the first assertion fails, there is an indication to the test runner to continue executing the remainder of the unit test method. With this arrangement, we would be able to see both failure messages in a single presentation of the ABAP Unit Result Display report.

EXERCISES

At this point, take a break from reading and shift into exercise mode. Refer to the accompanying workbook to perform the 16 exercises associated with workbook **Section 20: ABAP Unit Testing 503 – Gaining Control Over Message Statements.**

Using the Service Locator to Manage List Processing Statements

The Chapter 5 section titled "Challenges Presented by Classic List Processing Statements" described how a unit test encountering a classic list processing statement, such as WRITE and ULINE, would cause the resulting list output (a) to be presented to the user during the unit test and (b) to be preceded by lines generated by the test runner highlighted in red containing a warning against using such statements. The presentation of such output during a unit test requires manual intervention by the user to press a key enabling the unit test to run to completion. This violates one of the basic principles of xUnit testing – that the tests run to completion without requiring any monitoring or action by the user. This section addresses this issue.

Suppose a program is written to accept some selection criteria specified by the user and then produce a corresponding summary report of accounts payable, similar to the example report shown in Figure 10-1.

```
Vendor                         City                   Amount Currency
-------------------------      -----------      ---------------  --------
Amalgamated Materials          Toronto          2,571,909.06     CAD
Associated Manufacturers       Melbourne          184,396.26     AUD
General Industries LTD         London               6,005.72     GBP
Innovative Solutions           New York            12,545.80     USD
```

Figure 10-1. Example report

Part of the program is the subroutine shown in Listing 10-26 which uses classic list processing statements to produce the content of the report.

Listing 10-26. Subroutine producing report using classic list processing statements

```
form create_report using report_rows type report_list.
  data report_row like line of report_rows.
  loop at report_rows into report_row.
    new-line.
    write: report_row-vendor,
           report_row-city,
           report_row-amount,
           report_row-currency_key.
  endloop.
endform.
```

Notice the subroutine consists of a loop through the rows of the report, with each row formatted to appear on the report using the classic list processing statements NEW-LINE and WRITE.

Listing 10-27 shows the unit test class written for testing subroutine create_report.

Listing 10-27. Unit test class for testing subroutine create_report

```
class create_report_tester definition
                           for testing
                           risk level harmless.
  private section.
    methods create_report for testing.
    methods create_test_data
      exporting report_rows type report_list.
endclass.
class create_report_tester implementation.
  method create_report.
    data report_rows type report_list.
    create_test_data(
      importing report_rows = report_rows
      ).
```

```
    clear sy-msgty.
    perform create_report using report_rows.
    cl_abap_unit_assert=>assert_equals(
      act = sy-msgty
      exp = space
      ).
  endmethod.
  method create_test_data.
    data report_row like line of report_rows.
    report_row-vendor       = 'Amalgamated Materials'.
    report_row-city         = 'Toronto'.
    report row-amount       = 2571909.06.
    report_row-currency_key = 'CAD'.
    append report_row to report_rows.
    report_row-vendor       = 'Associated Manufacturers'.
    report_row-city         = 'Melbourne'.
    report row-amount       = 184396.26.
    report_row-currency_key = 'AUD'.
    append report_row to report_rows.
    report_row-vendor       = 'General Industries LTD'.
    report_row-city         = 'London'.
    report row-amount       = 6005.72.
    report_row-currency_key = 'GBP'.
    append report_row to report_rows.
    report_row-vendor       = 'Innovative Solutions'.
    report_row-city         = 'New York'.
    report row-amount       = 12545.80.
    report_row-currency_key = 'USD'.
    append report_row to report_rows.
  endmethod.
endclass.
```

There are a few things to notice about this unit test class. First, notice that it has two methods but only one of them is marked with the "for testing" clause. During unit test execution, only the method with the "for testing" clause will be called by the test runner. Notice also that the creation of test data has been delegated to helper method create_test_data. This utility method has many lines devoted to the creation of the test data to be used when method create_report calls subroutine create_report. These lines of code could easily have been included directly within method create_report, but then the purpose of the test would have become obscured by all the lines of code creating the test data to be used. As currently written, it is clear to see that method create_report calls a method to have its test data created for it, then clears system variable sy-msgty, then calls subroutine create_report, and finally asserts that sy-msgty was not affected by the activity performed by the subroutine.

If the unit test shown in Listing 10-27 were to be executed, it would be interrupted with the report shown in Figure 10-2 presented to the user.

```
+-------------------------------------------------------------------------
|Internal Session for Isolated Test Class Execution
+-------------------------------------------------------------------------
|Warning
|=======
|Program: <program name>
|Class:   <test class name>
|This window is displayed because your test case has triggered
|a list command like follows:
|- new page
|- leave to list processing
|- uline
|- write
|- new page
|- ...
|This as any interactive technique is not permitted !!
+-------------------------------------------------------------------------
|Please avoid the use of these statements. To locate them in the source
|code setting break-points on the mentioned statements should help.
+-------------------------------------------------------------------------
Amalgamated Materials          Toronto          2,571,909.06    CAD
Associated Manufacturers       Melbourne          184,396.26    AUD
General Industries LTD         London               6,005.72    GBP
Innovative Solutions           New York            12,545.80    USD
```

Figure 10-2. *Report presented when automated unit test shown in Listing 10-27 is executed*

The unit test will remain suspended at this point until the user presses a key enabling it to resume. This needs to be avoided so the unit test can run to completion with no help at all from the user.

We've already seen how encapsulating the production of ALV reports into a class enables defining that class with a test double to be used during execution of the unit test path. A similar approach will be used with classic list processing statements. The full solution will involve the following changes to the production path of the program:

- Define a class having public methods that can be called to issue classic list processing statements.

- Change the service locator to be able to manage the service provided by this class.

- Replace each explicit classic list processing statement in the program with a call to the corresponding service managed by the service locator.

The class having public methods that can be called to issue classic list processing statements will implement an interface defining those methods. Listing 10-28 shows an interface defining methods correlating to the classic list processing statements new-line and write.

Listing 10-28. Interface defining methods for classic list processing statements new-line and write

```
interface report_writable.
    types value_type  type c length 100.
    types format_type type c length 100.
    methods new_line.
    methods write
      importing
        format
          type report_writable=>format_type
        value
          type report_writable=>value_type.
endinterface.
```

Notice that this interface specifies signature parameters for indicating both a format and a value to be accepted by method write. This interface is implemented by the class shown in Listing 10-29.

Listing 10-29. Class implementing interface report_writable

```
class report_writer definition.
  public section.
    interfaces report_writable.
    aliases new_line for report_writable~new_line.
    aliases write    for report_writable~write.
endclass.
class report_writer implementation.
  method new_line.
    new-line.
  endmethod.
  method write.
    constants default_format type sy-msgv1 value 'SY-MSGV1'.
    data value_formatting_field type ref to data.
    field-symbols <value_formatting_field> type any.
    try.
      create data value_formatting_field type (format).
    catch cx_sy_create_data_error.
      create data value_formatting_field type (default_format).
    endtry.
    if value_formatting_field is bound.
      assign  value_formatting_field->*
          to <value_formatting_field>.
    endif.
    if <value_formatting_field> is assigned.
      <value_formatting_field> = value.
      write <value_formatting_field>.
    else.
      write value.
    endif.
  endmethod.
endclass.
```

Notice the implementation for method new-line simply contains the new-line statement. Notice also the implementation for method write will dynamically define a data field with the same type specified by the format parameter provided by the caller and then will move the value specified by the value parameter into this field so it can be formatted correctly when used with the write statement. It contains processing to accommodate the failure to dynamically define a field according to the type specified by the format parameter and to use a corresponding default format instead, as well as processing to accommodate the failure to assign a reference to the dynamically defined field.

Listing 10-30 is a copy of the service locator from Listing 10-13 changed to accommodate a classic list report service as a reference to an interface, with changes highlighted in bold.

Listing 10-30. Service locator from Listing 10-13 changed to accommodate managing a classic list report writer service

```
class service_locator definition create private.
  public section.
    class-methods class_constructor.
    methods       set_ticket_sales_examiner
                     importing ticket_sales_examiner
                       type ref to ticket_sales_examinable.
    methods       set_ticket_sales_reporter
                     importing ticket_sales_reporter
                       type ref to ticket_sales_reportable.
    methods       set_alv_report_function_module
                     importing alv_function_module_name
                       type funcname.
    methods       set_message_dispatcher
                     importing message_dispatcher
                       type ref to message_dispatchable.
    methods       set_report_writer
                     importing report_writer
                       type ref to report_writable.
    class-data singleton type ref to service_locator read-only.
    data ticket_sales_examiner type ref to ticket_sales_examinable
```

```abap
                                                 read-only.
    data ticket_sales_reporter type ref to ticket_sales_reportable
                                                 read-only.
    data alv_function_module_name type funcname read-only.
    data message_dispatcher type ref to message_dispatchable read-only.
    data report_writer type ref to report_writable read-only.
endclass.
class service_locator implementation.
  method class_constructor.
    create instance singleton.
  endmethod.
  method set_ticket_sales_examiner.
    me->ticket_sales_examiner = ticket_sales_examiner.
  endmethod.
  method set_ticket_sales_reporter.
    me->ticket_sales_reporter = ticket_sales_reporter.
  endmethod.
  method set_alv_report_function_module.
    me->alv_function_module_name = alv_function_module_name.
  endmethod.
  method set_message_dispatcher.
    me->message_dispatcher = message_dispatcher.
  endmethod.
  method set_report_writer.
    me->report_writer = report_writer.
  endmethod.
endclass.
```

Notice that there is now a new public read-only attribute named report_writer and a corresponding public setter method for it. These changes are similar to the changes required to enable the service locator to manage a message dispatch service and were just as easy to implement.

Listing 10-31 shows a subroutine for creating an instance of class report_writer and registering it with the service locator as the report_writer service.

Listing 10-31. Subroutine creating report writer service and registering it with the service locator

```
form create_report_writer.
  data report_writer type ref to report_writable.
  create object report_writer type report_writer.
  service_locator=>singleton->set_report_writer( report_writer ).
endform.
```

The subroutine shown in Listing 10-31 would be called at some point during the initial execution of the program to register the report writer to be used for producing a report with production path executions. With components defined as shown in Listings 10-28, 10-29, 10-30, and 10-31, it becomes possible to replace classic list processing statements new-line and write with corresponding calls through the public attribute of the service locator providing the report writer service.

Listing 10-32 shows how the subroutine in Listing 10-26 would be changed to do this, with changes highlighted in bold.

Listing 10-32. Subroutine producing classic report with classic list processing statements replaced with equivalent calls to a service managed by the service locator

```
form create_report using report_rows type report_list.
  data report_row like line of report_rows.
  loop at report_rows into report_row.
    new-line.
    service_locator=>singleton->report_writer->new-line( ).
    write: report_row-vendor,
           report_row-city,
           report_row-amount,
           report_row-currency_key.
    service_locator=>singleton->report_writer->write(
      exporting format =        'report_row-vendor'
                value  = conv #( report_row-vendor )
      ).
    service_locator=>singleton->report_writer->write(
      exporting format =        'report_row-city'
```

```
                value   = conv #( report_row-city )
      ).
    service_locator=>singleton->report_writer->write(
      exporting format =           'report_row-amount'
                value   = conv #( report_row-amount )
      ).
    service_locator=>singleton->report_writer->write(
      exporting format =           'report_row-currency_key'
                value   = conv #( report_row-currency_key )
      ).
  endloop.
endform.
```

Notice that each explicit classic list processing statement has been replaced with a call to a method of a service managed by the service locator. The calls to method write require specifying parameters to indicate the format to be used in addition to the value, but the format specified is simply the apostrophe-bounded name of the same field providing the value. Also, the fields providing the values for the value parameters of method write all are shown using the constructor operator "conv #" so that the value in the supplying field is converted to a value compatible with the type assigned to the value parameter, averting syntax errors otherwise raised by type mismatches and eliminating the need to define local helper variables to facilitate this conversion. This would not be needed in all cases but certainly would be necessary for the call to method write where the value is supplied by a numeric field, such as the use of field report_row-amount shown in the preceding example.

Listing 10-33 is a copy of Listing 10-32 without the highlighting and stricken lines:

Listing 10-33. Listing 10-32 without the highlighting and stricken lines

```
form create_report using report_rows type report_list.
  data report_row like line of report_rows.
  loop at report_rows into report_row.
    service_locator=>singleton->report_writer->new-line( ).
    service_locator=>singleton->report_writer->write(
      exporting format =           'report_row-vendor'
                value   = conv #( report_row-vendor )
      ).
```

```
    service_locator=>singleton->report_writer->write(
      exporting format =          'report_row-city'
                value  = conv #( report_row-city )
      ).
    service_locator=>singleton->report_writer->write(
      exporting format =          'report_row-amount'
                value  = conv #( report_row-amount )
      ).
    service_locator=>singleton->report_writer->write(
      exporting format =          'report_row-currency_key'
                value  = conv #( report_row-currency_key )
      ).
  endloop.
endform.
```

At this point, the task could be undertaken to replace any other NEW-LINE and WRITE statements in the program with corresponding calls to the report_writer service managed by the service locator. Once that has been completed, the program can be considered designed for testability. This is because a unit test would now be able to register with the service locator an instance of a test double implementing the report_writer interface, one that *does not* use classic list processing statements, guaranteeing no more interruptions of unit tests with lines generated by the test runner preceding a classic list report and requiring manual intervention by the user to enable the test to run to completion.

Listing 10-34 shows such a test double.

Listing 10-34. Test double for class report_writer

```
class report_writer_test_double definition.
  public section.
    interfaces report_writable.
    aliases new_line for report_writable~new_line.
    aliases write    for report_writable~write.
endclass.
class report_writer_test_double implementation.
  method new_line.
```

```
  endmethod.
  method write.
  endmethod.
endclass.
```

Notice the implementations for both methods are empty – neither contains any classic list processing statements. This makes it possible to write a unit test class for testing subroutine create_report that can run to completion without user intervention. Listing 10-35 shows how the unit test from Listing 10-27 would be adjusted to do this, with changes highlighted in bold.

Listing 10-35. Adjusted unit test class for testing subroutine create_report

```
class create_report_tester definition
                           for testing
                           risk level harmless.
  private section.
    methods setup.
    methods create_report for testing.
    methods create_test_data
      exporting report_rows type report_list.
endclass.
class create_report_tester implementation.
  method setup.
    data report_writer type ref to report_writable.
    create object report_writer type report_writer_test_double.
    service_locator=>singleton->set_report_writer( report_writer ).
  endmethod.
  method create_report.
    data report_rows type report_list.
    create_test_data(
      importing report_rows = report_rows
      ).
    clear sy-msgty.
    perform create_report using report_rows.
    cl_abap_unit_assert=>assert_equals(
      act = sy-msgty
      exp = space
      ).
```

```
  endmethod.
  method create_test_data.
    data report_row like line of report_rows.
    report_row-vendor       = 'Amalgamated Materials'.
    report_row-city         = 'Toronto'.
    report row-amount        = 2571909.06.
    report_row-currency_key = 'CAD'.
    append report_row to report_rows.
    report_row-vendor       = 'Associated Manufacturers'.
    report_row-city         = 'Melbourne'.
    report row-amount        = 184396.26.
    report_row-currency_key = 'AUD'.
    append report_row to report_rows.
    report_row-vendor       = 'General Industries LTD'.
    report_row-city         = 'London'.
    report row-amount        = 6005.72.
    report_row-currency_key = 'GBP'.
    append report_row to report_rows.
    report_row-vendor       = 'Innovative Solutions'.
    report_row-city         = 'New York'.
    report row-amount        = 12545.80.
    report_row-currency_key = 'USD'.
    append report_row to report_rows.
  endmethod.
endclass.
```

Notice that this unit test class has a setup method which will create an instance of class report_writer_test_double and then register that instance with the service locator as the instance to be used to provide the classic report writer service. The setup method is automatically called prior to executing the method defined as "for testing."

Executing this program normally with the corresponding selection criteria would produce the classic list report shown in Figure 10-1 at the top of this section. Executing the automated unit test of this program as shown in the preceding text would indicate a passing test for test method create_report and would not be interrupted prior to its completion by the presentation of a classic list report, despite calling the very same subroutine that causes the classic list report produced by the production path.

Upon further examination, it might be concluded that the unit test of Listing 10-34 is not very robust because it does not really test what the subroutine does but rather what it does not do – specifically, the test asserts the subroutine does not change the value of system variable sy-msgty. Listing 10-36 is a copy of Listing 10-34 and changed so that the report writer test double keeps track of the number of report rows that would result from the calls made to its methods, with changes highlighted in bold.

Listing 10-36. Listing 10-34 changed to track number of resulting report rows

```
class report_writer_test_double definition.
  public section.
    interfaces report_writable.
    aliases new_line for report_writable~new_line.
    aliases write    for report_writable~write.
    data number_of_lines_written type int4 read-only.
  private section.
    data new_line_pending type abap_bool value abap_true.
endclass.
class report_writer_test_double implementation.
  method new_line.
    new_line_pending = abap_true.
  endmethod.
  method write.
    if new_line_pending = abap_true.
      add 01 to number_of_lines_written.
      new_line_pending = abap_false.
    endif.
  endmethod.
endclass.
```

Notice that there is now a public read-only attribute to retain the number of report lines that would be written. In addition, a new private section defines a Boolean attribute indicating whether a new line is pending. Notice also that both methods now have non-empty implementations: method new_line will now set the private Boolean attribute to true to indicate that a new row of the report is pending; and method write will now increment public attribute number_of_lines_written when the private attribute indicates that a new line is pending and then will set the private attribute to false. Accordingly, each time method write is called after method new_line has been called, it will indicate another line written to the report. This change transforms class report_writer_test_double into a test spy which can be interrogated to determine how many report lines resulted from calls to methods new_line and write.

Listing 10-37 is a copy of unit test method create_report from Listing 10-35 changed to show how this method could assert the correct number of lines was written by the called subroutine, with changes highlighted in bold.

Listing 10-37. Listing 10-35 changed to assert the number of report lines caused by the subroutine

```
method create_report.
  data report_rows type report_list.
  data report_writer_test_double type ref to report_writer_test_double.
  create_test_data(
    importing report_rows = report_rows
    ).
  clear sy-msgty.
  perform create_report using report_rows.
  try.
    report_writer_test_double ?=
      service_locator=>singleton->report_writer.
  catch cx_sy_move_cast_error.
    cl_abap_unit_assert=>fail(
      msg = 'specializing cast has failed'
      ).
  endtry.
  cl_abap_unit_assert=>assert_equals(
    act = report_writer_test_double->number_of_lines_written
    exp = lines( report_rows )
    ).
endmethod.
```

Notice the additional local variable defined as a reference to class report_writer_test_double. This is used in the try-endtry block to enable the class instance occupying public read-only attribute report_writer of the service locator, defined as a reference to interface report_writable, to be regarded as an instance of class report_writer_test_double. If the

specializing cast works, then the assertion compares the value in attribute number_
of_lines_written of class report_writer_test_double and the number of lines in internal
table report_rows for equality, improving the unit test from asserting something the
subroutine does not do to something that it does do.

This solution may be considered by many as a long way to go to enable unit testing
a program producing a classic list report. Since the rows of the report in this example
already are contained within an internal table, it might be easier simply to convert from
using a classic list report to using an ALV report. This would eliminate from the program
the use of deprecated statements, as well as instantly providing users with new report
analyzing capabilities. So why bother with such heavy refactoring to enable automated
unit testing when ALV offers a much better approach to reporting and arguably is more
conducive to implementing its associated automated unit tests?

The answer is that some ABAP developer somewhere is working at a site full of
users who will moan and complain about every change made to the software they use.
Despite the benefits of ALV over classic lists, these users will revolt should the developer
have the temerity to make such an improvement to their beloved classic list reports
without their approval. Perhaps you know some users at your own site who fit this
description. So for those developers who find themselves in such a situation, this section
offers the less preferred alternative to implementing unit tests with reports, one for
which the associated changes would not be apparent to a user base intent on thwarting
improvements to the software they use on a daily basis.

EXERCISES

At this point, take a break from reading and shift into exercise mode. Refer to the
accompanying workbook to perform the ten exercises associated with workbook **Section 21:
ABAP Unit Testing 504 – Gaining Control Over List Processing Statements.**

Summary

This chapter showed how the service locator introduced in the previous chapter can be leveraged to manage

1. Services provided through global classes

2. Services provided through function modules

It also demonstrated how the service locator can be instrumental in providing solutions to the problems arising from those ABAP statements and features presenting challenges to automated unit testing – specifically

3. How it can be used to manage an ABAP MESSAGE statement service for which a unit test can provide a test double that can circumvent the otherwise automatic test failures when encountering messages of severities error and higher

4. How it can be used to manage a classic list statement service for which a unit test can provide a test double that can avoid the manual intervention otherwise required by the presentation of the classic report output during the execution of the unit test

Examples were provided showing how to resolve each of these challenges.

CHAPTER 11

Test-Driven Development

Test-Driven Development, known by its acronym TDD, is one of the many development approaches to have gained traction through the Agile software development movement. It is based on the idea of developing software using a test-first perspective: first, a failing executable test is written; then production software is written capable of passing the test. Accordingly, as its name suggests, the *development* of production software is being *driven* by the *test*. This chapter explores TDD.

The TDD Cycle

A developer utilizing TDD follows a cycle consisting of the following steps:

1. Write a new executable test.

2. Run all tests to confirm the new test fails.

3. Write production code to make the new test pass.

4. Run all tests to confirm they all pass.

5. Refactor code as necessary and rerun all tests.

6. Repeat from step 1.

This cycle implies a distinction between production code and test code. Whereas only the production code will be executed in a production environment, code used for its testing is not only developed along with it but the test code is written first before the corresponding production code it tests is written.

© James E. McDonough 2021
J. E. McDonough, *Automated Unit Testing with ABAP*, https://doi.org/10.1007/978-1-4842-6951-0_11

Roy Osherove summarizes the process:

You begin by writing a test that fails; then you move on to creating the production code, seeing the test pass, and continuing on to either refactor your code or create another failing test.[1]

Those who champion its use readily point out that with TDD it is virtually impossible not to have an associated test for every shred of production code and furthermore that the test code describes the functionality of the production software far more accurately than any external specification document possibly could simply because the tests must pass while an external specification documentation can eventually get out of synchronization with the software for a variety of reasons, including reengineering, postponed or canceled updates, and even loss of the specification. Indeed, having a robust testing harness for production software means that developers can refactor the software with the confidence that no new problems will be introduced with the new changes.

The Three Laws of TDD

Robert C. Martin has emerged as one of the leading advocates of using TDD, so much so that he formulated the *three laws of TDD*:

> **First Law** You may not write production code until you have written a failing unit test.

> **Second Law** You may not write more of a unit test than is sufficient to fail, and not compiling is failing.

> **Third Law** You may not write more production code than is sufficient to pass the currently failing test.[2]

Observing the TDD discipline in developing software enables adhering to what is known as the red-green-refactor cycle, which Martin puts into perspective for us:
The rules of this cycle are simple.

1. Create a unit tests that fails.

2. Write production code that makes that test pass.

3. Clean up the mess you just made.[3]

---

[1]Osherove, Roy, *The Art of Unit Testing*, second edition, Manning, 2014, p. 15
[2]Martin, Robert C., *Clean Code: A Handbook of Agile Software Craftsmanship*, Prentice Hall, 2009, p. 122
[3]https://blog.cleancoder.com/uncle-bob/2014/12/17/TheCyclesOfTDD.html

The red-green-refactor cycle gets its name from the feedback produced by many of the xUnit testing frameworks. A failing test generally is reported using the color red, whether it is a failure message with red background, a red flag associated with the failing unit test method, or a red traffic light in a report. A successful test generally is reported using the color green. Refactoring the code has no associated color, but once the refactoring is complete, the subsequent unit test execution will either continue to pass (green) or fail (red) indicating that something changed during the refactoring process has resulted in a failing unit test:

> *The red/green concept is prevalent throughout the unit testing world and especially in test-driven development. Its mantra is "Red-Green-Refactor," meaning that you start with a failing test, then pass it, and then make your code readable and more maintainable.*[4]

For developers who have been writing in a procedural style for most of their careers, the thought of writing the tests first may be perceived as backward at best and thoroughly confusing at worst. It represents a testing format that may be regarded as the antithesis of common sense and apt to cause a conflict with their comfort level. Indeed, some could sense a feeling of revulsion toward such a jarring change as elevating testing to the more prominent position within the development cycle that TDD demands of it. However, after having tried TDD, I have become an advocate of this development process since it forces the programmer to design the productive code in a way that it can be tested, perhaps the most significant benefit it has to offer.

Though it may feel uncomfortable at first, it eventually provides its own "Aha!" moments as developers come to understand the power it places at their disposal. It is not unlike other evolutionary improvements that have been discovered over the centuries that first were ignored, shunned, and ridiculed as folly, such as the change from the concept of a flat earth to one of a spherical planet and, by the supplanting of Newtonian physics, the theory of mechanics that had reigned throughout the world for two centuries, with Einstein's Theory of Relativity.

---

[4]Osherove, Roy, *The Art of Unit Testing*, second edition, Manning, 2014, p. 31

The Benefits of TDD

Programmers using the TDD approach to developing software will find themselves in a red-green-refactor cycle lasting only about half a minute. As Robert C. Martin describes it in his book *The Clean Coder*

> *The three laws lock you into a cycle that is, perhaps, thirty seconds long. ... Round and round the cycle you go. Adding a bit to the test code. Adding a bit to the production code. The two code streams grow simultaneously into complementary components. The tests fit the production code like an antibody fits an antigen.*[5]

Through the use of this cycle, development organizations reap what Martin describes as "The Litany of Benefits"[6] listed as follows:

- Certainty

  Using TDD enables a developer to be certain that a production solution produces the intended results. The test simply will continue to fail until it passes. This certainty instills in the developer the confidence that the solution implemented satisfies the associated requirement.

- Low defect injection rate

  When code is being changed, introducing new bugs into it can be avoided when there are associated unit tests available for it. Tests that suddenly fail after implementing a new change would identify a defect that would have made its way into production had there been no corresponding unit tests.

- Courage

  Most of us have encountered bad code during our careers. Too often we leave this bad code unchanged, despite the excessive time it might have required for us to determine how it works, because we fear we don't understand it well enough, even now,

---

[5]Martin, Robert C., *The Clean Coder: A Code of Conduct for Professional Programmers*, Prentice Hall, 2011, p. 80

[6]Ibid

to be certain of the conclusions we have drawn about it and changing it might introduce bugs that don't exist now. This trepidation disappears when there are accompanying unit tests exercising the bad code. It gives us the courage to refactor the bad code into good code because the unit tests will tell us whether we have broken anything in the process.

- Documentation

    Unit tests provide excellent examples of the ways in which a procedure can be called. Need to learn how some procedure parameter affects its operation? Consult a unit test using that parameter to see its effect in an executable context. Martin sums it up well by stating

The unit tests are documents. They describe the lowest-level design of the system. They are unambiguous, accurate, written in the language that the audience understands, and are so formal they execute. They are the best kind of low-level documentation that can exist.[7]

- Design

    Because the unit test must be written first, the corresponding production code written to cause the test to pass is implicitly designed for testability. This eliminates the possibility of finding that tests written later will expose design incompatibilities requiring the production code to be refactored. In short, using TDD promotes good program design.

Following the TDD Cycle

So let's run through the motions of implementing production code using the TDD model. Based on the pseudo-code we had encountered in the Chapter 4 section titled "Writing xUnit Tests," Listing 11-1 shows what might be the minimal compilable code we could write at the start for an ABAP program as we follow the TDD session.

---

[7]Ibid, p. 82

Listing 11-1. Minimal compilable code to start a TDD session

```
report.
" production code starts here
" production code ends here
" unit testing code starts here
class sign_tester definition.
  private section.
    methods test_positive for testing.
endclass.
class sign_tester implementation.
  method test_positive.
    data sign type c length 1.
    cl_abap_unit_assert=>assert_equals(
      act = sign
      exp = '+'
      ).
  endmethod.
endclass.
" unit testing code ends here
```

Here we see an ABAP report having no production code but having a single unit test class named sign_tester defining a single unit test method test_positive. The unit test method contains only the definition for a field named sign and a call to method assert_ equals of static class cl_abap_unit. When this source code is subjected to automated unit testing, we should expect a failure. The code is now in the red phase of the red-green-refactor cycle.

Next, we'll provide the minimal amount of production code to enable the unit test to pass, as shown in Listing 11-2, with changes from Listing 11-1 highlighted in bold.

Listing 11-2. Minimal production code to enable unit test to pass

```
report.
" production code starts here
class sign_setter definition.
  public section.
    types sign type c length 1.
```

```
    methods get_sign importing number type int4
                    returning value(sign) type sign.
endclass
class sign_setter implementation.
  method get_sign.
    sign = '+'.
  endmethod.
endclass.
" production code ends here
" unit testing code starts here
class sign_tester definition.
  private section.
    methods test_positive for testing.
endclass.
class sign_tester implementation.
  method test_positive.
    data sign type c length 1.
    data sign_setter type ref to sign_setter.
    create object sign_setter.
    sign = sign_setter->get_sign( 55 ).
    cl_abap_unit_assert=>assert_equals(
      act = sign
      exp = '+'
      ).
  endmethod.
endclass.
" unit testing code ends here
```

Here we have added to the production code a new class named sign_setter having a single method named get_sign. The implementation for get_sign consists of a single statement setting the returning value to '+'. We've also changed the implementation of unit test method test_positive of unit test class sign_tester in the following way:

- Defined local variable sign_setter as a reference to an instance of class sign_setter

- Created an instance of class sign_setter into local variable sign_setter

- Invoked method get_sign of the class referenced by local variable sign_setter, passing the value 55 for the number parameter and accepting the returned value in local variable sign

When this source code is subjected to automated unit testing, we should expect it to pass. The code is now in the green phase of the red-green-refactor cycle.

Next, we'll clean up the code as shown in Listing 11-3, with changes from Listing 11-2 highlighted in bold.

Listing 11-3. Result of cleaning the code after the unit test passes

```
report.
" production code starts here
class sign_setter definition.
  public section.
    types sign type c length 1.
    types integer type int4.
    constants positive_sign type sign value '+'.
    methods get_sign importing number type integer
                      returning value(sign) type sign.
endclass
class sign_setter implementation.
  method get_sign.
    sign = positive_sign.
  endmethod.
endclass.
" production code ends here
" unit testing code starts here
class sign_tester definition.
  private section.
    methods test_positive for testing.
endclass.
class sign_tester implementation.
  method test_positive.
    constants positive_number type sign_setter=>integer value 55.
    data sign type sign_setter=>sign.
    data sign_setter type ref to sign_setter.
```

```
    create object sign_setter.
    sign = sign_setter->get_sign( positive_number ).
    cl_abap_unit_assert=>assert_equals(
      act = sign
      exp = sign_setter=>positive_sign
      ).
  endmethod.
endclass.
" unit testing code ends here
```

Here we have changed production class sign_setter by adding to its public section a new types statement defining a type named integer, a new constant defining a positive sign value, and changed the signature of method get_sign to indicate type integer for its number parameter. Method get_sign was also changed to use the newly defined public constant instead of a character literal to set the returning value.

We also have changed unit test class sign_tester by defining a local constant positive_number in unit test method test_positive, defining it using the public type integer provided by class sign_setter and assigning it the value 55, as well as changed the type associated with local variable sign to use the public type defined by class sign_setter. In addition, the numeric literal on the call to method get_sign has been replaced with the local constant, and the value specified on the exp parameter of the assertion statement now uses the public constant defined by class sign_setter instead of the character literal value it had used. At this point, all the local data fields and parameter values of unit test method test_positive are defined in terms of types and constants provided by class sign_setter. The code now is in the refactor phase of the red-green-refactor cycle. Running the unit test again will determine whether the refactoring changes applied have caused the unit test to fail. If so, we would need to address this failure by altering our refactored code to the point where the unit test passes once again.

You may already have come to the conclusion that the implementation provided for method get_sign is hardly acceptable since it always provides the same value back to the caller. While this is true, the fact remains that the single unit test we have written passes. Meanwhile, we also recognize that method get_sign should be able to provide a negative sign for a negative number and a blank sign for zero. These are two more unit tests that we need to write during our TDD session.

Let's start with writing the unit test to determine whether method get_sign is capable of providing a negative sign for a negative number. Listing 11-4 shows the code with changes from Listing 11-3 highlighted in bold.

Listing 11-4. The code after adding new unit test method negative_test

```
report.
" production code starts here
class sign_setter definition.
  public section.
    types sign type c length 1.
    types integer type int4.
    constants positive_sign type sign value '+'.
    methods get_sign importing number type integer
                      returning value(sign) type sign.
endclass
class sign_setter implementation.
  method get_sign.
    sign = positive_sign.
  endmethod.
endclass.
" production code ends here
" unit testing code starts here
class sign_tester definition.
  private section.
    methods test_positive for testing.
    methods test_negative for testing.
endclass.
class sign_tester implementation.
  method test_positive.
    constants positive_number type sign_setter=>integer value 55.
    data sign type sign_setter=>sign.
    data sign_setter type ref to sign_setter.
    create object sign_setter.
    sign = sign_setter->get_sign( positive_number ).
    cl_abap_unit_assert=>assert_equals(
```

```
      act = sign
      exp = sign_setter=>positive_sign
      ).
  endmethod.
  method test_negative.
    constants negative_number type sign_setter=>integer value '-55'.
    data sign type sign_setter=>sign.
    data sign_setter type ref to sign_setter.
    create object sign_setter.
    sign = sign_setter->get_sign( negative_number ).
    cl_abap_unit_assert=>assert_equals(
      act = sign
      exp = '-'
      ).
  endmethod.
endclass.
" unit testing code ends here
```

Here we have cloned unit test method test_positive as unit test method test_negative, changing the name and respective value of the local constant, as well as changing the expected value to be used with the call to method assert_equals of static class cl_abap_unit_assert. Now when this source code is subjected to automated unit testing, we should expect unit test method test_positive to pass and unit test method test_negative to fail. The code is once again in the red phase of the red-green-refactor cycle.

So next we'll provide the minimal amount of production code to enable both unit tests to pass, as shown in Listing 11-5, with changes from Listing 11-4 highlighted in bold.

Listing 11-5. The code after changing class sign_setter to be able to handle both positive and negative numbers

```
report.
" production code starts here
class sign_setter definition.
  public section.
    types sign type c length 1.
    types integer type int4.
```

```
      constants positive_sign type sign value '+'.
      constants negative_sign type sign value '-'.
      methods get_sign importing number type integer
                        returning value(sign) type sign.
endclass
class sign_setter implementation.
  method get_sign.
    if number > 0.
      sign = positive_sign.
    else.
      sign = negative_sign.
    endif.
  endmethod.
endclass.
" production code ends here
" unit testing code starts here
class sign_tester definition.
  private section.
    methods test_positive for testing.
    methods test_negative for testing.
endclass.
class sign_tester implementation.
  method test_positive.
    constants positive_number type sign_setter=>integer value 55.
    data sign type sign_setter=>sign.
    data sign_setter type ref to sign_setter.
    create object sign_setter.
    sign = sign_setter->get_sign( positive_number ).
    cl_abap_unit_assert=>assert_equals(
      act = sign
      exp = sign_setter=>positive_sign
      ).
  endmethod.
  method test_negative.
    constants negative_number type sign_setter=>integer value '-55'.
```

```
    data sign type sign_setter=>sign.
    data sign_setter type ref to sign_setter.
    create object sign_setter.
    sign = sign_setter->get_sign( negative_number ).
    cl_abap_unit_assert=>assert_equals(
      act = sign
      exp = '-'
      ).
  endmethod.
endclass.
" unit testing code ends here
```

Here we have changed class sign_setter to define a new public constant to represent a negative sign and changed the implementation of its method get_sign to return a positive sign only when the number parameter indicates a positive number and to return a negative sign for all other values. Now when the unit tests are run, both of them pass. The code is once again in the green phase of the red-green-refactor cycle.

Listing 11-6 shows how we would refactor the code to keep it clean, again with changes from Listing 11-5 highlighted in bold.

Listing 11-6. Result of cleaning the code after both unit tests pass

```
report.
" production code starts here
class sign_setter definition.
  public section.
    types sign type c length 1.
    types integer type int4.
    constants positive_sign type sign value '+'.
    constants negative_sign type sign value '-'.
    methods get_sign importing number type integer
                     returning value(sign) type sign.
endclass
class sign_setter implementation.
  method get_sign.
    if number > 0.
      sign = positive_sign.
```

```
    else.
      sign = negative_sign.
    endif.
  endmethod.
endclass.
" production code ends here
" unit testing code starts here
class sign_tester definition.
  private section.
    methods test_positive for testing.
    methods test_negative for testing.
endclass.
class sign_tester implementation.
  method test_positive.
    constants positive_number type sign_setter=>integer value 55.
    data sign type sign_setter=>sign.
    data sign_setter type ref to sign_setter.
    create object sign_setter.
    sign = sign_setter->get_sign( positive_number ).
    cl_abap_unit_assert=>assert_equals(
      act = sign
      exp = sign_setter=>positive_sign
      ).
  endmethod.
  method test_negative.
    constants negative_number type sign_setter=>integer value '-55'.
    data sign type sign_setter=>sign.
    data sign_setter type ref to sign_setter.
    create object sign_setter.
    sign = sign_setter->get_sign( negative_number ).
    cl_abap_unit_assert=>assert_equals(
      act = sign
      exp = sign_setter=>negative_sign
      ).
  endmethod.
endclass.
" unit testing code ends here
```

Here the only difference is that we changed the expected value of the assertion in unit test method test_negative to use the public constant defined by class sign_setter so that the unit test code continues to be defined in terms of the public attributes provided by class sign_setter. The code is again in the refactor phase of the red-green-refactor cycle. Once more, we would need to run the unit tests to determine whether the refactoring changes applied have caused either of the unit tests to fail.

You may already have noticed the weakness of the implementation provided for method get_sign. If not, then examine it again carefully. This leads us to yet another unit test for method get_sign, whether it is able to provide the correct sign for a value that is neither positive nor negative - that is, zero.[8]

So let's write the unit test to determine whether method get_sign is capable of providing a blank value as the sign for the number zero. Listing 11-7 shows the code with changes from Listing 11-6 highlighted in bold.

Listing 11-7. Result after adding unit test to check sign returned for value zero is space

```
report.
" production code starts here
class sign_setter definition.
  public section.
    types sign type c length 1.
    types integer type int4.
    constants positive_sign type sign value '+'.
    constants negative_sign type sign value '-'.
    methods get_sign importing number type integer
                     returning value(sign) type sign.
endclass
class sign_setter implementation.
  method get_sign.
```

---

[8]In the context of computer science, an argument can be made that a binary integer value of zero is a positive number because its high-order bit is 0, just as it is for all positive integers. Even more absurd is the argument that can be made for packed decimal numbers: that a value of zero is positive when the low-order nibble of its final byte is the binary equivalent of hexadecimal value "A" or "C," negative when that low-order nibble represents hexadecimal "B" or "D," and unsigned when representing either "E" or "F." Here we will simply agree that a value of zero is to have neither a positive nor negative sign. See www.sfu.ca/sasdoc/sashtml/lrcon/z1265705.htm

```abap
    if number > 0.
      sign = positive_sign.
    else.
      sign = negative_sign.
    endif.
  endmethod.
endclass.
" production code ends here
" unit testing code starts here
class sign_tester definition.
  private section.
    methods test_positive for testing.
    methods test_negative for testing.
    methods test_zero      for testing.
endclass.
class sign_tester implementation.
  method test_positive.
    constants positive_number type sign_setter=>integer value 55.
    data sign type sign_setter=>sign.
    data sign_setter type ref to sign_setter.
    create object sign_setter.
    sign = sign_setter->get_sign( positive_number ).
    cl_abap_unit_assert=>assert_equals(
      act = sign
      exp = sign_setter=>positive_sign
      ).
  endmethod.
  method test_negative.
    constants negative_number type sign_setter=>integer value '-55'.
    data sign type sign_setter=>sign.
    data sign_setter type ref to sign_setter.
    create object sign_setter.
    sign = sign_setter->get_sign( negative_number ).
    cl_abap_unit_assert=>assert_equals(
      act = sign
```

```
      exp = sign_setter=>negative_sign
      ).
  endmethod.
  method test_zero.
    constants zero type sign_setter=>integer value 0.
    data sign type sign_setter=>sign.
    data sign_setter type ref to sign_setter.
    create object sign_setter.
    sign = sign_setter->get_sign( zero ).
    cl_abap_unit_assert=>assert_equals(
      act = sign
      exp = space
      ).
  endmethod.
endclass.
" unit testing code ends here
```

Here we have cloned unit test method test_negative as unit test method test_zero, changing the name and respective value of the local constant, as well as changing the expected value to be used with the call to method assert_equals of static class cl_abap_unit_assert. Now when this source code is subjected to automated unit testing, we should expect unit test methods test_positive and test_negative to pass and unit test method test_zero to fail. The code is once again in the red phase of the red-green-refactor cycle.

Once again we'll provide the minimal amount of production code to enable all unit tests to pass, as shown in Listing 11-8, with changes from Listing 11-7 highlighted in bold.

Listing 11-8. The code after changing class sign_setter to be able to handle positive, negative, and zero numbers

```
report.
" production code starts here
class sign_setter definition.
  public section.
    types sign type c length 1.
    types integer type int4.
```

```
    constants positive_sign type sign value '+'.
    constants negative_sign type sign value '-'.
    constants zero_sign     type sign value space.
    methods get_sign importing number type integer
                     returning value(sign) type sign.
endclass
class sign_setter implementation.
  method get_sign.
    if number > 0.
      sign = positive_sign.
    else.
      if number < 0.
        sign = negative_sign.
      else.
        sign = zero_sign.
      endif.
    endif.
  endmethod.
endclass.
" production code ends here
" unit testing code starts here
class sign_tester definition.
  private section.
    methods test_positive for testing.
    methods test_negative for testing.
    methods test_zero     for testing.
endclass.
class sign_tester implementation.
  method test_positive.
    constants positive_number type sign_setter=>integer value 55.
    data sign type sign_setter=>sign.
    data sign_setter type ref to sign_setter.
    create object sign_setter.
    sign = sign_setter->get_sign( positive_number ).
    cl_abap_unit_assert=>assert_equals(
```

```
      act = sign
      exp = sign_setter=>positive_sign
      ).
  endmethod.
  method test_negative.
    constants negative_number type sign_setter=>integer value '-55'.
    data sign type sign_setter=>sign.
    data sign_setter type ref to sign_setter.
    create object sign_setter.
    sign = sign_setter->get_sign( negative_number ).
    cl_abap_unit_assert=>assert_equals(
      act = sign
      exp = sign_setter=>negative_sign
      ).
  endmethod.
  method test_zero.
    constants zero type sign_setter=>integer value 0.
    data sign type sign_setter=>sign.
    data sign_setter type ref to sign_setter.
    create object sign_setter.
    sign = sign_setter->get_sign( zero ).
    cl_abap_unit_assert=>assert_equals(
      act = sign
      exp = space
      ).
  endmethod.
endclass.
" unit testing code ends here
```

Here we have changed class sign_setter to define a new public constant to represent a sign for a zero value and changed the implementation of its method get_sign to return a positive sign only when the number parameter indicates a positive number, to return a negative sign only when the number parameter indicates a negative number, and to return a zero sign for all other values. Now when the unit tests are run, all of them pass. The code is once again in the green phase of the red-green-refactor cycle.

Listing 11-9 shows how we would refactor the code to keep it clean, again with changes from Listing 11-8 highlighted in bold.

Listing 11-9. Result of cleaning the code after all unit tests pass

```
report.
" production code starts here
class sign_setter definition.
  public section.
    types sign type c length 1.
    types integer type int4.
    constants positive_sign type sign value '+'.
    constants negative_sign type sign value '-'.
    constants zero_sign      type sign value space.
    methods get_sign importing number type integer
                     returning value(sign) type sign.
endclass
class sign_setter implementation.
  method get_sign.
    if number > 0.
      sign = positive_sign.
    else.
      if number < 0.
        sign = negative_sign.
      else.
        sign = zero_sign.
      endif.
    endif.
  endmethod.
endclass.
" production code ends here
" unit testing code starts here
class sign_tester definition.
  private section.
    methods test_positive for testing.
    methods test_negative for testing.
    methods test_zero     for testing.
```

```abap
endclass.
class sign_tester implementation.
  method test_positive.
    constants positive_number type sign_setter=>integer value 55.
    data sign type sign_setter=>sign.
    data sign_setter type ref to sign_setter.
    create object sign_setter.
    sign = sign_setter->get_sign( positive_number ).
    cl_abap_unit_assert=>assert_equals(
      act = sign
      exp = sign_setter=>positive_sign
      ).
  endmethod.
  method test_negative.
    constants negative_number type sign_setter=>integer value '-55'.
    data sign type sign_setter=>sign.
    data sign_setter type ref to sign_setter.
    create object sign_setter.
    sign = sign_setter->get_sign( negative_number ).
    cl_abap_unit_assert=>assert_equals(
      act = sign
      exp = sign_setter=>negative_sign
      ).
  endmethod.
  method test_zero.
    constants zero type sign_setter=>integer value 0.
    data sign type sign_setter=>sign.
    data sign_setter type ref to sign_setter.
    create object sign_setter.
    sign = sign_setter->get_sign( zero ).
    cl_abap_unit_assert=>assert_equals(
      act = sign
      exp = sign_setter=>zero_sign
      ).
  endmethod.
endclass.
" unit testing code ends here
```

Again the only difference is that we changed the expected value of the assertion in unit test method test_zero to use the public constant defined by class sign_setter so that the unit test code continues to be defined in terms of the public attributes provided by class sign_setter. The code is again in the refactor phase of the red-green-refactor cycle. Once more we would need to run the unit tests to determine whether the refactoring changes applied have caused any of the unit tests to fail.

We now have a program that was constructed completely using the TDD cycle. Every shred of production code is covered by a corresponding passing unit test; and every unit test was written, and failed, before ever writing a shred of its corresponding production code.

Upon considering the time it took to maneuver through each phase of the TDD cycle, perhaps it might have taken about two minutes – 120 seconds – to write the code shown in Listing 11-1 due to the fact that we were starting from scratch. Then to include the changes shown in Listing 11-2 might also have taken about two minutes to write due to the fact that we needed to write an entirely new class from scratch and modify the unit test accordingly. Thereafter, the changes shown by Listings 11-3 through 11-9 each might have taken only a few seconds to apply since we simply were adding new functionality to the existing method of the production class and adding a new unit test method to the existing unit test class. We might conclude from this that it should be expected to take less time with each new unit test written to test the same chunk of production code.

EXERCISES

At this point, take a break from reading and shift into exercise mode. Refer to the accompanying workbook to perform the 19 exercises associated with workbook **Section 22: ABAP Unit Testing 601 – Detecting Missing Service Locators.**

Summary

The concept of Test-Driven Development (TDD) was introduced with accompanying explanation addressing how it can be used to insure that all production code is covered by a corresponding automated unit test. The three laws of TDD govern the short development cycle of red-green-refactor; and TDD's "Litany of Benefits," as described by Robert C. Martin, are summarized as

- Certainty that changes made to the production code are correct
- A low rate of defect injection resulting from new changes
- Instilling in developers the courage to refactor poorly written code
- Tests serving as system documentation
- Promotion of good program design

A sequence of examples walked the reader through a development scenario based on TDD, illustrating how the three laws of TDD apply to an ABAP development environment.

CHAPTER 12

Configurable Test Doubles

Chapter 8 covered the details of creating test doubles and using them during automated unit tests, describing how to define a test double either as a subclass inheriting from a base class or as a class implementing an interface. This chapter introduces configurable test doubles.

Isolation Frameworks

You'll be happy to know that manually defining your own test double is not the only way to facilitate using one. Many programming languages now provide frameworks for defining configurable test doubles for the associated unit tests, each framework capable of magically generating a test double *during the execution of the unit test*. ABAP is no exception.

Roy Osherove refers to these as *isolation frameworks*:

> *… a reusable library that can create and configure [test double] objects at runtime.*[1]

> *An isolation framework is a set of programmable APIs that makes creating [test double] objects much simpler, faster, and shorter than hand-coding them.*[2]

With ABAP, there are two configurable test double frameworks from which to choose:

- mockA

- ABAP Test Double Framework

---

[1]Osherove, Roy, *The Art of Unit Testing*, second edition, Manning, 2014, p. 90
[2]Ibid, p. 91

© James E. McDonough 2021
J. E. McDonough, *Automated Unit Testing with ABAP*, https://doi.org/10.1007/978-1-4842-6951-0_12

mockA

The mockA framework is open source software. Written primarily by Uwe Kunath, it was made available in 2013 at a time when there was not yet any configurable test double framework available with ABAP Unit testing. It is compatible with NetWeaver releases starting with 7.01.[3] More information about this mocking framework for ABAP can be found at the following websites:

- `https://github.com/uweku/mockA`

- `http://uwekunath.wordpress.com/2013/10/16/mocka-released-a-new-abap-mocking-framework`

The first website listed in the preceding list has links to others providing further information about how the framework can be used.

ABAP Test Double Framework

The ABAP Test Double Framework is the configurable test double framework provided by SAP. Known better by its acronym ATDF, it is available with NetWeaver release 7.40 SP9 and higher. Since it already is available to the development environment so long as the site has upgraded to a compatible release of NetWeaver, it is the framework most developers will use simply because it requires no extra effort to install as would be required with open source software.

Using this framework with automated unit tests means you can avoid having to define your own test doubles. With only a few configuration statements, it is able to *simulate* the presence of an actual test double. Not only that, but its configuration for simulating a test double occurs *while* the unit test is underway! It even comes with its own ability to verify the results of the calls made to the test double it is pretending to be. Well, what a wonderful utility! It does not yet have the capability to brew a cup of coffee for you, but perhaps some future release might even include that as a feature. Meanwhile, just think of all the time and effort spent coding test doubles that you can save by utilizing this framework instead!

---

[3]`https://blogs.sap.com/2015/01/05/abap-test-double-framework-an-introduction/`
 `#comment-246058`

However, with the great expectations you may have for the ATDF to eliminate the necessity for you to write your own test doubles, it might dampen your enthusiasm to learn that the ATDF is compatible only with global interfaces – that is, it cannot be used to define a test double based on a global class, a local class, or a local interface.[4] Furthermore, even if it could support local interfaces and both local and global classes, it would not be suitable for defining a test spy because it has no facility to recognize attributes and methods beyond those available publicly to the interface or class for which it is serving as a test double.

As a reminder of how a test spy works, refer back to Listing 10-36 in which test spy class report_writer_test_double includes public attribute number_of_lines_written, an attribute it explicitly defines in addition to the public methods it receives by implementing interface report_writable. An ATDF test double based on interface report_writable would not be able to reference this attribute because it is not defined by the interface.

Despite these limitations, you may find it useful for your unit testing purposes. Therefore, an example of its use is presented here describing how the unit test class of the ticket sales program shown in Listing 9-11 would be changed to use the ATDF instead of class ticket_sales_examiner_tstdbl.

Listing 12-1 shows local interface ticket_sales_examinable from Listing 9-11.

Listing 12-1. Local interface ticket_sales_examinable from Listing 9-11

```
interface ticket_sales_examinable.
    types stadium_identifier_range type range of zticket_sales-stadium_id.
    types event_date_range         type range of zticket_sales-event_date.
    methods get_total_tickets_sold
       importing stadium_identifier type stadium_identifier_range
                 event_date         type event_date_range
       exporting tickets_sold       type sy-dbcnt.
endinterface.
```

Since the ATDF requires a global interface on which to base its test doubling capabilities, assume that interface ticket_sales_examinable has been migrated to the global interface repository and now goes by the name zif_ticket_sales_examinable.

---

[4]At the time of this writing

Listing 9-14 showed the improved version of unit test class tester from Listing 9-11, so Listing 12-2 shows how this unit test class would be changed to use the ATDF to configure a test double to replace class ticket_sales_examiner_tstdbl, with changes from Listing 9-14 highlighted in bold.

Listing 12-2. Unit test class tester from Listing 9-14 changed to use ATDF

```
class tester definition for testing risk level harmless.
  private section.
    constants constant_tickets_sold type sy-dbcnt value 591.
    data stadium       type
                       zif_ticket_sales_examinable=>stadium_identifier_range.
    data event_date_type zif_ticket_sales_examinable=>event_date_range.
    methods setup.
    methods report_total_tickets_sold for testing.
    methods validate_test_results.
endclass.
class tester implementation.
  method setup.
    data ticket_sales_examiner type zif_ticket_sales_examinable.
    data ticket_sales_reporter type ticket_sales_reportable.
    data test_double_configurer type ref to if_abap_testdouble_config.
    create object ticket_sales_examiner type ticket_sales_examiner_tstdbl.
    ticket_sales_examiner ?=
      cl_abap_testdouble=>create( 'zif_ticket_sales_examinable' ).
    test_double_configurer =
      cl_abap_testdouble=>configure_call( ticket_sales_examiner ).
    test_double_configurer = test_double_configurer->set_parameter(
      name = 'tickets_sold'
      value = constant_tickets_sold
      ).
    ticket_sales_examiner->get_total_tickets_sold(
      exporting
        stadium_identifier = stadium_identifier_range
        event_date         = event_date_range
      ).
```

```
    create object ticket_sales_reporter type ticket_sales_reporter_tstdbl.
    service_locator=>singleton->set_ticket_sales_examiner(
      ticket_sales_examiner ).
    service_locator=>singleton->set_ticket_sales_reporter(
      ticket_sales_reporter ).
  endmethod.
  method report_total_tickets_sold.
    data stadium     type ticket_sales_examinable=>stadium_identifier_range.
    data event_date type ticket_sales_examinable=>event_date_range.
    perform report_total_tickets_sold using stadium
                                             event_date.
    validate_test_results( ).
  endmethod.
  method validate_test_results.
    data ticket_sales_reporter_tstdbl type ref
                                      to ticket_sales_reporter_tstdbl.
    data last_caller_tickets_sold type sy-dbcnt.
    try.
      ticket_sales_reporter_tstdbl ?=
        service_locator=>singleton->ticket_sales_reporter.
      ticket_sales_reporter_tstdbl->get_last_caller_tickets_sold(
        importing
          tickets_sold = last_caller_tickets_sold
        ).
    catch cx_sy_move_cast_error.
      cl_abap_unit_assert=>fail(
        msg = 'specializing cast has failed'
        ).
    endtry.
    cl_abap_unit_assert=>assert_equals(
      act = last_caller_tickets_sold
      exp = ticket_sales_examiner_tstdbl=>constant_tickets_sold
      ).
  endmethod.
endclass.
```

First, notice that the unit test class now has a private constant named constant_tickets_sold. It was simply copied from the corresponding public attribute of class ticket_sales_examiner_tstdbl. The assertion at the end of method validate_test_results was changed to reference this new field instead of the constant provided by test double ticket_sales_examiner_tstdbl.

Next, notice that the local variables defined in method report_total_tickets_sold have been removed from the method and elevated to private attributes of the class. This was necessary because these variables are now referenced also by the setup method.

Finally, notice that method setup now has a new variable named test_double_configurer and its statement creating an instance of class ticket_sales_examiner_tstdbl has been removed and replaced with four new statements configuring a dynamically defined test double using ATDF. Each of these four statements is described here in more detail:

```
ticket_sales_examiner ?=
    cl_abap_testdouble=>create( 'zif_ticket_sales_examinable' ).
```

The preceding statement calls static method create of ATDF class cl_abap_testdouble to return to reference variable ticket_sales_examiner the reference to an instance of a dynamically generated test double based on interface zif_ticket_sales_examinable. This instance will substitute for the instance of test double class ticket_sales_examiner_tstdbl that had been created by the removed "create object" statement.

```
test_double_configurer =
    cl_abap_testdouble=>configure_call( ticket_sales_
    examiner ).
```

The preceding statement calls static method configure_call of ATDF class cl_abap_testdouble to return to reference variable test_double_configurer a reference to an instance of a class capable of configuring the dynamically generated test double. Notice that the parameter value passed to this method is the reference to the instance of the dynamically generated test double created by the previous statement. The name of method configure_call may be misleading because no call is being configured with this statement. Instead, the instance being returned has the ability to configure calls to methods of a test double based on interface zif_ticket_sales_examinable. Method name get_call_configurer might have made it clearer what this statement is actually doing, but there is a reason why the name of the method is configure_call, a reason that will become clear later.

```
test_double_configurer = test_double_configurer->set_parameter(
    name = 'tickets_sold'
    value = constant_tickets_sold
).
```

The preceding statement calls method set_parameter of instance test_double_configurer to return an updated instance of itself after having established that the ATDF test double is to return the value constant_tickets_sold to the parameter named tickets_sold of a call to method get_total_tickets_sold. That is too much to take in a single gulp, so it needs some further explanation.

First, how is the relationship established between the parameter named tickets_sold and the unspecified method get_total_tickets_sold? In this case, it could be attributed to the fact that the interface zif_ticket_sales_examinable, upon which this ATDF test double has been based, contains only a single method, named get_total_tickets_sold. But suppose the interface had more than one method. Then how would the test_double_configurer know which of those methods is applicable? The fact is that it does not know. At this point, it simply knows that value constant_tickets_sold is the response to be provided through parameter tickets_sold for whatever method of interface zif_ticket_sales_examinable makes a call to it. This statement effectively registers the answer to be given to a question that has yet to be asked.

Second, what is the idea behind a method call resulting in an instance being returned to the very same reference variable providing access to the called method? The methods of the class providing for the configuration of an ATDF test double are

defined by interface if_abap_testdouble_config, as evident by
the type used to define new variable test_double_configurer.
The signatures of these methods are defined to enable method
chaining. Such method chaining is a characteristic of what is
known as the Builder[5] design pattern, which is a pattern for
building an object into its final state a single step at a time. Despite
the ATDF test configurer supporting method chaining, it is not
being used with the preceding statement.

An example of method chaining using the ABAP syntax is shown
in the following example:

```
some_builder=>configure( )->set_min( 5 )->set_max
( 9 )->set_limit( 15 ).
```

In this example, methods set_min, set_max, and set_limit had
been defined to indicate a returning parameter of the same type
of instance created by the configure method. That returning
instance is passed from one method to the next through the chain
of methods, each one contributing its applicable value to the final
state of the object being built.

```
ticket_sales_examiner->get_total_tickets_sold(
    exporting
    stadium_identifier = stadium_identifier_range
    event_date         = event_date_range
).
```

The preceding statement calls instance method get_total_tickets_
sold on the ATDF test double referenced by ticket_sales_examiner,
passing empty values to the two parameters defined for this
method. Notice that this call is being made without a value
associated with outbound parameter tickets_sold defined for this
method. The ATDF test double registers the call to this method

---

[5]For more information, see *Design Patterns: Elements of Reusable Object-Oriented Design*,
Gamma, Helm, Johnson, Vlissides, Addison-Wesley, 1995, p. 97

using these inbound parameter values as the call to trigger the response recorded by the previous statement. This represents the question asked to which the previously recorded answer is to be given. It establishes the values of the inbound calling parameters that are to trigger that answer. What might be confusing about this is that this configuration statement appears exactly the same as an actual call to a test double without parameter tickets_sold, an implicitly optional parameter anyway having been defined in the method signature as an exporting parameter.

One last observation to be made about all these changes is that the statement near the end of the setup method calling the service locator to register an instance to provide the ticket sales examination service did not change in any way, despite registering a test double instantiated and configured through the ATDF.

Listing 12-3 shows the ticket sales program from Listing 9-11 with the version of class tester from Listing 9-14 and modified to incorporate all the subsequent ATDF changes described in this section, with changes highlighted in bold.

Listing 12-3. Copy of Listing 9-11 modified to incorporate ATDF changes described in this section

```
report.
interface ticket_sales_examinable.
    types stadium_identifier_range type range of zticket_sales-stadium_id.
    types event_date_range         type range of zticket_sales-event_date.
    methods get_total_tickets_sold
      importing stadium_identifier type stadium_identifier_range
                event_date         type event_date_range
      exporting tickets_sold       type sy-dbcnt.
endinterface.

interface ticket_sales_reportable.
    methods show_total_tickets_sold
      importing descriptor         type string
                tickets_sold       type sy-dbcnt.
endinterface.
```

```
class service_locator definition create private.
  public section.
    class-methods class_constructor.
    methods        set_ticket_sales_examiner
                     importing ticket_sales_examiner
                       type ref to zif_ticket_sales_examinable.
    methods        set_ticket_sales_reporter
                     importing ticket_sales_reporter
                       type ref to ticket_sales_reportable.
    class-data singleton type ref to service_locator read-only.
    data ticket_sales_examiner type ref to zif_ticket_sales_examinable
                                                       read-only.
    data ticket_sales_reporter type ref to ticket_sales_reportable
                                                       read-only.
endclass.
class service_locator implementation.
  method class_constructor.
    create instance singleton.
  endmethod.
  method set_ticket_sales_examiner.
    me->ticket_sales_examiner = ticket_sales_examiner.
  endmethod.
  method set_ticket_sales_reporter.
    me->ticket_sales_reporter = ticket_sales_reporter.
  endmethod.
endclass.

class ticket_sales_examiner definition.
  public section.
    interfaces zif_ticket_sales_examinable.
    aliases get_total_tickets_sold
            for zif_ticket_sales_examinable~get_total_tickets_sold.
endclass.
class ticket_sales_examiner implementation.
  method get_total_tickets_sold.
    select count(*)
```

```abap
        into tickets_sold
        from zticket_sales
      where stadium_id in stadium_identifier
        and event_date in event_date.
    endmethod.
endclass.

class ticket_sales_examiner_tstdbl definition.
  public section.
    constants constant_tickets_sold type sy-dbcnt value 591.
    interfaces ticket_sales_examinable.
    aliases get_total_tickets_sold
            for ticket_sales_examinable~get_total_tickets_sold.
endclass.
class ticket_sales_examiner_tstdbl implementation.
  method get_total_tickets_sold.
    tickets_sold = constant_tickets_sold.
  endmethod.
endclass.

class ticket_sales_reporter definition.
  public section.
    interfaces ticket_sales_reportable.
    aliases show_total_tickets_sold
            for ticket_sales_reportable->get_total_tickets_sold.
endclass.
class ticket_sales_reporter implementation.
  method show_total_tickets_sold.
    write / descriptor, tickets_sold.
  endmethod.
endclass.

class ticket_sales_reporter_tstdbl definition.
  public section.
    interfaces ticket_sales_reportable.
    aliases show_total_tickets_sold
            for ticket_sales_reportable->get_total_tickets_sold.
```

```
    methods get_last_caller_tickets_sold
      exporting
        tickets_sold type sy-dbcnt.
  private section.
    last_caller_tickets_sold type sy-dbcnt.
endclass.
class ticket_sales_reporter_tstdbl implementation.
  method show_total_tickets_sold.
    last_caller_tickets_sold = tickets_sold.
  endmethod.
  method get_last_caller_tickets_sold.
    tickets_sold = last_caller_tickets_sold.
  endmethod.
endclass.

class service_factory definition create private.
  public section.
    class-data singleton type ref to service_factory read-only.
    class-methods class_constructor.
    methods create_all_services.
    methods create_ticket_sales_examiner.
    methods create_ticket_sales_reporter.
endclass.
class service_factory implementation.
  method class_constructor.
    create instance singleton.
  endmethod.
  method create_all_services.
    create_ticket_sales_examiner( ).
    create_ticket_sales_reporter( ).
  endmethod.
  method create_ticket_sales_examiner.
    data ticket_sales_examiner type ref to ticket_sales_examinable.
    create object ticket_sales_examiner type ticket_sales_examiner.
    service_locator=>singleton->set_ticket_sales_examiner(
      ticket_sales_examiner ).
```

```
    endmethod.
    method create_ticket_sales_reporter.
      data ticket_sales_reporter type ref to ticket_sales_reportable.
      create object ticket_sales_reporter type ticket_sales_reporter.
      service_locator=>singleton->set_ticket_sales_reporter(
        ticket_sales_reporter ).
    endmethod.
endclass.

select-options stadium  for zticket_sales-stadium_id.
select-options evntdate for zticket_sales-event_date.

start-of-selection.
  service_factory=>singleton->create_all_services( ).
  perform report_total_tickets_sold using stadium
                                           evntdate.

form report_total_tickets_sold using stadium_identifier_range
                                     event_date_range.
  data tickets_sold type sy-dbcnt.
  call method
  service_locator=>singleton->ticket_sales_examiner->get_total_tickets_sold
    exporting
      stadium_identifier = stadium_identifier_range
      event_date         = event_date_range
    importing
      tickets_sold       = tickets_sold.
  call method
 service_locator=>singleton->ticket_sales_reporter->show_total_tickets_sold
    exporting
      descriptor         = 'total number of tickets sold:'
      tickets_sold       = tickets_sold.
endform.
```

```
class tester definition for testing risk level harmless.
  private section.
    constants constant_tickets_sold type sy-dbcnt value 591.
    data stadium      type
                      zif_ticket_sales_examinable=>stadium_identifier_range.
    data event_date_type zif_ticket_sales_examinable=>event_date_range.
    methods setup.
    methods report_total_tickets_sold for testing.
    methods validate_test_results.
endclass.
class tester implementation.
  method setup.
    data ticket_sales_examiner type zif_ticket_sales_examinable.
    data ticket_sales_reporter type ticket_sales_reportable.
    data test_double_configurer type ref to if_abap_testdouble_config.
    create object ticket_sales_examiner type ticket_sales_examiner_tstdbl.
    ticket_sales_examiner ?=
      cl_abap_testdouble=>create( 'zif_ticket_sales_examinable' ).
    test_double_configurer =
      cl_abap_testdouble=>configure_call( ticket_sales_examiner ).
    test_double_configurer = test_double_configurer->set_parameter(
      name = 'tickets_sold'
      value = constant_tickets_sold
      ).
    ticket_sales_examiner->get_total_tickets_sold(
      exporting
        stadium_identifier = stadium_identifier_range
        event_date         = event_date_range
      ).
    create object ticket_sales_reporter type ticket_sales_reporter_tstdbl.
    service_locator=>singleton->set_ticket_sales_examiner(
      ticket_sales_examiner ).
    service_locator=>singleton->set_ticket_sales_reporter(
      ticket_sales_reporter ).
  endmethod.
```

```abap
method report_total_tickets_sold.
  data stadium    type ticket_sales_examinable=>stadium_identifier_range.
  data event_date_type ticket_sales_examinable=>event_date_range.
  perform report_total_tickets_sold using stadium
                                           event_date.
  validate_test_results( ).
endmethod.
method validate_test_results.
  data ticket_sales_reporter_tstdbl type ref
                              to ticket_sales_reporter_tstdbl.
  data last_caller_tickets_sold type sy-dbcnt.
  try.
    ticket_sales_reporter_tstdbl ?=
      service_locator=>singleton->ticket_sales_reporter.
    ticket_sales_reporter_tstdbl->get_last_caller_tickets_sold(
      importing
        tickets_sold = last_caller_tickets_sold
      ).
  catch cx_sy_move_cast_error.
    cl_abap_unit_assert=>fail(
      msg = 'specializing cast has failed'
      ).
  endtry.
  cl_abap_unit_assert=>assert_equals(
    act = last_caller_tickets_sold
    exp = ticket_sales_examiner_tstdbl=>constant_tickets_sold
    ).
endmethod.
endclass.
```

Notice that interface ticket_sales_examinable has been deleted along with test double class ticket_sales_examiner_tstdbl. Notice also that classes service_locator and ticket_sales_examiner were changed to reflect the migration of interface ticket_sales_examinable to the global interface repository and now having the prefix "zif_".

Listing 12-4 shows a copy of Listing 12-3 without the highlighting and stricken lines.

Listing 12-4. Copy of Listing 12-3 without highlighting and stricken lines

```
report.
interface ticket_sales_reportable.
    methods show_total_tickets_sold
        importing descriptor        type string
                  tickets_sold      type sy-dbcnt.
endinterface.

class service_locator definition create private.
  public section.
    class-methods class_constructor.
    methods        set_ticket_sales_examiner
                     importing ticket_sales_examiner
                       type ref to zif_ticket_sales_examinable.
    methods        set_ticket_sales_reporter
                     importing ticket_sales_reporter
                       type ref to ticket_sales_reportable.
    class-data singleton type ref to service_locator read-only.
    data ticket_sales_examiner type ref to zif_ticket_sales_examinable
                                                           read-only.
    data ticket_sales_reporter type ref to ticket_sales_reportable
                                                           read-only.
endclass.
class service_locator implementation.
  method class_constructor.
    create instance singleton.
  endmethod.
  method set_ticket_sales_examiner.
    me->ticket_sales_examiner = ticket_sales_examiner.
  endmethod.
  method set_ticket_sales_reporter.
    me->ticket_sales_reporter = ticket_sales_reporter.
  endmethod.
endclass.
```

```abap
class ticket_sales_examiner definition.
  public section.
    interfaces zif_ticket_sales_examinable.
    aliases get_total_tickets_sold
              for zif_ticket_sales_examinable~get_total_tickets_sold.
endclass.
class ticket_sales_examiner implementation.
  method get_total_tickets_sold.
    select count(*)
      into tickets_sold
      from zticket_sales
     where stadium_id in stadium_identifier
       and event_date in event_date.
  endmethod.
endclass.

class ticket_sales_reporter definition.
  public section.
    interfaces ticket_sales_reportable.
    aliases show_total_tickets_sold
              for ticket_sales_reportable->get_total_tickets_sold.
endclass.
class ticket_sales_reporter implementation.
  method show_total_tickets_sold.
    write / descriptor, tickets_sold.
  endmethod.
endclass.

class ticket_sales_reporter_tstdbl definition.
  public section.
    interfaces ticket_sales_reportable.
    aliases show_total_tickets_sold
              for ticket_sales_reportable->get_total_tickets_sold.
    methods get_last_caller_tickets_sold
      exporting
        tickets_sold type sy-dbcnt.
```

```
    private section.
      last_caller_tickets_sold type sy-dbcnt.
endclass.
class ticket_sales_reporter_tstdbl implementation.
  method show_total_tickets_sold.
    last_caller_tickets_sold = tickets_sold.
  endmethod.
  method get_last_caller_tickets_sold.
    tickets_sold = last_caller_tickets_sold.
  endmethod.
endclass.

class service_factory definition create private.
  public section.
    class-data singleton type ref to service_factory read-only.
    class-methods class_constructor.
    methods create_all_services.
    methods create_ticket_sales_examiner.
    methods create_ticket_sales_reporter.
endclass.
class service_factory implementation.
  method class_constructor.
    create instance singleton.
  endmethod.
  method create_all_services.
    create_ticket_sales_examiner( ).
    create_ticket_sales_reporter( ).
  endmethod.
  method create_ticket_sales_examiner.
    data ticket_sales_examiner type ref to ticket_sales_examinable.
    create object ticket_sales_examiner type ticket_sales_examiner.
    service_locator=>singleton->set_ticket_sales_examiner(
        ticket_sales_examiner ).
  endmethod.
  method create_ticket_sales_reporter.
    data ticket_sales_reporter type ref to ticket_sales_reportable.
```

```
    create object ticket_sales_reporter type ticket_sales_reporter.
    service_locator=>singleton->set_ticket_sales_reporter(
       ticket_sales_reporter ).
   endmethod.
endclass.

select-options stadium  for zticket_sales-stadium_id.
select-options evntdate for zticket_sales-event_date.

start-of-selection.
   service_factory=>singleton->create_all_services( ).
   perform report_total_tickets_sold using stadium
                                            evntdate.

form report_total_tickets_sold using stadium_identifier_range
                                     event_date_range.
   data tickets_sold type sy-dbcnt.
   call method
   service_locator=>singleton->ticket_sales_examiner->get_total_tickets_sold
     exporting
       stadium_identifier = stadium_identifier_range
       event_date         = event_date_range
     importing
       tickets_sold       = tickets_sold.
   call method
  service_locator=>singleton->ticket_sales_reporter->show_total_tickets_sold
     exporting
       descriptor         = 'total number of tickets sold:'
       tickets_sold       = tickets_sold.
endform.

class tester definition for testing risk level harmless.
   private section.
     constants constant_tickets_sold type sy-dbcnt value 591.
     data stadium    type
                     zif_ticket_sales_examinable=>stadium_identifier_range.
     data event_date type zif_ticket_sales_examinable=>event_date_range.
```

```
    methods setup.
    methods report_total_tickets_sold for testing.
    methods validate_test_results.
endclass.
class tester implementation.
  method setup.
    data ticket_sales_examiner type zif_ticket_sales_examinable.
    data ticket_sales_reporter type ticket_sales_reportable.
    data test_double_configurer type ref to if_abap_testdouble_config.
    ticket_sales_examiner ?=
      cl_abap_testdouble=>create( 'zif_ticket_sales_examinable' ).
    test_double_configurer =
      cl_abap_testdouble=>configure_call( ticket_sales_examiner ).
    test_double_configurer = test_double_configurer->set_parameter(
      name = 'tickets_sold'
      value = constant_tickets_sold
      ).
    ticket_sales_examiner->get_total_tickets_sold(
      exporting
        stadium_identifier = stadium_identifier_range
        event_date         = event_date_range
      ).
    create object ticket_sales_reporter type ticket_sales_reporter_tstdbl.
    service_locator=>singleton->set_ticket_sales_examiner(
      ticket_sales_examiner ).
    service_locator=>singleton->set_ticket_sales_reporter(
      ticket_sales_reporter ).
  endmethod.
  method report_total_tickets_sold.
    perform report_total_tickets_sold using stadium
                                             event_date.
    validate_test_results( ).
  endmethod.
  method validate_test_results.
    data ticket_sales_reporter_tstdbl type ref
                                to ticket_sales_reporter_tstdbl.
```

```
    data last_caller_tickets_sold type sy-dbcnt.
    try.
      ticket_sales_reporter_tstdbl ?=
        service_locator=>singleton->ticket_sales_reporter.
      ticket_sales_reporter_tstdbl->get_last_caller_tickets_sold(
        importing
          tickets_sold = last_caller_tickets_sold
        ).
    catch cx_sy_move_cast_error.
      cl_abap_unit_assert=>fail(
        msg = 'specializing cast has failed'
        ).
    endtry.
    cl_abap_unit_assert=>assert_equals(
      act = last_caller_tickets_sold
      exp = constant_tickets_sold
      ).
  endmethod.
endclass.
```

The ATDF has many more test configuration options than just the simple example shown in the preceding text. Here is a list of just some of the other useful testing capabilities it offers:

- Ignore the values provided for specific parameters accompanying a method call.

- Ignore the values provided for all parameters accompanying a method call.

- Indicate the number of times a configured response is to be returned for calls to the corresponding method.

- Indicate the number of times a specific method is expected to be called.

- Raise an exception when a method is called.

- Request the ATDF to verify all testing expectations have been met with a single method call.

An example of using some of the configuration settings noted in the preceding text in a single chained method call to configure the ATDF test double is the following statement using fragments from the ticket sales program:

```
cl_abap_testdouble=>configure_call( ticket_sales_examiner
  )->set_parameter( name  = 'tickets_sold'
                    value = constant_tickets_sold
  )->times( 1
  )->ignore_all_parameters(
  )->and_expect(
  )->is_called_times( 1
  ).
```

The preceding statement is indicating to configure a call to a method of the ATDF test double to set the return parameter tickets_sold to the value constant_tickets_sold, to do this only once regardless of the parameter values supplied by the caller, and to expect that this response is called for only once. This example statement also makes it clear why the name of the method is "configure_call" – because a call to a method of a test double is being configured with this single chained method call statement.

The explanation following Listing 12-2 for the second of the four new statements that had been introduced in the setup method raised the point that the name of method configure_call was misleading because no configuration was occurring with that statement. However, when the configuration is achieved through a chained method call statement, it becomes possible to combine the new second and third statements in the setup method of Listing 12-2 into a single statement, and now the method name makes more sense. The following two consecutive statements from method setup of Listing 12-2

```
test_double_configurer =
  cl_abap_testdouble=>configure_call( ticket_sales_examiner ).

test_double_configurer = test_double_configurer->set_parameter(
  name = 'tickets_sold'
  value = constant_tickets_sold
  ).
```

appear awkward when the first of these statements is performing no configuration of a call as its name would suggest, but when the two statements are combined into a single chained method call statement, now it becomes clear that indeed it does represent the configuration of a call:

```
cl_abap_testdouble=>configure_call( ticket_sales_examiner
  )->set_parameter( name  = 'tickets_sold'
                    value = constant_tickets_sold
  ).
```

Accordingly, "configure_call" was chosen deliberately as the name for this method with the expectation that it would be used in a chained method call statement. Not only that, but as an added bonus, it eliminates the need to define variable test_double_ configurer since it is not used in the chained method call statement. Instead, the call to static method configure_call returns an instance of an object upon which the call to method set_parameter is made. Normally a call to a method that returns an instance would need a reference variable to receive the pointer to that instance, but when method chaining is involved, there is no need for such a variable.

EXERCISES

At this point, take a break from reading and shift into exercise mode. Refer to the accompanying workbook to perform the ten exercises associated with workbook **Section 23: ABAP Unit Testing 701 – Using the ABAP Test Double Framework.**

Summary

This chapter continued with the concept of test doubles, this time introducing configurable test double frameworks that can eliminate the need to manually define test doubles. Open source framework mockA was discussed briefly before moving on to a thorough explanation of the ABAP Test Double Framework supplied by SAP. An example of utilizing a configurable test double with an automated unit test was shown using the ABAP Test Double Framework. This is the final chapter having associated new exercise programs to be written.

CHAPTER 13

Obtaining Code Coverage Information Through ABAP Unit Testing

Writing automated unit tests is perhaps the most reliable way to insure that production code is designed properly. Failing unit tests will indicate areas of the production code in need of attention. With larger components, it can be difficult to determine which portions of the production code are covered by unit tests and which are not. This chapter covers the type of code coverage information that can be obtained via ABAP Unit.

Code Coverage Metrics

Fortunately for us, the ABAP Unit Testing Framework is capable not only of running unit tests but also of providing code coverage metrics for any component having at least one automated unit test for one of its procedures. The code coverage metrics provide the following statistics for production components:

- Procedure coverage
- Statement coverage
- Branch coverage

These metrics are generated only when explicitly requested as part of the unit test run and are presented as part of the ABAP Unit Result Display report even when all of the unit tests pass, typically a scenario causing the presentation of the ABAP Unit Result Display report to be bypassed. While there are variations for issuing the command through which to produce a coverage metrics report, one can be produced from the standard ABAP editor (SE38) by selecting the following command path from the menu:

© James E. McDonough 2021
J. E. McDonough, *Automated Unit Testing with ABAP*, https://doi.org/10.1007/978-1-4842-6951-0_13

Program ➤ Execute ➤ Unit Tests With ➤ Coverage

Each category of metric has its own tab on the report such that clicking the tab brings that report forward.

Procedure coverage will list all of the procedures of the component, which include subroutines, methods of classes, and classic ABAP event blocks. The metrics provided include total procedures, number of procedures executed, number of procedures not executed, and percentage of procedure code covered by unit tests. Metrics shown for Total procedures is always 1 for subroutines, methods, and classic ABAP event blocks; but each method is shown subordinate to the class in which it appears, so the node entries for a class will indicate the sum total of methods defined for it.

Statement coverage will list the number of statements within each procedure of the component. The metrics provided include total number of statements in the procedure, number of statements executed by a unit test, number of statements not executed by a unit test, and a percentage of statements by procedure covered by unit tests. Total number of statements is not always accurate. It correctly shows the number of statements in subroutines and classic ABAP event blocks, but for methods it often indicates a count one greater than the actual number of statements in the method (release 7.4).

Branch coverage will reflect the number of logical paths within each procedure of the component. The metrics provided include total number of logical paths in the procedure, number of paths executed by a unit test, number of paths not executed by a unit test, and a percentage of paths by procedure covered by unit tests. Total number of paths is not always accurate in this report either, sometimes overstating the number of paths by one when any type of procedure contains conditional logic.

Not only is it possible to see the percentages of procedures, statements, and branches covered during the unit test run but it is also possible to drill into the report further to see the actual statements that were executed to produce those percentages. Double-clicking the node of a procedure name shown in the coverage metrics report will present the lines of code for that procedure highlighted to indicate which statements were executed as a result of running a unit test and which were not. Executed lines appear highlighted with green background, while lines not executed will appear with red background. This report also has its weaknesses since there are times when a scope terminator, such as endif or endloop, or a condition node, such as else, will not be highlighted at all even though code within its scope had been highlighted in red or green.

This highlighted code coverage report makes it possible to discover which lines of which procedures remain without an associated unit test to cover them. Then it becomes a simple task to write additional unit tests to cover the uncovered lines. Eventually the percentage for statement coverage will converge on 100%, even though there may be some cases in which it is impractical to expect to reach 100% coverage. Indeed, because they cannot be called by an automated unit test, classic ABAP event blocks will always show that none of their statements had been executed by a unit test. So we should expect percentages presented in procedure, statement, and branch coverage for classic ABAP event blocks to always show 0%.

EXERCISES

At this point, take a break from reading and shift into exercise mode. Refer to the accompanying workbook to perform the exercise associated with workbook **Section 24: Obtaining ABAP Unit Test Code Coverage Information.**

Summary

This chapter briefly described how the ABAP Unit Testing Framework is capable of providing statistics on the code coverage offered through the corresponding automated unit tests, describing each of the statistics presented in the resulting report as well as showing how to initiate a unit test run to cause code coverage statistics to be produced. Using these statistics and the highlighted code coverage, the developer is able to see which parts of a program remain without sufficient unit testing. This is the final chapter for which an exercise is to be performed, one that does not require writing any new code.

CHAPTER 14

Cultivating Good Test Writing Skills

Writing automated unit tests is a skill that must be honed and nurtured just as carefully as the skills developers acquire over their careers writing production software. Indeed, a new programming model is involved with writing tests, one where the prime directive is to insure the stability and accuracy of production software. This chapter addresses some of the topics related to the development of those skills.

The Pillars of Good Unit Tests

Perhaps you've heard tales of developers at other software organizations experiencing difficulties keeping their automated unit tests in a passing state, some even deciding to abandon those tests once they came to be regarded as a hindrance instead of a help.[1] Often such situations arise from poorly written tests. So how do we determine whether the unit tests we write are any good? Roy Osherove offers guidance with what he calls the *pillars of good unit tests*:

> *The tests that you write should have three properties that together make them good:*

- *Trustworthiness*

- *Maintainability*

- *Readability*[2]

---

[1]For examples, see 1) Osherove, Roy, *The Art of Unit Testing*, second edition, Manning, 2014, p. xix, and 2) Meszaros, Gerard, *xUnit Test Patterns: Refactoring Test Code*, Addison Wesley, 2007, p. xxii

[2]Osherove, Roy, *The Art of Unit Testing*, second edition, Manning, 2014, p. 151-152

© James E. McDonough 2021
J. E. McDonough, *Automated Unit Testing with ABAP*, https://doi.org/10.1007/978-1-4842-6951-0_14

Osherove further explains that trustworthiness addresses the collective confidence felt by members of the development staff in accepting the results of the tests, which are neither riddled with bugs nor test the wrong things; that maintainability addresses the diligence required during repeated modification efforts to prevent tests from spiraling out of control to the point where the staff ceases to maintain them; and that readability addresses the ease with which the next programmer can quickly understand the intent of the test, having a detrimental ripple effect on both trustworthiness and maintainability when a test becomes difficult to understand.

None of us suddenly becomes an expert with a skill simply because we have read the books or had a competent instructor, so it should be expected that our initial experience writing automated unit tests will not be perfect. It will take some time to become proficient at writing unit tests. Insuring the automated unit tests you write conform to these pillars may spare you coming to the painful conclusion that the tests are impeding development instead of aiding it.

Test Simplicity

With production code, it is possible to write large complex procedures to achieve the desired result. Some procedures start off small but grow so large over repeated maintenance cycles they no longer are easily understood without exhaustive examination. Perhaps you are familiar with such a procedure at your site, one that induces dread with each new change requirement.

The ABAP language seems to place virtually no limits on the number of lines a procedure may have or the number of nesting levels of scope-terminated constructs such as if, case, and while. This presents the possibility of single procedures having thousands of lines containing many levels of deeply nested constructs, procedures that defy comprehension simply due to their size and complexity. Despite the horror stories you might have heard about code like that at other sites, perhaps you are fortunate enough to work on a development staff where the programmers never, ever, *ever* write such monstrous procedures or allow one to emerge through repeated maintenance updates.

In contrast to what typically is found in production code, a unit test should be devoid of all conditional logic. That means it should have no if statements and no case statements. Since the unit test should execute *exactly the same way every time*, the inclusion of conditional logic presents the possibility of multiple outcomes based on the associated conditions. Roy Osherove elaborates on this issue:

If you have any of the following inside a unit test, your test contains logic that shouldn't be there:

- [case], if, or else statements
- ... for or while loops

A test that contains logic is usually testing more than one thing at a time, which isn't recommended, because the test is less readable and more fragile. But test logic also adds complexity that may contain a hidden bug.[3]

Following the Four-Phase Test model proposed by Gerard Meszaros, the intent of the test should be readily evident to the reader. According to Robert C. Martin, test readability is paramount:

What makes a clean test? Three things: Readability, readability, readability. Readability is perhaps even more important in unit tests than it is in production code.[4]

Roy Osherove and Gerard Meszaros offer their perspectives on readability:

Readability is one of the most important aspects when writing a test. As far as possible, it has to read effortlessly, even to someone who's never seen the test before, without needing to ask too many questions – or any questions at all.[5]

Without readability the tests you write are almost meaningless. Readability is the connecting thread between the person who wrote the test and the poor soul who has to read it a few months later. Tests are stories you tell the next generation of programmers on a project.[6]

... tests must be simple – simple to read and simple to write. They need to be simple to read and understand because testing the automated tests themselves is a complicated endeavor.[7]

---

[3]Osherove, Roy, *The Art of Unit Testing*, second edition, Manning, 2014, p. 157

[4]Martin, Robert C., *Clean Code: A Handbook of Agile Software Craftsmanship*, Prentice Hall, 2009, p. 124

[5]Osherove, Roy, *The Art of Unit Testing*, second edition, Manning, 2014, p. 31

[6]Ibid, p. 180

[7]Meszaros, Gerard, *xUnit Test Patterns: Refactoring Test Code*, Addison Wesley, 2007, p. 27

This means that to avoid diminishing the readability of a unit test, any complicated processing for establishing the conditions necessary to run the test or to the subsequent assertion of the test outcome should be encapsulated into helper methods.

A test should be designed such that it tests only a single outcome of a procedure. The best way to do this is for the test to contain only a single assertion, but this is not possible when the procedure has multiple outbound parameters defined for its signature or changes global variables. In such cases, it may be necessary to have multiple assertions in the unit test, with each assertion testing some result of a single call to the procedure. Robert C. Martin puts this into perspective:

> *There is a school of thought that says that every test function in a [unit] test should have one and only one assertion. This rule may seem draconian ... Perhaps a better rule is that we want to test a single concept in each test function.*[8]

Test Coverage

Ideally, a production procedure should have maximum test coverage for it. This means that each statement in the procedure has been exercised by an automated unit test. Achieving 100% coverage is not often attainable, but we should strive to get as close to 100% as possible. Indeed, if you abide by the advice offered in this book, then you will have test doubles that mimic production components during a unit test, meaning that the production components being mimicked may have no coverage at all, as expected, since executing them may cause the unit test to fail or to be interrupted and require manual intervention – exactly the reasons why the test double was used in the first place.

A given procedure may have multiple logic paths that can be traversed. Avoid writing a single unit test that sequentially tests multiple paths through the same procedure. In such cases, the procedure should have as many unit tests for it as there are unique paths of logic to be taken. Why not have multiple paths of a procedure tested by a single unit test? Here are a few reasons why this is not a good idea:

1. The single name of the unit test method cannot do justice in describing all the paths it is responsible for testing.

---

[8]Martin, Robert C., *Clean Code: A Handbook of Agile Software Craftsmanship*, Prentice Hall, 2009, p. 130–131

2. When a unit test failure does occur, it is not abundantly clear which path resulted in the failure. Meszaros refers to such a situation as emanating the smell *Assertion Roulette*.[9]

3. Execution of one path could set the conditions causing the test of the next path to fail when it should pass or to pass when it should fail, another example of Interacting Tests.

4. Unless the quit=no parameter is used with all the assertions being issued after testing a specific path, it would cause some paths not to be tested when one of the paths causes a failure.

5. When the component under test changes and now has fewer paths to test, it is easier and safer to remove an entire unit test method testing that path than to remove only those applicable lines of code from an existing unit test method testing multiple paths.

With a unit test per procedure path, it can be determined at a glance which paths pass and which ones fail. All of the unit tests for a single procedure should be contained within a single unit test class. In some cases, it may make sense for a single unit test class to contain unit tests only for a single procedure.

SAP Recommendations and Constraints When Writing Unit Tests

SAP has made the following recommendations for writing unit tests:

- Place all ABAP Unit local test class code after all code of the object under test. This provides the test classes with access to all data and procedures of the object under test.[10]

---

[9]Meszaros, Gerard, *xUnit Test Patterns: Refactoring Test Code*, Addison Wesley, 2007, p. 224
[10]https://help.sap.com/viewer/ba879a6e2ea04d9bb94c7ccd7cdac446/1709%20000/
en-US/49250ce64d7216b5e10000000a42189d.html

- Define all test methods in the private section or, if inherited, the protected section.[11] Methods in the public section are applicable only when a test executes the tests of other unit test classes. Local test classes may inherit from an abstract global test class.

SAP also has established the following constraints:

- Global test classes, if defined, must be defined with their instantiation property set to "abstract." When this is not the case, a warning is issued when the global class itself is subjected to unit testing.

- A local test class inheriting from a global test class must specify a compatible attribute for risk level. A local class can raise the risk level assigned to the global class but cannot lower it.

Tips for Writing Unit Tests

Over the years, I have implemented some ABAP Unit testing techniques I later came to regret. Accordingly, here are some tips I can offer for avoiding some of the pitfalls I had encountered:

1. Do not define components in the code under test which are used solely by its unit testing code. Examples of such components are the following:

   - Types and data definitions, including those for structures and internal tables

   - Constants

   - Text elements

   - Messages defined via Message Maintenance (SE91)

2. Do not elevate the visibility of a class member simply to make it accessible to the local class containing its unit testing code. The correct way to facilitate this capability, when it becomes necessary, is via class friendship.

---

[11]https://help.sap.com/doc/saphelp_nw74/7.4.16/en-us/49/25686a29ac16b7e10000000a42189d/content.htm?no_cache=true

Note   The accompanying exercise programs provide an example showing how to use friendship in this way.

3. Hard-coded staging data is permissible within the unit test class for the preparation of unit test execution. Avoid defining such hard-coded values in the production code.

    •   Any hard-coded staging data related to Personally Identifiable Information (PII) should be composed of mock values and not based on real values.

4. There may be times when you want to disable a unit test method. You can do this easily by commenting out the "for testing" clause on its method definition. If the unit test method needs to be disabled for an extended period of time, then I would suggest a different approach, which is to place a call to method fail of class cl_abap_unit_assert as the first executable statement in the method, set its level parameter to tolerable, and include a message such as "Unit test has been disabled." These test methods still will be counted as executed tests but will appear with warnings in the ABAP Unit Result Display report. This way it will be easy to distinguish those tests that are truly failing from those that are simply disabled, and because they trigger the ABAP Unit Result Display report, you cannot forget to go back and address the reason why disabling them had become necessary.

5. Define all ABAP Unit tests initially as deliberately failing tests. This will enable running the ABAP Unit test feature to see which unit test methods still remain to be completed. Listing 14-1 illustrates this with an example of a report consisting of three subroutines and a test class named test_all_subroutines having corresponding unit test methods for testing each of the three subroutines.

Listing 14-1. Example program with deliberately failing unit tests

```
report.
    o
    o

form calculate_gross_weight using ...
    o
    o
endform.

form calculate_net_weight using ...
    o
    o
endform.

form calculate_overweight_penalty using ...
    o
    o
endform.

class test_all_subroutines definition.
  private section.
    methods calculate_gross_weight      for testing.
    methods calculate_net_weight        for testing.
    methods calculate_overweight_penalty for testing.
endclass.
class test_all_subroutines implementation.
  method calculate_gross_weight.
    cl_abap_unit_assert=>fail(
      msg = 'No ABAP Unit test code implemented'
      ).
  endmethod.
  method calculate_net_weight.
    cl_abap_unit_assert=>fail(
      msg = 'No ABAP Unit test code implemented'
      ).
  endmethod.
```

```
method calculate_overweight_penalty.
  cl_abap_unit_assert=>fail(
    msg = 'No ABAP Unit test code implemented'
    ).
  endmethod.
endclass.
```

Issues Related to Testing Object-Oriented Code

For years there has been a debate raging on the Internet on the topic of writing unit tests for non-public members of classes. This controversy originated over the testing practices associated with purely object-oriented languages such as Java and C++, so its relevance to ABAP is restricted to the object-oriented aspects of the language.

Those who advocate *against* it suggest that only the public interface of a class should have associated tests, meaning only the public methods and public attributes of a class should be accessed during a unit test, that class members assigned a visibility level other than public should be exempt from direct testing. Their position is that any class members that are not public should be exercised through the process of testing the public members. Roy Osherove makes the case this way:

> When you test a private method, you're testing against a contract internal to the system, which may well change. Internal contracts are dynamic, and they can change when you refactor the system. When they change, your test could fail because some internal work is being done differently, even though the overall functionality of the system remains the same.[12]

In contrast, those who advocate *for* it argue that even non-public members, such as protected and private methods, may be sufficiently complex to warrant their own unit tests. It may be the processing performed by a non-public member that causes the failure for a test of a public member, so restricting unit tests only to public members makes finding those problems more difficult. Their position is that any class member should be a candidate for a unit test.

As demonstrated by the exercise programs, ABAP certainly provides the ability to make non-public members of a class accessible to unit tests.

---

[12]Osherove, Roy, *The Art of Unit Testing*, second edition, Manning, 2014, p. 161

In the past, I have written unit tests against private methods. Lately I have been swayed by the argument presented by advocates against unit testing of non-public members, who raise the credible point that a class that has such complexity in its non-public methods is an example of a class that needs to be split into two classes. The result of extracting out part of one such class into a new class would cause former non-public members now to become public members, for which unit tests could now be written and restricted only to its public interface.

Indeed, a case can be made that restricting unit tests to only the public interface of a class will have the positive effect of making classes smaller, with the associated benefit of them now being easier to understand and maintain. Defining smaller classes is a recommendation made by Robert C. Martin:

> *The first rule of classes is that they should be small. The second rule of classes is that they should be smaller than that. ... smaller is the primary rule when it comes to designing classes.*[13]

> *You can also express yourself by keeping your functions and classes small. Small classes and functions are usually easy to name, easy to write and easy to understand.*[14]

Summary

This chapter offered advice on acquiring and developing good unit test writing skills. After explaining the characteristics that make a unit test most effective, it elaborated on the programming skills associated with writing automated unit tests and how these skills differ from those used for writing production software. Various test writing tips were offered, and arguments for and against writing tests for non-public members of object-oriented classes were presented.

---

[13]Martin, Robert C., *Clean Code: A Handbook of Agile Software Craftsmanship*, Prentice Hall, 2009, p. 136

[14]Ibid, p. 175

CHAPTER 15

Welcome to Autropolis

I hope by now you are convinced that the automated unit testing framework will simplify your ABAP testing efforts and free you from the agony to be endured through manual testing. The fact that tests can be written as executable code just might be the catalyst needed for transforming reluctant manual testers into enthusiastic automated testers. This chapter presents some further commentary on the topic of automated unit testing.

One Small Step for Manual Toward Automated

Now that you are familiar with the ways an ABAP component can be brought under the control of automated unit tests, you may feel as though you are facing a daunting challenge when you consider the amount of work it would take to retrofit existing programs with such tests. Instead of trying to implement a comprehensive set of tests for every nook and cranny of an ABAP component all in one gulp, it may be better to simply add unit tests as maintenance is performed. For instance, the next time you need to change a subroutine to accommodate a new user requirement, write one small automated unit test method for that changed subroutine. Over time the number of unit tests for the component will grow and cover more of a percentage of the code. Eventually you'll be able to use the coverage tool of the ABAP Unit Testing Framework to identify where there remain procedures in the code having little or no test coverage.

© James E. McDonough 2021
J. E. McDonough, *Automated Unit Testing with ABAP*, https://doi.org/10.1007/978-1-4842-6951-0_15

The Right Tool for the Job

The Extended Program Check and the Code Inspector are two valuable tools for insuring that ABAP code contains no statement usage considered obsolete, prone to error, or potentially inefficient. Most developers use these automated tools to identify portions of code to be analyzed further in the quest for high-quality software. They've been around much longer than the new kid on the block: the ABAP Unit Testing Framework. However, these older tools were not designed to insure that ABAP code produces the correct business results.

In episodes of *Star Trek*, there are often scenes where a ship's component is subjected to an immediate diagnosis to determine its effectiveness, such as the one resulting from this exchange heard one fine day on the bridge of the USS Enterprise:

> **Lieutenant Uhura:** Captain, we've received a subspace communication from the USS Excalibur that multiple Klingon warships have taken positions along the neutral zone.
>
> **Captain Kirk:** Spock, can you confirm that?
>
> **Commander Spock:** No, captain, our long-range scanners show no unusual activity along the neutral zone.
>
> **Captain Kirk:** Ensign Chekov, run a Level 1 Diagnostic on the long-range scanners.
>
> **Ensign Chekov:** Aye aye, captain!

Give some consideration toward designating the *self-checking automated unit tests* of ABAP Unit as your preferred Level 1 Diagnostic tool for your development efforts. The Extended Program Check and the Code Inspector can occupy positions as diagnostic tools at level 2 and level 3, respectively, after first running the automated unit tests to determine that the code is producing the correct results. It will enable you to avoid the embarrassment, finger-pointing, unconvincing explanations, and ensuing scramble to address the associated issues arising from the following exchange when the captain of your organization looks to you for immediate confirmation that the code is working as expected:

> **Lieutenant Uhura:** Captain, we've received an intercompany communication from a user that the rabblefrang report is producing incorrect results.
>
> **Captain Kirk** Spock, can you confirm that?

Commander Spock: No, captain, the rabblefrang report seems to be working properly.

Captain Kirk: Ensign Chekov, run a Level 1 Diagnostic on the rabblefrang report.

Ensign Chekov: [after a momentary pause] Captain, the rabblefrang report has no Level 1 Diagnostic capability.

Resistance Is Futile

The software industry is constantly changing. New development and deployment processes such as DevOps[1] and Continuous Integration[2] (CI), enabling software development staffs to release changes to production multiple times *per day*,[3] have moved to the forefront, displacing older models based on larger releases made at intervals of months or years. Automated unit testing plays a central role in these processes.

Although such processes had been adopted long ago by many in the software industry, their use is not yet commonplace among ABAP development organizations. However, the software development tide is surging in that direction, and adopting a policy of automated unit testing will move your organization one step closer to being able to continuously integrate changes into production.

There are those who are content with their software development process being based on manual testing and see no reason why it needs to change. Perhaps it never occurs to them that there are better, faster, cheaper ways to deliver effective, robust, user-friendly, efficient, and easily maintainable software. Those who resist change and insist on continuing with a manual testing process are choosing to use stone-age tools to build and maintain a modern software infrastructure. But such resistance is futile. With the inexorable march of the software industry toward better tools to facilitate better software, it is inevitable that automated unit testing becomes such an integral part of ABAP development that programmers will consider it indispensable and wonder how they ever would be able to do their jobs without it.

---

[1]https://atarc.org/wp-content/uploads/2019/01/MITRE-ATARC-DevOps-White-Paper-2016-08-18.pdf

[2]http://cope.eecs.oregonstate.edu/papers/OpenSourceCIUsage.pdf

[3]https://dzone.com/articles/release-frequency-a-need-for-speed

Becoming the Agent for Change

The Chapter 1 section titled "Why This Book Was Written" recounts my experience being the pioneer with automated unit testing at the site I had been working. If you also find yourself in a situation where automated unit testing is not yet used by any of your development colleagues, then you also may find yourself to be the agent for change with introducing automated unit testing into your development process. Roy Osherove proposes two different ways to succeed with this challenge:

> *There are two main ways an organization or team can start changing a process: bottom up or top down (and sometimes both). The two ways are very different ... and either could be the right approach for your team or company.*[4]

Osherove elaborates on this point by stating Guerrilla Implementation is an example of a bottom-up process, one in which a small team of developers determined to improve their work processes pursues a new practice, obtains some encouraging results, and then shares their experience with others who might become convinced of the worthiness of the new practice and begin to adopt it to their own work processes, before long percolating up through the various levels of management. He also states that a top-down process is one where a manager will initiate a change in a work process, making the case to subordinates why the change would be beneficial to the team and then using their authority to enable the new practice to become part of the team's standard work process once it becomes embraced by a significant number of team members.

The experience I recounted previously was one based on both the top-down and bottom-up approaches – it was the recommendation of managers who attended one of my presentations to undertake a pilot project (top-down), the results of which could be used to convince other management personnel (bottom-up) of the merits of implementing automated unit testing.

---

[4]Osherove, Roy, *The Art of Unit Testing*, second edition, Manning, 2014, p. 193

Go Forth and Automate

You've reached the end of the book. Now it is up to you to decide when to begin automating your ABAP Unit testing efforts and how you will approach it. Harness the power of the computer to perform the boring and repetitive testing tasks for you. Dare to ascend from the depths of that dungeon of despair known as manual testing. Enlist the machine itself as your co-pilot as you depart Mutville for Autropolis, the destination famous for thorough automated unit testing for insuring high-quality software.

Summary

Retrofitting a complete set of automated unit tests to a legacy program at once is an intimidating prospect even for the most seasoned programmer. Instead of trying to attempt that forbidding challenge, make small steps simply by adding to that legacy program a new unit test each time it is updated in a subsequent maintenance cycle. Eventually the unit test collection grows to cover most of the program. Since it will indicate whether the business logic is operating as expected, consider using ABAP Unit as your primary tool for insuring software quality, to be supplemented by the Extended Program Check and Code Inspector.

To keep abreast of changes occurring in the software industry, developers in ABAP organizations soon may find themselves using new technologies such as DevOps and Continuous Integration. Since automated unit testing is a fundamental component of such technologies, get a head start by slowly abandoning manual unit testing in favor of its automated counterpart, and in the process reap the resulting rewards contributing to higher-quality software. You can become an agent of change in your development organization using a top-down or a bottom-up approach toward making automated unit testing a process accepted and embraced by your colleagues.

APPENDIX A

Requirements Documentation and ABAP Exercise Programs

The source code for this book is available on GitHub via the book's product page, located at www.apress.com/9781484269503.

It contains the following:

- The file containing the requirements document describing the associated ABAP exercise programs (.pdf).

- The file containing the supplemental source code described by the requirements document to be included in each new exercise program (.txt). Use this as the source for the code to copy and paste into each new exercise program because, unlike .pdf documents, it retains consecutive spaces used for maintaining proper formatting and alignment of the ABAP code.

- The files containing the source code for each of the associated ABAP exercise programs (.txt).

- The file containing the ABAP program for uploading all the exercise programs into your training system (.txt).

© James E. McDonough 2021
J. E. McDonough, *Automated Unit Testing with ABAP*, https://doi.org/10.1007/978-1-4842-6951-0

APPENDIX B

Answers to Chapter Quizzes

Answers to Quiz #1

Presented at the end of Chapter 4

Multiple Choice: Select the Best Answer

The correct answers to the multiple choice selections of Quiz #1 are the entries highlighted in bold.

1. xUnit describes

    A. Manual code–driven testing frameworks

    B. **Automated code–driven testing frameworks**

    C. Consolidated code–driven testing frameworks

2. xUnit enables testing at the

    A. Internet level

    B. System level

    C. **Module level**

3. xUnit facilitates

    A. **Test-Driven Development**

    B. Extreme programming

    C. Seat-of-the-pants development

© James E. McDonough 2021
J. E. McDonough, *Automated Unit Testing with ABAP*, https://doi.org/10.1007/978-1-4842-6951-0

4.   xUnit tests are implemented as

   A.   Breakpoints

   B.   Conditions

   C.   Assertions

5.   xUnit facilitates preparing a test through

   A.   Dynamic definition

   B.   Fixture

   C.   Collection

6.   The order in which xUnit tests are executed

   A.   Is the order in which they appear

   B.   Is dependent on test attributes

   C.   Should not matter

True or False

The answers to the True or False statements of Quiz #1 are shown to the right of the statements.

Advantages of using xUnit testing include

1. No need to remember what the test result should be	True
2. Elimination of user testing	False
3. Tests are automated	True
4. Reduction in requests for changes	False
5. No need to think about how to implement logic	False
6. No need to write the same test more than once	True
7. Can substitute for design discussions	False
8. Enables testing of peripheral systems	False

The phases of xUnit can be described using the word sequence

9. Ready, Set, Go	False
10. Arrange, Act, Assert	True (Osherove)
11. Setup, Exercise, Verify, Teardown	True (Meszaros)
12. Open, Test, Close	False

Answers to Quiz #2

Presented at the end of Chapter 5

Multiple Choice: Select the Best Answer

The correct answers to the multiple choice selections of Quiz #2 are the entries highlighted in bold.

1. ABAP Unit tests are written in

    A. SAPScript

    B. Java

    C. ABAP

2. ABAP Unit tests

    A. Must be implemented as local classes

    B. Must be implemented as global classes

    C. May be implemented as either local or global classes

3. ABAP Unit tests can be executed

    A. Only from the editor

    B. Only from the Code Inspector

    C. From either the editor or the Code Inspector

4. An ABAP Unit test class definition requires the class to be

    A. Marked as "for testing"

    B. Inherited from a globally defined static class provided by SAP

    C. Defined in a separate module

5. An ABAP Unit test validity is asserted by

    A. Using an ASSERT statement

    B. Invoking static methods of the class cl_abap_unit_assert

    C. Calling function module ASSERT_THIS

6. An ABAP Unit test may test

    A. Only code written using classes and methods

    B. Only classic procedural ABAP code

    C. Classic procedural ABAP code and code written using classes and methods

True or False

The answers to the True or False statements of Quiz #2 are shown to the right of the statements.

An ABAP Unit test may be defined for

1. Executable programs	True
2. Class pools	True
3. Interface pools	False
4. Module pools	True
5. Function groups	True
6. Configuration	False
7. Subroutine pools	True
8. Type groups	False

An ABAP Unit test

9. By default is compiled into all environments	False
10. Accommodates using a fixture	True
11. Is embedded with the object to be tested	True
12. Can generate the source code to comply with the test	False
13. May accept parameters	False
14. Is transported along with its tested object	True

Concepts Associated with Defining Local Test Classes

Although the ABAP Unit Testing Framework requires that a unit test be written as a local class, such a class requires the use of only a few of the many object-oriented ABAP statements. This section covers those concepts of object-oriented programming necessary to be known in order to define and use local test classes effectively. If you are reading this section, the assumption is that you know nothing about either object-oriented programming or the ABAP statements used to write object-oriented programs. We will concentrate only on what is required to be understood in order to use the object-oriented extensions to the ABAP language to define and execute local test classes.[1]

With object-oriented programming, the fundamental unit of design is called a *class*. A class is a complex data object consisting of *attributes* and *behaviors*. Collectively, attributes and behaviors are known as *members* of the class.

An attribute of a class is simply a data item. Each attribute is defined as a data field or as a constant, using the ABAP statement DATA or CONSTANTS, respectively. The TYPES statement also may be defined within the class to assist in defining the data fields and constants.

A behavior, also known as a *method*, is an action defined for a class that can be used to read or change the values of its attributes or to produce some other type of processing result. A method must be invoked to perform the action it provides, similar to using the PERFORM statement to call a subroutine that performs some action.

---

[1]For a comprehensive explanation of using object-oriented design in ABAP programs, refer to *Object-Oriented Design with ABAP: A Practical Approach* (McDonough, James E., Apress, 2017)

© James E. McDonough 2021
J. E. McDonough, *Automated Unit Testing with ABAP*, https://doi.org/10.1007/978-1-4842-6951-0

The following example, from the SAP online help,[2] shows a simple production class named *myclass* and a test class named *mytest*[3]:

```
* Production classes
CLASS myclass DEFINITION.
  PUBLIC SECTION.
    CLASS-DATA text TYPE string READ-ONLY.
    CLASS-METHODS set_text_to_x.
ENDCLASS.

CLASS myclass IMPLEMENTATION.
  METHOD set_text_to_x.
    text = 'U'.
  ENDMETHOD.
ENDCLASS.

* Test classes
CLASS mytest DEFINITION FOR TESTING.
  PRIVATE SECTION.
    METHODS this_test FOR TESTING.
ENDCLASS.

CLASS mytest IMPLEMENTATION.
  METHOD this_test.
    myclass=>set_text_to_x( ).
    cl_abap_unit_assert=>assert_equals( act = myclass=>text
                                        exp = 'X' ).
  ENDMETHOD.
ENDCLASS.
```

As with all classes defined using the ABAP language, each class has both a definition component and an implementation component. The definition component of a class specifies its attributes as well as the names and signatures of its methods; it begins

---

[2]https://help.sap.com/saphelp_snc700_ehp01/helpdata/en/49/180619005338a1e100000 00a421937/content.htm?no_cache=true

[3]With this example, I have taken the liberty to change the name of the method defined in class mytest from *mytest* to *this_test* simply to avoid confusion with a class and one of its methods having the same name

with the CLASS … DEFINITION statement and ends with the ENDCLASS scope terminator statement. The implementation component contains an implementation for each of the methods specified in the definition component; it begins with the CLASS … IMPLEMENTATION statement and ends with the ENDCLASS scope terminator statement. The statements METHOD and ENDMETHOD are functionally equivalent to the statements FORM and ENDFORM found with classic ABAP. Both the definition and implementation components together represent a complete class.

In the preceding example, class *myclass* has been defined to contain a static attribute (CLASS-DATA) called *text* and a static method (CLASS-METHODS) called *set_text_to_x*. These are both defined in the PUBLIC SECTION, which assigns public visibility to any attributes and methods following this section header. Public visibility means that any external entity has access to these members – can read or change the attribute and can call the method. Effectively, external entities can *see* these class members. However, in this case the attribute *text* also carries the READ-ONLY qualifier, which means external entities can read its value but cannot change it. The implementation for its method *set_ text_to_x* uses a simple ABAP assignment statement to set its attribute *text* to the value 'U'. This is about the simplest example of how a class could be defined which has both an attribute and a method.

By comparison, class *mytest* has been defined to contain no attributes but with only a method called *this_test*. The method is defined on a METHODS statement in the PRIVATE SECTION, which assigns private visibility to any attributes and methods following this section header. Private visibility means that only the class itself has access to these members – can read or change the attribute and can call the method. Effectively, external entities cannot see these class members and so have no access to them.

In addition to the usual ABAP statements (CLASS, ENDCLASS, PUBLIC SECTION, PRIVATE SECTION, METHODS, METHOD) used to define any type of class, *mytest* also includes ABAP statement words that specifically designate the class as an ABAP Unit test class. These are

- The additional clause FOR TESTING appearing on the class definition statement

- The additional clause FOR TESTING appearing on the methods definition statement

There are other ABAP statement words and clauses also associated solely with defining ABAP Unit test classes, but the FOR TESTING clause on the class definition statement is the only one necessary to designate the entire class as a test class.

Using the preceding example, class *mytest* is dependent upon class *myclass* – that is, class *mytest* knows about class *myclass*, but class *myclass* knows nothing about class *mytest*. This dependency exists because class *mytest* includes a statement in its implementation of method *this_test* to call the static method *set_text_to_x* of class *myclass*:

```
myclass=>set_text_to_x( ).
```

This statement makes use of the functional syntax for invoking a method of a class. Prior to the introduction into the ABAP language of the functional syntax for invoking methods of classes, there was the original, and still supported, syntax for doing so:

```
call method myclass=>set_text_to_x.
```

Though it uses more words, this syntax variation for invoking a method of a class has similarities with the syntax of the CALL FUNCTION statement to invoke a function module to perform some action, and indeed the concept of calling a method of a class via the call method statement is comparable to calling a function module of a function group via the call function statement.

In addition to invoking method *set_text_to_x* of class *myclass*, the implementation for method *this_test* of class *mytest* also has a statement calling static method *assert_equals* of *class cl_abap_unit_assert*:

```
cl_abap_unit_assert=>assert_equals( act = myclass=>text
                                    exp = 'X' ).
```

Here again the call to this method of this class uses the more recent functional syntax. Had the original method invocation syntax been used, the statement would have looked like this:

```
call method cl_abap_unit_assert=>assert_equals
    exporting
        act = myclass=>text
        exp = 'X'.
```

The call effectively requests an assertion that the actual value (parameter *act*) found in attribute *text* of class *myclass* is equal to the expected value (parameter *exp*) of 'X'. Our conclusion that the expected value should be 'X' is based not so much on knowing anything about how method *set_text_to_x* of class *myclass* is implemented but is based simply on the name of the method itself – we expect that when we call a method named *set_text_to_x*, an attribute named *text* will be set to the value 'X', just as the method name suggests. If indeed the value found in attribute *text* of class *myclass* is equal to 'X', then the assertion passes; otherwise, the assertion fails.

Before continuing, look again at the code defining these two classes and determine for yourself whether you think the assertion call in method *this_test* will pass or fail.

When we request to execute an ABAP Unit test for a program containing these two classes, the ABAP Unit Testing Framework will be invoked, which eventually will determine that method *this_test* of class *mytest* is to be invoked. When method *this_test* of class *mytest* does gain control, the first thing it will do is call method *set_text_to_x* of class *myclass*. This will have the effect of setting attribute *text* of class *myclass* to the value 'U'. The next thing method *this_test* will do is to call the method *assert_equals* of class *cl_abap_unit_assert*, requesting it to assert that the value in attribute *text* of class *myclass* is equal to the value 'X'. This assertion will fail because the actual value 'U' in attribute *text* of class *myclass* is not equal to the expected value 'X'.

Index

387

© James E. McDonough 2021
J. E. McDonough, *Automated Unit Testing with ABAP*, https://doi.org/10.1007/978-1-4842-6951-0

U, V, W

X, Y, Z

Printed in the United States
by Baker & Taylor Publisher Services